BIBLE KEY WORDS

VOLUME III

Previously Published:

BIBLE KEY WORDS—Volume I

four books in one:

BIBLE KEY WORDS—Volume II

four books in one:

BIBLE KEY WORDS
Volume III

from *GERHARD KITTEL'S*
THEOLOGISCHES WÖRTERBUCH
ZUM NEUEN TESTAMENT

TRANSLATED AND EDITED BY

DOROTHEA M. BARTON, P. R. ACKROYD,
and A. E. HARVEY

A ONE-VOLUME EDITION CONTAINING
TWO BOOKS:

I. FAITH
by **Rudolf Bultmann** *and* **Artur Weiser**

II. SPIRIT OF GOD
by **Eduard Schweizer** *and others*

Harper & Brothers, Publishers, New York

BIBLE KEY WORDS—VOL. III

Copyright © 1960, 1961 by A. & C. Black Ltd
Printed in the United States of America

Library of Congress catalog card number: 51-11930

I

FAITH

BY

RUDOLF BULTMANN

AND

ARTUR WEISER

Translated
from the German
by Dorothea M. Barton

edited by P. R. Ackroyd

EDITOR'S PREFACE

THIS book is a translation of the article Πίστις, written by Professors Rudolf Bultmann and Artur Weiser in the *Theologisches Wörterbuch zum Neuen Testament* (TWNT), begun by G. Kittel and now edited by G. Friedrich, Vol. VI, pp. 174-230. Apart from some abbreviations in Chapters II and III, and some curtailing of footnotes, the whole text is here translated. The order of the material differs by the placing of the Old Testament chapter first; cross-reference to the German text may readily be made since the chapter subdivisions coincide.

The 'Word Books' in this series which have already appeared (and others are to follow) make available to the English reader some part of the immense assemblage of material in TWNT, material of great interest to any student of the Old and New Testaments. But a word of caution may not be out of place. Some years ago, a New Testament scholar was heard to remark that the articles in TWNT were being regarded in some circles as providing the last word in the study of biblical terms, and their authority was being too readily accepted as absolute. This is, of course, a misuse of the material, and far from representing the intentions of the authors. In these matters, new approaches and understandings continually become necessary, and, in any case, a distinction must be made between the presentation of factual material (lexical material, information about the usage of words) and the theological interpretations placed upon this. The summary to the Old Testament chapter here (pp. 31 ff.), and the many points of comment in the New Testament chapter, represent conclusions drawn by Professors Weiser and

Bultmann. But these conclusions must be carefully examined if further progress is to be made towards understanding the biblical words and ideas. A forthcoming book by Professor James Barr of Edinburgh (see the Bibliography) contains furthermore some trenchant criticism of the methods and assumptions of TWNT, and this points to the need for careful scrutiny of the evidence and its presentation.

But this is all to the good. For so central an idea as that of Faith will not readily find exhaustive treatment. The chapters of this book provide some of the material which needs to be taken into account if we are to approach an understanding of what was in the minds of biblical writers of many periods when they used words which may be reasonably translated by this word.

Reference may also appropriately be made here to Martin Buber's contrast of the 'faith of Abraham' with the 'faith of Paul' (*Two Types of Faith*, 1951), and to the discussion of this by Hans Urs von Balthasar (*Martin Buber and Christianity*, 1961).

All Hebrew words have been transliterated (unattractive though this is to the Hebraist) and, where necessary, translated. The non-Hebraist will observe that where the root of a word is cited, this is done without vowels, e.g. *'mn*, but where a particular word is mentioned, the vowels are added, e.g. *'emet*. It will not normally be difficult for the connexion between different words to be recognised from the occurrence of the root letters (sometimes partly concealed as in the example just given). Four forms of the Hebrew verb are mentioned; the *qal* which is the simple form; the *niph'al* which is strictly reflexive, but often passive in meaning; the *hiph'il* which is often though not exclusively causative in meaning; the *pi'el*, the intensive form.

Greek words are not transliterated. It is not really so very difficult for the reader with no Greek to make himself familiar with the letters, and if he will work with a Bible open, he will quickly recognise the phrases which appear in Greek here. Where quotations are given from elsewhere than the New Testament (or Septuagint) a translation has been given.

P. R. A.

CONTENTS

ix

BIBLIOGRAPHY

GENERAL

Reference may be made to the general Theologies of the Old and
New Testaments

M. FLACIUS: *De voce et re fidei* (1549).

H. HOELEMANN: *Bibelstudien, I: Die biblischen Grundbegriffe der
Wahrheit* (1859), pp. 1-53.

J. B. LIGHTFOOT: *Epistle to the Galations* (1865, [10]1890), pp. 154-64.
(Reprinted 1957 by Zondervan, U.S.A.)

H. H. WENDT: 'Der Gebrauch der Wörter ἀλήθεια, ἀληθής und
ἀληθινός im NT auf Grund des alttestamentlichen Sprach-
gebrauchs', ThStKr, 56 (1883), pp. 511-47.

A. POTT: *Das Hoffen im NT in seiner Beziehung zum Glauben* (1915).

A. NAIRNE: *The Faith of the NT* (1920).

R. GYLLENBERG: *Pistis*, I, II (Swedish) (1922).

A. SCHLATTER: *Der Glaube im NT* ([4]1927).

B. B. WARFIELD: *Biblical Doctrines* (1929), pp. 465-508.

W. G. KÜMMEL: 'Der Glaube im NT', ThBl, 16 (1938), pp. 209-21.

J. DUPONT: *Gnosis* (1949), pp. 250-2, 260 f., 398-409, *et passim*.

V. WARNACH: *Agape* (1951), pp. 581-5 *et passim*.

C. H. DODD: *The Bible and the Greeks* (1935), pp. 65-75.

J. GUILLET: *Thèmes Bibliques* (1951) esp. chs. II, III.

P. VALLOTTON: *Le Christ et la Foi* (1960).

C. F. D. MOULE: *An Idiom Book of NT Greek* (1953).

J. J. von ALLMEN: *Vocabulary of the Bible* (1958).

JAMES BARR: *The Semantics of Biblical Language* (Oxford, to be
published shortly), esp. Chapter VII on 'Faith and Truth'
and the literature there discussed.

CHAPTER I

L. BACH: 'Der Glaube nach der Anschauung des AT', BFTh, 4
(1900), pp. 1-96.

J. PEDERSEN: *Israel, its life and culture*, I-II (1926), pp. 336-48.

K. H. FAHLGREN: *Sedaka nahestehende und entgegengesetzte Begriffe
im AT* (1932).

K. J. CREMER: 'Oudtestamentische Semasiologie', *Gereformeerd
Theologisch Tijdschrift*, 48 (1948), pp. 193-200; 49 (1949),
pp. 1-15, 79-99.

S. Virgulin: 'La fede nel profeta Isaia', *Biblica*, 31 (1950), pp. 346-64, 483-503.

J. C. C. van Drossen: *De derivata van den stam 'mn in het Hebreeuwsch van OT* (1951).

G. J. Botterweck: ' "Gott erkennen" im Sprachgebrauch des AT', *Bonner Bibl. Beiträge*, II (1951).

CHAPTER II

R. Reitzenstein: *Die Hellenistischen Mysterienreligionen* (³1927).

R. Walzer: *Galen on Jews and Christians* (1949), pp. 48-56.

CHAPTER III

W. Bousset: *Die Religion des Judentums im späthellenistischen Zeitalter*, ed. H. Gressmann (³1926), pp. 193-6 *et passim*.

G. F. Moore: *Judaism* (1927-30).

H. L. Strack and P. Billerbeck: *Kommentar zum NT aus Talmud und Midrasch* i-v (²1956), see iii, 187-201.

P. Volz: *Die Eschatologie der jüdischen Gemeinde im neutestamentlichen Zeitalter* (²1934), pp. 80 f.

CHAPTER III, B, 3

H. Windisch: *Die Frömmigkeit Philos* (1909), pp. 23-29.

W. Bousset: *Kyrios Christos* (²1921), pp. 145-7.

Bousset-Gressmann, pp. 447 f.

M. Peisker: *Der Glaubensbegriff bei Philon* (Dissertation, Breslau 1936).

E. Käsemann: *Das wandernde Gottesvolk* (1939), pp. 48-52.

CHAPTER IV, B

M. Dibelius: *Jesus* (²1949), pp. 106 f.

E. Käsemann: *Das wandernde Gottesvolk* (1939), pp. 19-27.

CHAPTER IV, C

W. H. P. Hatch: *The Pauline Idea of Faith in its relation to Jewish and Hellenistic Religion* (1917).

W. Bousset: *Kyrios Christos* (²1921), pp. 145-54.

E. Wissmann: *Das Verhältnis von πίστις und Christusfrömmigkeit bei Paulus* (1926).

W. Michaelis: 'Rechtfertigung aus Glauben bei Paulus' in *Festgabe für A. Deissmann* (1927).

E. Lohmeyer: *Grundlagen paul. Theologie* (1929).

K. Mittring: *Heilswirklichkeit bei Paulus* (1929).

M. Dibelius: 'Glaube und Mystik bei Paulus', *Neue Jahrbücher für Wissenschaft und Jugendbildung*, 7 (1931), pp. 683-99.

W. Mundle: *Der Glaubensbegriff des Paulus* (1932).

R. Gyllenberg: 'Glaube bei Paulus', ZSTh, 13 (1937), pp. 612-30.

M. Hansen: *Om Trosbegrebet hos Paulus* (1937).

R. Schnackenburg: *Das Heilsgeschehen bei der Taufe nach dem Apostel Paulus* (1950), pp. 115, 188 f., *et passim*.

Chapter IV, D

J. O. Buswell: 'The Ethics of "Believe" in the Fourth Gospel', *Biblica Sacra*, 80 (1923), pp. 28-37.

W. H. P. Hatch: *The Idea of Faith in Christian Literature from the Death of St. Paul to the Close of the Second Century* (1926).

J. Huby: 'De la connaissance de foi dans Saint Jean', *Recherches de Science religieuse*, 21 (1931), pp. 385-421.

R. Schnackenburg: *Der Glaube im vierten Evangelium* (Dissertation, Breslau 1937).

W. F. Howard: *Christianity according to St. John* ([3]1947), pp. 151-65.

C. H. Dodd: *The Interpretation of the Fourth Gospel* (1953), pp. 179-86.

ABBREVIATIONS

ATD	Das Alte Testament Deutsch (Commentary series ed. by A. Weiser, Göttingen.
BFTh	*Beiträge zur Förderung christlicher Theologie.*
BH	*Biblia Hebraica,* ed. R. Kittel (3rd edition).
Bousset-Gressmann	W. Bousset, *Die Religion des Judentums im späthellenistischen Zeitalter, ed.* H. Gressmann (^{3}1926).
EVV	English versions.
Ges.-K.	Gesenius-Kautzsch, *Hebrew Grammar.*
NGG	*Nachrichten von der Gesellschaft der Wissenschaften zu Göttingen.*
Pr-Bauer	E. Preuschen, *Griechisch-deutsches Wörterbuch . . . NT* ed. W. Bauer (^{5}1958) ET of ed. 4 (1949ff.) by W. F. Arndt and F. W. Gingrich (1957).
Str.-B.	Strack-Billerbeck, cf. Bibliography.
Theod.	Theodotion.
ThBl	*Theologische Blätter.*
ThStKr	*Theologische Studien und Kritiken.*
TWNT	*Theologisches Wörterbuch zum Neuen Testament,* ed. G. Friedrich.
VB	J. J. von Allmen ed. *Vocabulary of the Bible* (1958).
ZKG	*Zeitschrift für Kirchengeschichte.*
ZNW	*Zeitschrift für die neutestamentliche Wissenschaft.*
ZSTh	*Zeitschrift für die systematische Theologie.*

Works which appear in the Bibliography are referred to in the text and footnotes by the author's name either alone or with an abbreviated title.

I. THE OLD TESTAMENT CONCEPT

A. *General considerations*

IF faith is understood in quite general terms as the relationship and attitude of man towards God, then the OT statements concerning faith do not occupy a very prominent position. Interest in man is usually overshadowed by the centrality of God. Faith as interpreted by the OT is always the response of man to the primary activity of God. In addition to this, OT religion in early times was a matter for the community[1] and it is difficult for expression to be given to the personal inner life of the community. Hence the language only begins to develop a wealth of such expressions when the individual emerges from his dependence on the community and examines the attitude of man towards God with particular interest as a result of his own inner experience. So it was the prophets who provided a fresh stimulus to the development of the language, with its wealth of metaphors treating of faith, by giving greater depth to their content; and the resources of the language available for describing faith can be found at their richest in the Psalms, where the piety of the individual has the opportunity of expressing itself most clearly.

A study of faith in the OT cannot fail to observe the striking fact that in describing man's relationship to God two fundamentally different and indeed contrasting groups of ideas are employed, namely fear and trust. The contradiction between them is felt down to a late period and yet they stand side by side and pass

---

[1] See Baumgärtel, *Die Eigenart der at.lichen Frömmigkeit* (1932), pp. 20-25, 49-63, 95-103.

over into each other, so that the fear of God is often
simply the term for faith.[1] This tension and polarity
in man's relationship to God, expressed in the antithetic quality of the words in common use, is of fundamental significance for the OT attitude to faith.[2]

The following picture is obtained by counting the
number of times in which the individual groups of
words are employed. The word groups denoting fear
and trust to express the relationship to God are evenly
balanced (they both occur about 150 times). In the
case of the verbal stems of the second group, *bṭh* is most
frequently used: it occurs 57 times in a religious sense
(of which 37 are in the Psalms and 3 apply to idols),
60 times in profane usage. Next comes *ḥsh*: 34 times
in a religious sense (24 times in the Psalms), 5 times in
profane usage. Taking the verbs of hope, we find *qwh*
32 times referring to God (12 times in the Psalms), 11
times in profane use; *yḥl* 15 times in reference to God,
14 times in profane use, *ḥkh* 6 times referring to God,
8 times in profane use; on the other hand the *hiph'īl* of
'*mn* (the LXX uses the stem πίστις and its derivatives
for this alone) is applied directly to God only 15 times.
It is combined 10 times in a religious sense with God's
word, command or action, or used absolutely, besides
occurring 23 times in profane usage. The *niph'al* is used
45 times, 12 times of God himself but only 3 times of
the relationship of man to God.

This survey leads to the following question. Does the
fact that, according to the statistics of the uses of the

[1] e.g. Gen. xx.11, xxii.12; Isa. viii.13, xi.2; Prov. i.7; Ps. xix.10,
cxi.9 *et passim*.

[2] J. Hempel, *Gott und Mensch im AT* (BWANT,[2] 1936), pp. 4-33,
233-49. I intentionally avoid Hempel's expressions 'consciousness
of being both at a distance and in association', because for the OT
fear is more than this, namely the awareness that one's own
existence is threatened and might be annihilated, and confident
faith transcends association and includes a special quality of being.

individual verbal stems, the stem 'mn—πιστεύειν only comes in the fourth place, give a correct picture of the qualitative weight of the individual stems in the OT? For in that case the use of πιστεύειν in the LXX and the NT would appear to represent an arbitrary choice of a stem of minor importance in the OT. Or, on the other hand, did not the NT after all link up with a form which was vital and fundamental for the conception of faith in the OT, and bring into prominence an expression which had been most completely and fully stamped with the depth of the OT conception of faith? None of the verbal stems named is of specifically religious origin, and their use in religion seems to have arisen out of profane roots. Consequently in order to determine their meaning we must first ascertain the particular significance of the individual verbal stems by drawing on their profane usage. We can then attempt to give a historical sketch of the changes and developments in their meaning.

B. *The root 'mn and related expressions*[1]

1. The *qal*, which occurs only as a participle, has a strictly limited range of meaning. It is used of a child's mother, nurse, attendant in II Sam. iv.4, Ruth iv.16, Num. xi.12; to denote a guardian, a foster-father in II Kings x.1, 5; Esther ii.7; (Isa. xlix.2). The passive participle in Lam. iv.5 describes the child that is *wrapped in* purple, the *niph'al* in Isa. lx.4 the child that is *carried* by its mother on her hip in the fold of her garment. The noun *'omnā* occurs in Esther ii.20 in an abstract feminine formation with the meaning of *education, nurture*. It is not possible to reach a definite conclusion from these passages whether the customary translation of carrying, holding, or the close association

---

[1] cf. ἀλήθεια, *truth*, in TWNT, I, pp. 233 ff. for a discussion of *'emet.*

in general between mother, nurse, attendant, guardian
and the child comes nearest to the original meaning.
It is just as difficult to ascertain whether there is a
connexion between this employment of the word and
its religious usage, and if so, what it is (cf. below,
pp. 7, 11 f.).[1]

2. The range of the use of the *niph'al* is considerably
wider. Its usual translation as *firm*, *certain* and *reliable*
is no more than an approximation and does not represent its ultimate and fundamental meaning.[2] This can
be recognised most readily in those passages in which
the profane use of the verb is connected with a thing.
Thus it is associated with a place in Isa. xxii.23, in order
to express its suitability for a particular purpose *I will
fasten it as a tent peg in a māqōm ne'emān (sure place)*, or of
a dynasty (descendants) in order to say that it will not
die out (I Sam. ii.35, xxv.28; II Sam. vii.16; I Kings
xi.38).[3] In Deut. xxviii.59 the participle is used for
lasting afflictions and grievous diseases and includes not
only the persistent continuance but also the devastating
effect. The LXX proves that in this last case the usual
translation does not cover the whole meaning, for it finds
itself forced to use the paraphrase θαυμαστός (*wondrous*).
In Isa. xxiii.16 the participle means the drinking water
that will not fail; in Jer. xv.18 the *niph'al* is employed in a
parallel passage as a contrast to the *deceitful brook of
waters* which does not perform what it promises.[4]

---

[1] Nothing positive can be said about the meaning of *'ōmenōt* in
II Kings xviii (usually translated as *door-posts*) and about its connexion with *'mn* (? = *to carry*).

[2] The LXX translates it 29 times with πιστός, 9 times with
πιστοῦν, once each with ἀξιότιστος, ἐμπιστεύειν, πίστιν ἔχειν,
and θαυμαστός.

[3] In the same sense *šālōm we'emet* I Kings xx.19 *peace and security
in my days* (RSV).

[4] A similar interpretation must be given to Exod. xvii.12: *His*
(Moses') *hands were 'emūnā = did not sink down*, and Jer. ii.21 where

Finally the *niph'al* is used in Gen. xlii.20 of the statement which is proved to be true because it corresponds with the facts of the case.[1] These examples show clearly that an unvarying translation with only one word is impossible[2]; thus *ne'emān* does not express a quality which is added to the subject concerned and which could equally well be attached to something else, but *'mn* is shown to be a general concept the content of which is determined differently in each case by the particular thing it describes. It declares that in any given instance the qualities to be attributed to the subject in question are actually present. Thus here *'mn* contains perhaps something which might be defined as 'specific' and means that the quality which is characteristic of the particular subject concerned is related to reality. In accordance with the OT idea of completeness this implies not only one particular

zera' 'emet = true choice plant, is contrasted with *nokriyyā = an alien, wild one*.

[1] Similarly the Aramaic passive participle *mehēmān* of the interpretation of dreams in Dan. ii.45.

[2] The difficulties which this causes in the Versions can be observed already in the LXX which adopts different methods at its several stages. The earliest—the Pentateuch and the translations influenced by it in early days, such as Isaiah in particular—give simply the appropriate meaning. The later stage which afterwards culminated in Aquila, prefers a definite equivalent for each word in the original text in order to reproduce that text as precisely (and mechanically) as possible, and then leaves the interpretation to those qualified for it (P. Katz, *Philo's Bible* (1950), especially 34 f., 42 f., 64-67, 83 ff., 149). Consequently in Exod. xvii.12 the LXX renders *yādāw 'emūnā* intelligibly with ἐστηριγμέναι, the metaphor being replaced by the concrete term, as in the Targums. On the other hand Aquila has πίστις which is not a 'literal' translation, but simply his regular word for *'emūnā*, whatever its sense may be in the context. Another example of the mechanical methods of the later translators is provided by the rendering of *'emūnā official duty* in I Chron. ix. In v. 22 *be'emūnā* is translated by τῇ πίστει αὐτῶν (cf. also vv. 26.31, Katz).

feature, but all the features taken together which pertain to this subject. Moreover the nature of the Hebrew genius demands that this relationship between concept and reality should be seen not as an abstraction of logical thought, but always as a practical experience drawn from life. Thus in the formal concept what belongs to it is conceived, felt and experienced each time together with it, and in this way the logical relationship invariably involves also a practical relationship with life. The particular meaning in any given case can be intensified or extended according to the strength of the demands or the acuteness of the power of observation.[1]

It is with these results in mind that the application of the *niph'al* to persons must be judged. It is used of a servant in I Sam. xxii.14 and in Num. xii.7 (Moses); of witnesses in Isa. viii.2, and in Jer. xlii.5 where the word expresses not only the truthfulness of the statement but includes also the capacity to observe, the understanding and the gift of description[2]; of the messenger[3] in Prov. xxv.13; of a prophet in I Sam. iii.20 where *ne'emān* is used to describe Samuel as the ideal of a prophet, 'as he ought to be'; also of a priest in I Sam. ii.35; of a city pictured as a wife in Isa. i.21, 26[4]; of officers in charge in Neh. xiii.13.[5] The conclusions reached above can without difficulty be applied to these examples, for in these too the same form of the word describes qualities quite different in themselves. The same word is used in every case because the same relationship, determined by the sense,

---

[1] We may perhaps think of the different characteristics which make up the concept of a genuine choice plant.

[2] cf. *'emūn* in Prov. xiv.5.

[3] *'emūn* appears for this in Prov. xiii.17; and in Prov. xx.6 of a friend.

[4] cf. Zech. viii.3 'city of *'emet*'.

[5] cf. the Aramaic passive participle, in Dan. vi.5.

exists between the qualities demanded by the conception of the subject and those which are actually
present. This and the variability of the content in any
given case comes out with special clarity in Prov. xi.13
where, as contrasted with the slanderer who betrays
secrets, the man is *ne'eman ruaḥ* whose behaviour
corresponds to the meaning of a secret, namely he
keeps it to himself.[1]

These examples throw light also on the religious use
of the verbal stem. The nature of its form makes it
possible, when it is predicated of God, for the rich
abundance of the different manifestations of God's
activity to be summed up in the same term *'mn*. Thus
in Deut. vii.9 the *faithful* God is He who keeps covenant
and *ḥesed* with those who love Him and obey His commandments, He who performs the oath which He
swore to the fathers. In Isa. xlix.7 the word is used to
mean the performance of God's promise to His servant
with reference to his election. The *niph'al* is used to
denote that God's word has come into force, has become actuality, both as a promise (I Kings viii.26;
I Chron. xvii.23 f.; II Chron. i.9, vi.17; Isa. lv.3;
Ps. lxxxix.29) and also as a threat (Hos. v.9)[2]; for it is
part of the nature of a promise or threat that it is
fulfilled. The word is employed, in a similar sense, of
precepts (Ps. cxi.7) and of the law (Ps. xix.8), where
in the parallel phrases *established for ever and ever*, to be
performed with *'emet* and *yōšer*, *the work of his hands are
'emet and mišpāṭ*, or in the series of terms in Ps. xix, we
can see that the concept includes the whole of the
features which are to be expected of the law in order
that it may achieve its purpose as the manifestation of

---

[1] In Job xii.20 *ne'emān* used absolutely denotes the well-trusted,
experienced, true man, paralleled by elders and princes.

[2] In Ps. xciii.5 the *decrees* are probably meant to be understood
as promises and threats.

the divine will for shaping human life. The OT speaks
in the same way of God's *'emet* and *'emūnā*[1]; the basic
meaning here too is the 'essential' = that which makes
God to be God. The more precise definition of its
content which is always in mind at the same time
depends in each individual case on the particular
conception of God or on that aspect of God which
happens to be to the fore. Thus for example in the
phrase *ḥesed we'emet*[2] or *ḥesed we'emūnā*, which became a
fixed liturgical form, the word *ḥesed* (*love, mercy*) provides a more precise definition of its content, whilst
'emet (*'emūnā*) (*faithfulness and constancy in His disposition
and in the expression of His love*) represents the more formal
element.

The *niph'al* is used of the relationship of man to God[3]:
Neh. ix.8 in *thou didst find his* (Abraham's) *heart ne'emān
before thee and didst make with him a covenant*, an allusion
to *he'emīn* in Gen. xv.6; Ps. lxxviii.37 of the Israelites in
the time of Moses *lō' ne'emenū biberītō*, to which the
parallel is *their heart was not steadfast toward him*, alluding
to the covenant relationship; and Ps. lxxviii.8 *lō'
ne'emenū 'et-'ēl rūḥō*, referring to the disobedience towards the commandments. In these passages the idea
of *'mn* expresses the attitude of man towards God which
corresponds to the claim of God in the case concerned;
it denotes not only the correctness of the external behaviour, but just as much the disposition, and it is not
restricted to a single action performed once only, but
applies to the whole of a man's relationship to God.

3. The usage of the verbal adjective *'āmēn* points in
the same direction[4]; by its use in I Kings i.36 to confirm

---

[1] cf. p. 3, n. 1.

[2] cf. A. Weiser, *Die Psalmen* (ATD, [4]1955) 28. For *'emet* cf. the
similar noun *'ōmen* in Isa.xxv.1; probably also in lxv.16.

[3] Hos. xii.1 is uncertain.

[4] Similarly the adverbs *'omnām truly* in II Kings xix.17; Isa.

a royal command; in Num. v.22, Deut. xxvii.15-26,
Jer. xi.5, Neh. v.13 to accept (God's) curse; in Jer.
xxviii.6 after a prediction of restoration; and implies
the wish that these will be fulfilled. In Neh. viii.6;
Ps. xli.13 (Heb. 14), lxxii.18, xxxix.52 (Heb. 53),
cvi.48; I Chron. xvi.36, it is used as a concluding
liturgical formula after a doxology. When in I Kings
i.36 Benaiah replies '*āmēn* to the king's command to
anoint Solomon as king, this implies that Benaiah has
understood the command, agrees with it and desires
that Yahweh may bring the king's word to pass, but
also at the same time expresses his own obligation to
contribute himself all he can to the execution of the
order. Thus in '*āmēn* too the idea is present of the
relationship between the claim made by the saying and
its realisation, an idea which brings out the fact that
all that is involved in the order (or curse, or doxology)
and its consequences are to be realised. This aspect is
still clearly reflected in the LXX, in which '*āmēn* is
translated 14 times by γένοιτο and is transliterated only
3 times as ἀμήν.[1] But beside this objective connexion
between idea and actual fact, we must not overlook the
subjective relation of him who says '*āmēn* to that which
he reinforces with his *Amen*; this includes both the subjective (theoretical) knowledge and recognition, and
also at the same time the practical submission of the

xxxvii.18; Job ix.2, xii.2, xix.4 f., xxxiv.12, xxxvi.4; Ruth iii.12
and '*umnam* in questions *indeed*? Gen. xviii.13, Num. xxii.37,
I Kings viii.27; II Chron. vi.18, Ps. lviii.1 (Heb. 2), and '*omnā*
Gen. xx.12, Josh. vii.20.

[1] (cf. TWNT, I, 340, on ἀμήν in the NT, and Allmen VB, pp.
15 f.) In Jer. xxxv (Heb. and EVV xxviii).6 the LXX reads
ἀληθῶς. In Num. v.22 and Deut. xxvii. 15-26 Symmachus and
Theodotion have the transliteration ἀμήν, probably favoured by
liturgical custom, whilst Aquila prefers an etymological translation,
usually πεπιστωμένως, but in Jer. xxxv (xxviii).6 πιστωθήτω (so
Katz privately).

whole person with his understanding, will and attitude
to the obligations of the command (or curse, or doxology) in question. Thus the term *'mn*, when used in this
form, comprises a double reference: the knowledge and
recognition of the relation between the obligation and
its realisation, and the fact that this obligation with all
its practical consequences is binding on him who says
Amen.

4. With this in mind, the *hiph'il he'emin to believe*,[1]
rendered in the LXX 15 times as πιστεύειν, 5 times as
ἐμπιστεύειν, once as καταπιστεύειν and once as πειθέσθαι,
can be defined (cf. below pp. 55 f.) most simply as 'saying Amen to something with all the consequences for the
subject and the object'. This expresses both that the
objective relation of the idea to the object is recognised
to be an actual one, and also that there is subjective
connexion between the subject holding the idea and
the object of it; thus when combined with the preposition *le* or with *kī* (for) (also *le* with infinitive),[2]
it is rather the action itself which is emphasised, when
combined with the preposition *be* it is the general
attitude.[3] Thus in profane usage *to believe* a word, a
report, a piece of news, means first to be aware of and to
accept as true the thing reported, but at the same time
it includes an attitude appropriate to the thing reported
(Gen. xlv.26, Exod. iv.1, 8 f.,[4] I Kings x.7 = II Chron.
ix.6, Jer. xl.14, Isa. liii.1, Hab. i.5 [Prov. xiv.15],
II Chron. xxxii.15). Whilst in these cases the stress falls
on the single act, the use of *he'emin* towards persons

---

[1] Dan. vi.24 Aramaic *hēmīn*.

[2] The combination with *'et* (not the sign of the accusative but
the preposition *with*) in Judges xi.20 should be translated *to make
an agreement with* . . . = *to permit*; perhaps with the following infinitive construct *le* has dropped out owing to haplography.

[3] In Ps. cvi.24, cf. v.12 (also lxxviii.32), it seems as if this
distinction is no longer made.

[4] Here the profane usage merges into the religious usage.

emphasises rather the basic attitude which is associated in English too with the word 'trust'. Trust with regard to the vassal (I Sam. xxvii.12), the friend (Mic. vii.5, Jer. xii.6), the flatterer (Prov. xxvi.25), the servant (Job iv.18), the holy one (Job xv.15), includes on the one hand the recognition of the claim contained in the name of friend, servant, etc., and on the other hand at the same time also the fact that this claim is binding on the man who himself trusts. Thus it is the reciprocal relationship which makes trust what it really is and not merely a one-sided connexion, that is comprised in the word *he'emin*. Moreover the OT uses it only for a personal relationship; for also behind the word which is trusted there stands the man who is trusted.[1]

The *hiph'il* is employed analogously to express the relationship of man to God. Here too it is not used in a causative sense, but is declarative[2]: it pronounces God to be *ne'eman* or, if we may paraphrase, it says Amen to God. But even this does not embrace the whole of the meaning. Firstly in this sphere of its usage *he'emin* appears as a formal term signifying to recognise and to acknowledge the relationship into which God enters with man, i.e. to put oneself into this relationship. Thus here too the reciprocal relationship between God and man is part of the essence of faith.[3] Moreover it is

---

[1] Of the exceptions, Job xxxix.12: *Do you have faith in the wild ox that he will return?*, the phrase in Deut. xxviii.66 and Job xxiv.22: *to have assurance of life*, the first is probably to be understood as a metaphorical transference of a human relationship, while in the other two passages the negative meaning *there is no assurance of life* demonstrates just the impossiblity of a personal relationship to life. Perhaps too there may be an assimilation of *he'emin* to the originally different meaning of *bṭḥ to be sure* (cf. below, pp. 19 ff.).

[2] cf. Ges.-K §53d. [Ges.-K. actually describes the declarative usage in §53c, and subsequently classifies *he'emin* among internal Hiph'ils, in §53e. Cf. J. Barr, op. cit. on p. xi.]

[3] This meaning suggests the need to consider whether this religious usage has not its linguistic root in the concrete form

such that—even in those cases in which faith indicates
a human activity for which man can be made responsible (the demand for faith)—man is never the one to
initiate this reciprocal relationship. Even in passages
where faith is not expressly mentioned, the assumption
is always present that God is the real originator of the
relationship between God and man.[1] In each individual case the manner in which the content is determined depends on the particular aspect of the reciprocal
relationship which is brought to the fore. When a command, order, or commandment is concerned (Deut.
ix.23, Ps. cxix.66 [II Kings xvii.14[2]]), then faith means
the acknowledgement of the demand and man's
obedience. When attention is concentrated on God's
promise (Gen. xv.6 [Ps. cvi.12]), then *he'emin* expresses the acknowledgement of the promise and of the
power of God to perform it, and includes the honour-
ing of God as the mighty Lord (Num. xx.12).[3] The
two themes of promise and obligation seem to be combined in *he'emin* in Exod. iv.1, 8 f. and in Ps. cvi.24.

But even this does not exhaust the range of the word.
By virtue of its formal nature, *he'emin* possesses further
possibilities of being extended and deepened. These are

given in the *qal* of the relationship between the mother, nurse,
etc. and the child. (cf. above, p. 3).

[1] The fact that the term *'mn* includes a reciprocal relationship
seems to me still to appear in the translation of Ps. xxxi.23 (Heb.
24) where it is difficult to decide between *Yahweh preserves faith*
(LXX, F. Hitzig, *Die Psalmen* (1863), ad loc.; E. König, *Die
Psalmen* [1921], ad loc.) and *Yahweh preserves the faithful* (B. Duhm,
'Die Psalmen' in *Kurzer Hand. Kommentar zum AT*, 14[3] (1922),
ad loc.; R. Kittel, 'Die Psalmen' in *Komm. zum AT*, 13[1,2] (1914),
ad loc.; Kautzsch, ad loc.; H. Gunkel, 'Die Psalmen', in *Göttinger
Hand. Komm. zum AT*, II, 2 [1926], ad loc.), according to whether
the relationship is seen from the point of view of God or of man.

[2] cf. the Qumran Hab. Commentary ii.14 f.

[3] The shade of meaning in the concept of faith when faced with
God's wondrous deeds in Ps. lxxviii.32.

specially directed towards including the whole relationship between God and man (Exod. xiv.31, xix.9; Num. xiv.11; Deut. i.32; Ps. lxxviii.22; perhaps already in Gen. xv.6).[1] When it is God who is in view, then all those characteristics are included which just make God to be God, and one who wishes to establish a relationship with Man: His might, His power to work miracles, His purpose in choosing His people, His disposition to love, the constancy and fidelity of His conduct, the realisation of His word and His plan, His demands, His justice; for *hesed, mišpāṭ* and *ṣ^edēqā* are in fact frequently used in the OT to characterise the divine *'^emet* more precisely. Accordingly the OT religious usage of *he'^emīn* suggests the meaning of 'to take God as God with complete seriousness', and thus includes as an essential factor the exclusiveness of the divine relationship. This can also be perceived from the fact that in the language of the OT 'not to believe' is often the equivalent of 'to become an apostate' (*pš^'*).[2] Since the idea of apostasy is derived from the OT ideology of the covenant and is significant only in this context, it is already apparent that the setting and origin of the religious usage of the stem *'mn* is to be sought in the OT tradition of the sacral covenant of Yahweh. Corresponding to the extensive exclusiveness there is an intensive one in so far as the term *'mn* sums up all the ways by which men express in their lives their relationship to God. Thus *he'^emīn* is used with different shades of meaning. In Isa. xliii.10, when paralleled by *yd'* (*know*) and *bīn* (*understand*) *that they may believe that before me no god was formed nor shall there by any after me*, the relation-

---

[1] In Jonah iii.5 the heathens' faith in God (Yahweh) too must be understood to mean the whole of their religion (cf. faith in the *divine covenant* Hab. Comm. ii.4).

[2] cf. Deut. xxxii.20, where *children in whom is no 'ēmūn* has idolatry as its parallel.

ship to God is emphasised from the point of view of
knowing him. In Hos. iv.1, in addition to knowledge, a
strong element of emotion appears in the triad *da'at*
'elōhīm, 'emet, ḥesed. The aspect of the will is already
prominent in those passages already cited in which
belief is to be understood as indicating obedience. In
Exod. xiv.31, Jos. xxiv.14, II Chron. xix.9, Ps. lxxxvi.11
the impulse of fear is associated with the idea of faith.[1]
Similarly the fact that, in behaviour and disposition,
the relationship to God excludes all others, is shown by
the expression used in Hos. x.2 to describe the attitude
which is the opposite of faith: *ḥālaq lēb* (probably = *to
have a divided heart*), whilst conversely the phrase *with
all your heart and with all your soul*, of which Deuteronomy
is particularly fond (cf. Deut. vi.5 *et passim*), leaves no
doubt how the OT wishes the attitude of faith to be
understood. Moreover the fact that both extensive and
intensive exclusiveness is a basic quality of the relationship of faith in the OT, is made clear in the passages in
which it is defined more precisely with *šālēm* (*undivided* =
to surrender oneself completely)[2] for here the *complete
loyalty of faith* is expressed by *to follow Yahweh fully*[3] or
to be blameless before Yahweh.[4] In all these passages there
is evident a real understanding of what is meant in the
OT by faith, which exhibits the course which the use
of *hè'emīn* has followed: a relationship to God which

[1] Isa. viii.13 *Yahweh Sabaoth, him you shall regard as holy, let him be
your dread* should also be mentioned in this connexion in addition
to the prophet's demand for faith. Cf. Ps. lxxviii.22 with vv. 32 ff.

[2] cf. I Kings viii.61, xi.4, xv.3, 14; II Chron. xvi.9 (with *'el*).
Cf. also II Kings xx.3; Isa. xxxviii.3; II Chron. xix.9 in each case
paralleled with *'emet, 'emūnā*; I Chron. xxviii.9, xxix.9 (19);
II Chron. xv.17, xxv.2; frequently directed against idolatry.

[3] *millē' 'aḥᵃrē yhwh* Num. xiv.24, xxxii.11; Deut. i.36; I Kings xi.6.

[4] *tāmīm 'im yhwh* Deut. xviii.13, Ps. xviii.24 = II Sam. xxii.24
(with *lᵉ* here); as a noun parallel with *'emet* in Josh. xxiv.14,
cf. I Kings ix.4.

embraces the whole man in every part of his outward behaviour and his inner life. Hence also *he'ᵉmīn* is nowhere used for the relationship with other gods, whilst *bṭḥ* and *ḥsh* are employed without hesitation in reference to idols also. This is intelligible; for only in a religion directed towards monotheism, such as the OT conception of the Yahweh covenant, is the idea of the reciprocal relationship between God and man possible with that comprehensive depth of meaning which we can discover in the usage of *he'ᵉmīn*.

It is the absolute use of *he'ᵉmīn* which exhibits its most significant development and intensification. It does so in the form which goes back to Isaiah.[1] It is the problem of how existence is possible, the question of faith and being, which is the centre of Isaiah's interest. The idea of the remnant, the hope for Zion, the founding of a religious community among his disciples—all this must probably be understood with this problem in mind and is most closely associated with the prophet's general conception of faith. This in its turn goes back to his personal encounter with God which took place within the framework of the cultic tradition (vi.1 ff.). The fact that faith is marked off from political considerations (vii.1 ff.[2]), from protection against dangers

---

[1] Ps. cxvi.10 may be connected with Isaiah's conception of faith. The profane usage in Job xxix.24 does not admit a similar view. The absolute usage of *he'ᵉmīn* in Isaiah has been disputed by J. Boehm, 'Der Glaube und Js.', ZAW (1923), pp. 84-93, but this view has rightly found no acceptance.

[2] This is not the place to enter into the much discussed question of the 'prophet and politics'; cf. on this in addition to the commentaries (in particular O. Procksch, *Js.*, Vol. I (Komm. AT 9), (1930), pp. 10-17; V. Herntrich, *Der Prophet Js.* (ATD 17²) (1954), pp. 11 f., 118-22); J. Hempel, 'Chronik', ZAW, 49 (1931), pp. 152 f.; F. Weinrich, *Der religiös-utopische Charakter der prophetischen Politik* (=Aus der Welt der Religion, Bibl. Reihe, Heft 7) (1932); K. Elliger, 'Prophet und Politik', ZAW, 53 (1935), pp. 3-22; J. Hempel, *Gott und Mensch im AT* (²1936), pp. 321 f.; K. Elliger,

(xxviii.14 ff.) and from reliance on human strength (xxx.15 ff.), shows, as well as the absolute use of *he'ᵉmîn*, that for Isaiah faith means an altogether special form of existence for those dependent on God alone, which becomes effective like the *might of a hero* (*gᵉbūrā*, xxx.15) and forms the foundation laid by God for the divine community[1] (xxxviii.16). In fact faith and existence are identical for Isaiah. In the well-known saying in Isa. vii.9 *'îm lō' ta'ᵃmînū kî lō' tē'āmēnū to be established*, referring to the whole of a man's life (cf. pp. 5 f.), is thought to be not just the reward of faith, so that faith would be the prerequisite of life, but—since *kî* (surely) must be understood as both demonstrative and explicative—it expresses by this phrase that faith and *to be established* (i.e. existence) are identical. If couched in positive terms the meaning of the saying would be: the people of God have their particular manner of being and are established through their faith.[2] This

'Nochmals "Prophet und Politik" ', ZAW, 55 (1937), pp. 291-6. with an addendum by J. Hempel; H. J. Kraus, 'Prophetie und Politik', *Theol. Existenz heute*, NF. 36 (1952); E. Würthwein, 'Js. vii.1-9. Ein Beitrag zu dem Thema "Prophetie und Politik" ', *Festschrift für K. Heim* (1954), pp. 47-63. G. von Rad, *Der heilige Krieg im alten Israel* (1952), pp. 56-61, attempts to explain Isa. vii.1 ff., xxx.15 ff., xxxi.1 ff. as a vivid presentation of the early sacral ordinances of the Holy War in which he seeks the origin of the OT faith and its Sitz im Leben (cf. p. 31), but he does not do justice to the breadth of the OT conception of faith (cf. A. Weiser, review in *Für Arbeit und Besinnung*, 7 [1953], pp. 158-60).

[1] The late Jewish interpretation of the *corner-stone* as the Messiah (cf. TWNT, IV, 276) which is found in Tg Jonathan and Rashi and was accepted by F. Delitzsch, *Komm. uber das Buch Js.* (⁴1889), p. 316, and by O. Procksch, *Js.*, Vol. I (Komm. AT 9) (1930), p. 358, cannot be inferred directly from the text itself. In I Pet. ii.6 f., Isa. xxviii.16, together with Ps. cxviii.22, is applied to Christ as the corner-stone of the primitive community (cf. TWNT, VI, p. 97).

[2] Procksch does not make this quite clear in *Theologie des AT* (1950), p. 181, when he defines faith as 'the condition of existence'.

and his refusal to fear (vii.1 ff.) and to trust in any way the might of men (xxx.15 f.) which after all is transient, as well as the inclusion of the fear of Yahweh alone in the relationship of faith, shows in addition that for Isaiah faith is the only possible mode of existence, and that this utterly excludes every other independent attitude for man or any obligation towards any one other than God. For Isaiah, the only thing which matters, whatever happens or is experienced, is Yahweh, His plan and His will and the appropriate attitude of man. From this derives the exclusive character of the relationship of faith in its external aspect. So too there is perfected the inner experience of this exclusive relationship by the intimate linking of faith and existence. There can thus be no further deepening of the meaning of this word. From this point of view too Isaiah deserves to be called the prophet of faith; for he has played a decisive part in giving the ultimate depth of meaning to the content of this word, as well as causing it to influence the further development of linguistic usage.

5. A short survey of the further development of the religious use of 'mn and its derivatives will show this. The crucial emphasis which Isaiah gave to this word and concept never dropped out of the later history of its usage. This is the main source of the strong qualitative influence of the meaning of he'emīn on the other roots used in the language of religion for the attitude of man towards God. Although the use of 'mn is of less account, so far as mere numbers are concerned, the meaning of the roots bṭḥ, ḥsh, qwh, yḥl, ḥkh, originally very limited, merged into the sense of he'emīn to express the exclusive relationship of a personal nature between man and God (cf. p. 19 ff.). Where the word itself is used, there is no mistaking the tendency to stretch it to include the most comprehensive range of meaning,

just as *'ᵉmūnā* too embraces the whole attitude to life
resulting from faith (Hab. ii.4,[1] II Chron. xix.9, Jer.
vii.28 [v.3]).[2] Finally *'ᵉmet*, corresponding to *'ᵉlōhē
'ᵉmet*='the true God' (II Chron. xv.3), comes to denote
true religion altogether (Dan. viii.12, ix.13, x.21)[3] and
thereby finally the idea of exclusiveness issues in a claim
to be absolute.

6. One question remains to be answered. Whence
came that strong religious impulse which by means of
the stem *'mn* gave expression to the peculiarity of OT
religion at its various stages? It seems to be connected
from the beginning most closely with the particular
character of the religious set-up and of the development
of thought in the Israelite religion of Yahweh. In the
'Succession History of David', written by a contemporary, the old saying has been handed down in
II Sam. xx.18 f.[4]: *Let them but ask at Abel and Dan
whether what the 'ᵉmūnē yisrā'ēl ordained has fallen into disuse.*
The intention is to reproach Joab with wishing to
destroy the 'heritage of Yahweh' by laying siege to Abel.
The fact that in this passage the designation the *faithful
ones of Israel* has been preserved in an old proverb and is
brought into a pertinent connexion with the religious
and dogmatic concept of the 'heritage of Yahweh'
suggests the conclusion that the original home of this

[1] In the original prophecy in Hab. ii.9 (see BH) *the righteous*
means the congregation. It was only by the change of the prophecy into a proverb, which occurred already in OT times, that
the particular interpretation 'a pious individual' arose. It is this
which underlies Paul's quotation in Rom. i.17 (cf. *Righteousness* in
this series, pp. 46 ff.), Gal. iii.11 (ibid., p. 24, 62). The LXX
ὁ δὲ δίκαιος ἐκ πίστεώς μου ζήσεται presupposes *be'ᵉmūnātī*, i.e.
God's faithfulness to his covenant, and by this change-over to the
theocentric outlook the word is given another meaning.

[2] On *'ēmūn* in this sense cf. Deut. xxvii.20.

[3] Similarly perhaps in Ps. xxv.5, xxvi.3, lxxxvi.11.

[4] According to the LXX which has preserved a better text here.

old usage of '*mn* was in the association of the Yahweh Covenant and its sacral tradition. Thus from the beginning the particular way in which the Israelites developed the Yahweh religion seems to have shaped the religious tone given to the term '*mn* in the OT. It is true that in the ordinary usage the more general term *bᵉrît* prevailed to denote the special relationship between Yahweh and Israel,[1] and not until Neh. ix.38 (x.1 in Heb.) is '*ᵃmānā* used to describe the declaration by which the covenant was renewed in the religious reform of Nehemiah.[2] But the fact that the majority of the passages in which the OT uses *heᵉᵉmîn* refer to the relationship to God of the Mosaic period (Exod. iv.8 f., xiv.31, xix.9; Num. xiv.11, xx.12; Deut. i.32, ix.23; II Kings xvii.14; Ps. lxxviii.22, 23, cvi.12, 24) after all shows clearly enough the close connexion between the special meaning of the term '*mn* and the sacral tradition concerning the beginnings of the Yahweh religion in Israel. The OT saw in the relationship described by *heᵉᵉmîn* the special religious attitude of the people of God to Yahweh.[3] This is all the more significant since this attitude provides the pattern according to which the OT religion was again and again regenerated and developed.

C. *The root bṭḥ*

1. In the case of *bṭḥ*, which the LXX translates mainly with πεποιθέναι and ἐλπίζειν, the position is the reverse of that of *heᵉᵉmîn*. The English 'to trust' is richer in meaning than the original meaning of the root. The

---

[1] On the 'covenant' cf. TWNT, II, pp. 120 ff., J. Pedersen, *Israel*, I-II (1926), pp. 263-310.

[2] cf. the use of '*ᵉmūnā* for the duties of those entrusted with the service of the temple cult in I Chron. ix.22, 26, 31.

[3] The use of *heᵉᵉmîn* in Gen. xv.6 does not contradict this, for in the perfect type of Abraham who believed, the author has given us a sketch of his own ideas of faith from the post-Mosaic time.

basic significance can still be recognised clearly in its
absolute use, especially in the early passage in Judges
xviii.7, 27, where *bōṭēaḥ* (*unsuspecting*) is explained by
šōqēṭ (*quiet*) and in v. 7 by *yōšebet lābeṭaḥ* (*dwelling in
security*) (LXX: ἡσυχάζειν); thus *bṭḥ* means *to be in a
state of security* (*beṭaḥ*). We find that in Judges xviii and
in Prov. xi.15 (LXX ἀσφάλεια) (Job xl.23) the objective
state is emphasised, whilst in Isa. xxxii.9-11, xii.21;
Jer. xii.5; Ps. xxvii.3; Prov. xiv.16, xxviii.1; Job vi.20,
xi.18 the subjective feeling of security, usually contrasted with fear, is emphasised.[1] As contrasted with
he'ᵉmīn, *bṭḥ* expresses, even when the means or the
author of the security is added with the prepositions
bᵉ, *'al* or *'el*, not a relationship but the condition,
corresponding perhaps most nearly to the translation:
to feel secure by reason of . . . (or *to base one's security on . . .*).
This is evident from passages where *bṭḥ* is used of confidence in a man's own resources (Ps. xlix.6 [Heb. 7],
Prov. xxviii.26), his own achievement (Hab. ii.18,
Jer. xlviii.7), his own righteousness (Ezek. xxxiii.13)
or in reference to such things as ambushes (Judges
xx.36), chariots (Hos. x.13 [LXXA], Isa. xxxi.1), cities
(Amos vi.1; Jer. v.17), walls (Deut. xxviii.52), bows
(Ps. xliv.6 [Heb. 7]), riches (Jer. xlix.4, Ps. lii.7 [Heb. 9];
Prov. xi.28), beauty (Ezek. xvi.15), oppression (Isa.
xxx.12, Ps. lxii.10 [Heb. 11]), wickedness (Isa. xlviii.
10), and where there can be no question of a reciprocal
relationship as in the case of *'mn*. Even where the word
is connected with persons, it appears from some earlier
passages, especially where it is used with *'al* (II Kings

---

[1] Similarly *mibṭāḥ* = 'basis, originator of security' (in the LXX
9 times ἐλπίς 3 times πεποιθέναι) especially in Isa. xxxii.18; Prov.
xiv.26; *kesel* = confidence Ps. xlix.13 (Heb. 14) (LXX has
σκάνδαλον); Job xxxi.24, viii.14 (*kislā* Job iv.6; LXX ἀφροσύνη);
in ritual language it has still preserved its original meaning = 'loins'
in Lev. iii.4, 10, 15 *et passim*.

xviii.20, 24) and with the ethical dative (II Kings xviii.21, 24 [Jer. vii.4, 8]), that here a subjective feeling of safety attributed to the individual must be distinguished from the concepts of relationship described by 'mn. The passive participle *bāṭūaḥ b*ᵉ*yhwh* too, *made safe by Yahweh* (Ps. cxii.7, Isa. xxvi.3) as well as the *hiph'il*: *Do not let Hezekiah make you rely on* ('el) *Yahweh* (II Kings xviii.30[1]) shows the same meaning of the stem. To this must be added the frequent use of the word in a derogatory sense in the prophets in order to express and to attack man's self-reliance (of the 30 cases in which *bṭḥ* is used of things, 20 are found in the prophetic writings; as many as 11 in Jeremiah, yet only once with a positive meaning, in xxxix.18). The fact that 'mn can never denote confidence in idols, whilst *bṭḥ* does so without hesitation (Isa. xlii.17, Jer. xlvi.25), may provide evidence for the difference between the meaning and use of *bṭḥ* and that of 'mn.[2]

2. Yet beside the use of *bṭḥ* meaning *to feel oneself secure* we may note an extension of meaning in its religious usage, namely in the direction of assimilating it to that of *he'*ᵉ*mīn* (Jer. xxxix.18, Zeph. iii.2 (Mic. ii.5)). This occurs especially often in Deuteronomy, where no difference is any longer made between *bṭḥ* and *he'*ᵉ*mīn*. In later additions to the prophetic literature also, *bṭḥ* has acquired the meaning of a term for relationship, even where occasionally the original meaning of the objective feeling of security is still dimly visible (Isa. i.10, Jer. xlvi.25[3]). This process goes so far that—above all in the Wisdom literature and in the Psalms—

[1] cf. Ps. xxii.9 (Heb. 10).

[2] Parallel with this *smk = to be stayed on*, in the passive participle of the *qal* in Isa. xxvi.3, Ps. cxii.8; in the *niph'al* in Ps. lxxi.6 (Isa. xlviii.2); the *niph'al* of *š*ᵉ*n* in profane usage in Isa. xxx.12, xxxi.1; Job viii.15, and in religious usage in Isa. i.10 (II Chron. xiii.18, xiv.11 [Heb. 10], xvi.7 f.; Mic. iii.11).

[3] Here the translation *to rely on* would really be most appropriate.

bṭḥ meaning *he'᾽emīn* has almost completely ousted the latter. Thus for example in Prov. iii.5 *trust* in Yahweh *with all your heart* is spoken of just as though it were faith. In Ps. lxxviii.22, xxxvii.3 *bṭḥ* and *he'᾽emīn* (*'᾽emūnā*) are used in parallel. In Ps. xl.3 (Heb. 4), lvi.4, xxvi.1, 3 fear is also included in the whole relationship to God. Further in those cases in which there is no direct parallel to *he'᾽emīn*, *bṭḥ* is used quite commonly for the *pious man* generally (Prov. xvi.20, xxviii.25, xxix.25; Ps. xxxii.10, cxxv.1; Jer. xvii.7); often also in the well-worn form for the attitude of prayer in liturgical opening and closing formulae (Ps. xci.2, lxxxiv.12 [Heb. 13], xxv.2, xxxi.6 [Heb. 7], *et passim*). The development of the usage here follows a line similar to that of *'mn*.

3. Since the development of the meaning of *'mn* took place without a change in its basic sense, the alteration of meaning of *bṭḥ* when compared with it requires an explanation. In general terms the following factors may be regarded as effective forces in the linguistic transformation: the evolution of the monotheistic faith in Yahweh in the tradition of the Yahweh cult, an evolution which asserted itself more and more definitely in its struggle with alien religions, the influence of the prophets and the pressure of history, the religious situation during the exile and political impotence also in the post-exilic period, the growing feeling of *being cast on God* (for this expression see Ps. xxii.10 [Heb. 11]), which seeks and finds its security in God alone. Besides these we may note the development of religious individualism, through which, in connexion with the transformation of the nation into a religious community, the piety of the laity called forth by the prophetic movement gains more and more ground. Moreover a decisive turning point in the use of *bṭḥ* for the whole attitude to faith may be fixed even more precisely. It arises from the influence of Isaiah on the shaping of

religious language, which can be illustrated from the significant passage in Isa. xxx.15. Isaiah too is well aware of the use of *bṭḥ* in the sense of man-made objective security (xxx.12, xxxi.1, xxxii.9 ff.), which he attacks; but in xxx.15 he employs the verbal stem with a positive meaning: *In returning (šūbā) and rest (naḥat) you shall be saved, in quietness (hašqēṭ) and trust (biṭḥā) shall be your strength (gᵉbūrā)*. The fact that Isaiah does not choose a form of the verb *bṭḥ* but creates two fresh formations, *biṭḥā* and *šūbā*[1] perhaps reveals his intention of distinguishing this word clearly from the meaning which he has rejected in other passages. In any case we can see here clearly his struggle to find language in which to express a content which represents something new as compared with the previous meaning of *bṭḥ*. It is true that in this passage too the old meaning of *feeling secure* can still be detected, but both *šūbā (returning)* and *gᵉbūratkem (your strength)* enable us to see beneath them the concept of faith of Isa. vii.9, xxviii.16, and what follows—*And you would not, and you said 'No. We will speed upon horses'*—shows clearly that *strength* here does not mean their own strength, but that which issues from the relationship with God (*biṭḥā*). At this point we can put our finger directly on the change of meaning: Isaiah filled the verbal stem with the content of his own concept of faith and by his creative action here too, as in the case of *'mn*, gave a fresh stimulus to the development of the verbal usage.

D. *The root ḥsh*

1. *Ḥsh to seek (find) refuge, to make oneself safe*[2] (the

---

[1] Both these formations occur only here in the OT. [Ed. It must, however, be observed that an argument based on hapax-legomena is never entirely satisfactory.]

[2] cf. *refuge ḥāsūt* in Isa. xxx.3; *maḥᵃseh* in Ps. civ.18; Job xxiv.8; Isa xxviii.15 in profane use (LXX καταφυγή, σκέπη, ἐλπίς); used of

Accadian *ḥisu* has the same meaning; in the LXX 20 times ἐλπίζειν, 9 times πεποιθέναι, 3 times εὐλαβεῖσθαι twice σκεπάζειν, once each σῴζειν and ἀντέχειν) shows a development similar to that of *bṭḥ*. It belongs to a somewhat more elevated style and compared with *bṭḥ* its original range of meaning is rather more restricted. For whilst *bṭḥ* can also mean self-reliance, based on one's own strength (cf. p. 20), *ḥsh* presupposes rather being dependent on protection and in need of help. The poetic root-meaning can still be seen in the use of the word in the simile of the tree in the shadow of which one *takes refuge* (Judges ix.15, Isa. xxx.2) *to take refuge in the protection of Egypt*; or in the simile of a bird with outstretched wings *under whose wings one takes refuge* (Ruth ii.12; Ps. xxxvi.7 [Heb. 8], lxi.4 [Heb. 5], xci.4). Moreover the second simile is found applied only to Yahweh. The primary meaning here too is not to be thought of as a reciprocal relationship between the one who seeks and the one who bestows protection, but the objective state of being protected or the action which seeks to reach such a condition. This is just as evident from its connexion with *taḥat* (*under*) (Ruth ii.12, Ps. xci.4), as from the phrase *finds refuge through his integrity* (Prov. xiv.32).[1] Like *bṭḥ* (cf. p. 21) *ḥsh* can also be applied to gods (Deut. xxxii.37).

2. As an expression for the relationship with Yahweh, *ḥsh* has also often still preserved the colouring of its original meaning, especially in the Psalms where the worshipper in all kinds of temptation and danger seeks his God (Ps. lvii.1 [Heb. 2], xci.4, xxv.20, lxi.4 [Heb. 5] *et passim*). But often—and this suggests the comparison with *bṭḥ*—especially in the opening and closing for-

Yahweh in Ps. xlvi.1 (Heb. 2), lxi.4, xc.9 *et passim* (LXX καταφυγή, ἐλπίς).

[1] Read with the LXX Syr *bᵉtummō* instead of *bᵉmōtō* (in his *death.*

mulae of the liturgy, the word has become hackneyed in use and its meaning has been extended to the whole relationship to God (Ps. vii.1 [Heb. 2], xvi.1, xviii.2 [Heb. 3], xxv.20, xxxi.2, ii.11 [Heb. 12], v.11 [Heb. 12], xxxiv.22 [Heb. 23]). It is used in parallel with *bṭḥ* in Ps. cxviii.8 f. [cf. xxv.2 and 20] and parallel to *fearing God* in xxxi.19 [Heb. 20]). The final stage of this linguistic development seems to be the absolute of the *qal* participle *hōsīm* meaning *the godly* (Ps. xvii.7[1]). The same tendency is seen in the extension of the meaning of *maḥseh* which was used originally of the *security*, of the *place* and the *giver of protection* in Ps. lxii.7 (Heb. 8), xciv.22; in lxxiii.28 *I have made Yahweh my refuge* is paralleled with *being near God* and is applied to the actual relationship to God. The depth of meaning in the word here does not fall short of Isaiah's concept of faith (cf. p. 28.)[2]

E.   *The roots qwh, yḥl, ḥkh*

An essential part of the OT attitude of faith, namely that part of it which looks toward the future, could not

---

[1] Yet the LXX adds ἐπί σέ.

[2] In a certain sense the development of the verbs *drš* and *bqš* (*to seek*) might be compared. They were originally restricted to religious usage in questions addressed to the divine oracle (Gen. xxv.22; I Sam. ix.9; I Kings xxii.8; II Kings xxii.13, 18; (to Baal) II Kings i.2 f., 6, 16; to a soothsayer in I Sam. xxviii.7; to the dead in Isa. viii.19, Deut. xviii.11), and also to seeking the face of the deity in the cult (II Sam. xxi.1; Ps. xxiv.6, xxvii.8, cv.4; Hos. v.[6], 15 [II Sam. xii.16, Zeph. i.6]), and finally as the expression of the whole relationship to God including its inward aspects, e.g. Amos v.4, Deut. iv.29 *to seek with all your heart and with all your soul*; similarly Jer. xxix.13; then as a participle frequently describing the godly generally, e.g. Ps. ix.10 (Heb. 11), xl.16 (Heb. 17), lxix.6 (Heb. 7) *et passim*. The fact that the prophets rejected the externalised worship of the cult and made the relationship with God deeper and more spiritual seems here too to have been the decisive factor in this change of meaning.

be appreciated if the stems of the verbs of hope[1] were not taken into account. They must be brought into the investigation of faith for another reason also, namely that in later times they are used in the OT in exactly the same sense as the verbs of believing. In spite of the fact that the basic meaning of the individual stems is different, a common treatment of this group of words is justified because the development through which they passed was similar, and also because the three stems often appear simply as alternatives. This is brought out by their being translated with the same words expressing *hope, waiting for*.

1. The basic meaning of these words is the concrete condition of tension. *qwh*, of which the stem is attested with the same meaning in Accadian, Arabic and Syriac and which has preserved its original meaning most clearly in *qaw, a measuring line*, and in *tiqwā* (Joshua ii.18, 21), *a twisted cord*, means in the first instance *to be stretched*. *yhl* seems to be connected with *ḥil to be in labour, to give birth to*.[2] This would also explain the stronger expression of feeling which is still noticeable in the later use of this verb; the basic meaning is *the state of painful expectation*. *ḥkh* seems to have preserved its fundamental sense most clearly in II Kings ix.3 where it means *to restrain oneself, to hesitate*, and probably also in Hos. vi.9 to express *tense lying in wait* (in a hostile sense).

In profane usage the original meaning also still shows through; thus *qwh* is used in Job vii.2 of the workman *who looks for his wage* or in Ps. lvi.6 (Heb. 7), cxix.95

---

[1] cf. *Hope* (ἐλπίς), to be published shortly in this series.

[2] Grammatically this may be a case of the tendency in the imperative and infinitive of the verbs beginning with *y* to represent an enlargement of the stems with two radicals into stems of three radicals. For this tendency cf. G. Beer, *Hebr. Grammatik*, II (1921), p. 42.

they *lie in wait to destroy me*. The painful undertone of waiting can still be heard in *yhl* in I Sam. xiii.8 where we are told that Saul *waited* seven days in vain for Samuel, or in the saying of Job xiv.14 *I would wait all the days of my service*. In each of these cases the subjective condition of waiting stands in the forefront of the meaning. Both of these last-named stems have their original meaning expanded, especially in Proverbs and Job where they are often used with the general sense of *vital hope (vital energy)*, and this usage reveals clearly the influence of reflexion on the concept (*qwh*: Job iii.9, xxx.26[1]; *yhl*: Job vi.11, xiii.15, xxx.26[2]).

2. In religious usage the verbs of hope are found first as the expression of the tension of looking to a definite goal, and in fact when used collectively of the godly usually with reference to the hope of salvation, frequently in the metaphorical phrase *hoping for light*: *qwh* in Jer. viii.15, xiii.16; Isa. lix.9, 11, lxiv.3 (Heb. 2); in Jer. xiv.19 paralleled with *ḥkh*; *yhl* in Ezek. xiii.6; *ḥkh* in Zeph. iii.8; Ps. cvi.13. In the case of individual godly men, it means hope for divine help in any kind of trouble, in prayers with reference to waiting to be heard, thus especially in Ps. cxix.81: of the hope of God's salvation; in vv. 74, 114, 147: of hope in God's word; in v. 43, in God's ordinances; in Ps. xxxiii.18, of His love. In the case of *qwh*, although Yahweh himself is named everywhere as the object of hope, yet sometimes a quite definite expectation lies behind this *hope in Yahweh*. Thus in Prov. xx.22 the hope for help, in Ps. xl.1 (Heb. 2) for prayer to be heard. It is probably the same in Ps. cxxx.5 as a parallel to *yhl* and in Ps. xxxiii.20

---

[1] cf. the abstract feminine formation *tiqwāh* with the same meaning in Prov. xxiii.18, xxiv.14, xxvi.12, xxix.20; Job v.16, viii.13, xi.18, 20, xiv.7, xvii.15, xix.10, xxvii.8; *miqweh* I Chron. xxix.15.

[2] cf. *tōḥelet* as a parallel to *tiqwāh* in Prov. x.28, xi.7.

where the three verbal stems *ḥkh*, *bṭḥ* and *yḥl* are used side by side in a similar sense.[1] The last-named passages do indeed show a usage, namely the waiting for God himself, which cannot be simply regarded as a direct transference of the basic meaning to the religious sphere. The root of this linguistic form, which occurs most commonly in the Psalms, may perhaps have lain in the expectation of a theophany, perhaps during the cult, perhaps in world events, as announced particularly by the prophets. From there the usage may have passed through Deutero-Isaiah[2] to that eschatological use which we meet in later Judaism and which is found in Dan. xii.12 *Blessed is he who waits . . . to the end of the days* (*ḥkh* Theod. ὑπομένειν cf. Matt. x.22, xxiv.13; Mark xiii.13). And in all passages in which hope in God includes a definite goal, the pronounced this-worldly character of OT piety with its particularly intense interest in the visible appearance of the divine rule, would seem to express itself in the form of a theophany of the kind already mentioned.

3. But besides this, yet another development emerges which has transformed *hope for God* into a distinct expression of faith as a general relationship to God. In fact, here too, as in the case of *'mn* (cf. pp. 15 ff.) and *bṭḥ* (cf. pp. 22 f.), it is Isaiah in whose writings there becomes apparent the decisive change of meaning in the verbs of hope towards their final depth of meaning in the OT. Isa. viii.17 shows us the prophet in an attitude of faith before the hidden God: *I will wait* (*ḥkh*) *for Yahweh who is hiding his face from the house of*

[1] The verb *šbr* is also used similarly (*qal* = *examine carefully* in Neh. ii.13, 15) in the *pi'el* = *hope* in Ps. civ.27, cxlv.15 in the sense of waiting on God as the giver of food, in Ps. cxix.166 of hope for help, in Isa. xxxviii.18 for hope of God's *'emet*; cf. the noun *śēber hope* for God's help, in Ps. cxlvi.5.

[2] Isa. li.5 *the isles* (RSV *coastlands*) *wait for me* (*qwh*) (lx.9); xlii.4 (*yḥl*) seems to mean 'waiting for the manifestation of God'.

Jacob and I will hope in him (*qwh*). The change we find here becomes plain when it is contrasted with II Kings vi.33. Here the king (Joram?) says to Elisha with regard to the famine in Samaria: *This trouble is from Yahweh! Why should I wait for Yahweh any longer* (*yhl*)? The difference is evident: the moment in which the king gives up hoping for Yahweh becomes for Isaiah the very moment in which he dares to 'hope' more than ever. The judgement and anger of God did not, it seems, interrupt for him the relationship with God which had existed up till then. Isaiah's faith continues to endure, but it endures—and this is the new factor in his realisation of faith in which the original meaning of *qwh* and *ḥkh* still shows through—in a tension, in a state when the strength of his faith is strained to the utmost, in the background of which the tension between fear and hope can be felt. This waiting and hoping is a faith which does not see and yet believes. The tension in the soul of the prophet, expressed in the basic meaning of the words *qwh* and *ḥkh*, springs from his knowledge of the tremendous daring of such a faith in view of his desperate external situation. It is not resignation with the faint ray of hope of a 'perhaps', but the heightened strength of a 'nevertheless', achieved after the ultimate struggle for certainty, that lies embedded in this 'tension' of faith.

No one understood the real depths of these struggles of Isaiah for faith better than Deutero-Isaiah, to whom we owe in Isa. xl.31 the classical formulation of the OT hope of faith. His conception is born out of a similar spiritual situation and points in the same direction: he too is concerned with the hidden God. Under the influence of their downfall in the exile, the people believe themselves to be forsaken by God (xl.27): *My way is hid from Yahweh and my right is disregarded by my God*. Deutero-Isaiah snatches these weary souls—and

in this we see the same 'nevertheless' as in Isaiah—
from the brink of their despair by pointing to just this
hidden God, to his unfathomable wisdom and his in-
exhaustible strength which he grants precisely to the
helpless (vv. 28 f.). It is in this situation that he coins
the saying *they who wait (qwh) for Yahweh shall renew*[1]
their strength (v. 31). Here the 'hope in Yahweh' is
recognised to be a new kind of existence and vital
energy, a superhuman miraculous power which makes
possible the impossible: the youths may be weary and
faint and the young men may break down (v. 30, note
the stylistic hyperbole!). He who waits for Yahweh
can run and not grow weary. Here is expressed clearly
the difference between physical life-force and the vital
energy of faith as a (spiritual) force of a different kind,
which confesses God in the face of all appearances and
in this relationship with God overcomes all temptations
and weakness. Deutero-Isaiah too knows this further
truth and thereby associates himself most closely with
Isaiah's conception of faith (cf. xxviii.16) that it is God
himself who bestows on man such strength through
faith (cf. xl.29). The whole of Deutero-Isaiah's prophecy, including the song in chapter liii, is the living
proof of the victorious power of the strength of faith,
which overcomes in man's soul the most dire mis-
fortunes of this life on earth and even death itself, because its roots lie in another, transcendent world.

4. An extension and intensification of the verbs of
hope in the direction indicated by its use by the two
Isaiahs can be observed also in later passages and
especially in the Psalms. In addition to the usage
already mentioned in the sense of hope for particular
aid or for answer to prayer and beside the strong
emotional tinge of longing, the word 'to hope' is em-

---

[1] *ḥlp pi'el* and *hiph'il = replace, change* (of clothing) in Gen. xli.14,
II Sam. xii.20.

ployed especially in the Psalms for the whole position with regard to man's relationship with God in general, as e.g. Ps. xlii.5 (Heb. 6), 11 (Heb. 12), xliii.5: *Hope (yhl) in God, for I shall again praise him, that he is the help of my countenance* (see BH) *and my God* (cf. Ps. cxxx.5 f.). In the course of this development the verbal stems of hope are used as synonyms of *bṭḥ* (Ps. xxv.3, 5, cf. v. 2, xxxiii.21 f.),[1] of *ḥsh* (Ps. xxv.21 cf. v. 20), and of *yr'* (*to fear*, cf. v. 14; xxxiii.22 cf. v. 8), without the possibility of establishing any difference in meaning. The apparently almost playful ringing of the changes in Ps. cxix[2] on the most varied verbs for the relationship to God is probably the clearest evidence for the fact that the linguistic usage in the OT flows through the most diverse tributaries into one main stream. What has been observed already in the case of the other verbal stems is confirmed also in the verbs of hoping, namely that at last they become stereotyped formulae and describe the attitude of the godly worshipper—especially in liturgical forms in Isa. xxxiii.2: *qwh*; in Ps. xxxiii.22, cxix.147: *yhl*; in Isa. xxx.18; Ps. xxxiii.20 *ḥkh*—or denote the godly in general as contrasted with the wicked in Ps. xxxvii.9.

F. *Summary*

If the development of OT usage as a whole is surveyed in the light of this study, the answer can be given to the question posed at the beginning: the LXX and the NT did after all see matters essentially correctly when they attached their concept of faith ($\pi\iota\sigma\tau\epsilon\acute{\upsilon}\epsilon\iota\nu$) to the OT stem '*mn*. For this is the one which brings out the peculiar quality and also the most profound thought in what the OT has to say about faith. Although if

[1] The case is the same when Yahweh is described as 'the hope' of the worshipper in Ps. lxxi.5; *tiqwātī* as a parallel to *mibṭāḥī*.

[2] cf. for this especially *to hope* in vv. 43, 49, 74, 147.

mere numbers are taken into account *he'ᵉmîn* is of less importance than other verbal stems, yet there is no doubt of its qualitative preponderance. This can be recognised from the notable fact that it is one of the most significant features of the linguistic development of the other verbal stems that they become assimilated to the meaning of *'mn*, involving a more or less pronounced change in their meaning. There are three reasons for this remarkable process. (1) Linguistically the root *'mn* shows itself to be by nature a concept of very wide range and flexibility as regards its meaning; thus it is able to admit more and more fresh elements without giving up its basic meaning. So in the *hiph'il* it includes the comprehensive, exclusive and personal reciprocal relationship between God and man. (2) Historically this meaning of the *'mn* concept came nearest to the peculiar connexion with God, that of Yahweh and Israel, and probably became already in early days the expression of that specifically OT relationship with God which was fostered in the covenant tradition. (3) Theologically the prophetic movement, especially Isaiah, through personal religious experience and meditation reached the ultimate depths of this relationship to God and of the knowledge of its nature, and gave to the usage a creative intensity and—within the range of OT thought—a completeness which was taken up by the piety of individuals and helped again and again in the inward mastering of historical catastrophes and personal troubles.[1] For the significance of the OT concept of faith lies in this, that it is the expression of the particular form of existence and

---

[1] The objective vividness felt from the beginning to be more definitely inherent in the stems *bṭḥ, ḥsh, qwh, yḥl, ḥkh* as compared with the term *he'ᵉmîn* may have contributed to the fact that these stems, especially after their meaning had become assimilated to that of *'mn*, outstripped the use of the latter numerically.

life of the people of God and of its members, who stood in an active relationship with God; that it embraces this relationship in its whole wide range and penetrates to its utmost depths. For these come into view only when, under the threat to human existence, divine assurance releases fresh forces of faith and life.

II. THE LINGUISTIC USAGE IN GREEK

A. *Classical usage*[1]

AMONGST the words formed with πισ-τ- the earliest attested is the verbal adjective πιστός with its privative formation ἄπιστος. It includes active and passive meanings *trusting* and *trustworthy* (*reliable*). In Homer only the latter sense appears; but since ἄπιστος is found there in the sense of *mistrustful* (e.g. *Od.* 14.150), it is clear that both these meanings are originally inherent in the word. They are both found again too in the noun πίστις.

1. In the literature we meet with πιστός with the meanings (*a*) *trusting* (Theogn. 283); it is used in poetic language of trust in weapons, or in skill in their use (Aesch. *Prom.* 915-17, *Pers.* 52-57); of trust in man (Theogn., and also Soph. *Oed. Col.* 1031, Dio C. 37.12. 1). In so far as trust can be a duty, πιστός can acquire the nuance of *obedient*. (*b*) πιστός in the sense of *trustworthy* is to start with a word used in the sacral and juristic sphere; *oaths* are designated as πιστά (Hom. *Il.* 2.124 etc.), similarly *proofs* (Aesch. *Suppl.* 53, etc.). The expression πιστὰ διδόναι καὶ λαμβάνειν signifies *to make a covenant*.[2] Τὰ πιστά is the *reliability* of those bound by the covenant (Aesch. *Ag.* 651; Xenoph. *An.* II.4, 7), *loyalty*; similarly τὸ πιστόν (Thuc. I.68.1). It is in keeping with this that πιστός (*trustworthy*, *loyal*) is used of persons who are connected with one another by a

[1] This chapter includes a discussion of only those principal meanings of πίστις etc. in Greek literature which are important for the history of the biblical concept or for a comparison with it.

[2] Xenoph. *An.* III.2.5, IV.8.7 etc. Also as late as P. Petr. II.19.1, 4 (third century B.C.): τά πιστὰ διδόναι *to give a firm guarantee*.

covenant[1]: the companion, the friend, the husband, the witness and the messenger, the guard and the slave, and others too are characterised as πιστός, and similarly the wife as πιστή. The meaning becomes generalised, so that τὸ πιστόν can signify *reliability* and *security* in general,[2] and that πιστός becomes the name for the quality of *loyalty* in general. Πιστός is not used of things in the strict sense, but only of people and of circumstances which are brought about by people or endured by them. The *reliability* of things is denoted by βέβαιος which can become partly synonymous with πιστός because it can be used also for persons and personal behaviour.[3] In special cases a word can be described as πιστός; and so too the tongue, so that in philosophy the λόγος (Plat. *Tim.* 498), the hypothesis (Plat. *Phaed.* 107b) or the proof (Plat. *Phaed.* 245c) can be called πιστός, and πιστός may be combined with *demonstrable* (ἀποδεικτικός) (Arist. *Rhet.* II.1, p 1377 b 23).

2. The meanings of ἄπιστος correspond to this: (*a*) *Mistrustful*, Homer (*Od.* 14.150 *et passim*) and frequently later. (*b*) *Disloyal, unreliable*, already in Homer and frequently thereafter. The unreliability of circumstances, like that of persons, can also be denoted by ἄπιστος (Thuc. I.120.4), and so too particularly the word or speech (Hdt. III.80; Plat. *Phaedr.* 245c). In this way ἄπιστος acquires the meaning of *unworthy of belief*.

3. Corresponding to the usage of πιστός, πίστις has (*a*) the (abstract) meaning of *trust, confidence*[4] and in fact

---

[1] cf. especially Xenoph. *Hist. Graec.* II.3.29. On a Syrian inscription πιστός appears simply as the designation of a *confidant*, see Lietzmann, *Komm. z. 1 Kor.* (vii.25).

[2] Occasionally πιστός can also mean *genuine*.

[3] On βέβαιος cf. TWNT, I, p. 600.

[4] cf. Hes. *Op.* 372; Theogn. 831; Soph. *Oed.* 950. The nouns in -τις (-σις) are originally *only* abstract; what are evidently concrete meanings must somehow be derived from them.

in this sense can be applied to circumstances (Thuc. I. 120.5) and to things (Plat. *Phaedr.* 275a) as well as to persons. Trust, in so far as it contains a factor of uncertainty which can be contrasted with knowledge (Soph. *Trach.* 588-93), can nevertheless also mean *conviction* and (subjective) *certainty*.[1] Parmenides contrasts πίστις ἀληθής (Fr. 1.30 [Diels, 7th ed., I.230.12]) *reliable truth* (literally: trust in what is real) with human opinions. Plato also speaks of the πίστις μόνιμος (*well-established belief, Rep.* VI.505e) and of opinions and beliefs which are assured and true, but which must nevertheless be distinguished from perception and knowledge (*Tim.* 37b, c). Similarly he contrasts right belief with knowledge (*Rep.* X.601e). But often the meaning of πίστις is *firm conviction* without any such distinction. (*b*) In accordance with the genius of the Greek language, πίστις can mean both the *trust that a man feels* as well as the *trust that he inspires*,[2] that is to say *trustworthiness*. This meaning is related to that of *reliability* (cf. p. 35), but must be carefully distinguished from it. It resembles rather that of the passive form πιστεύεσθαι. It is often emphasised that πίστις is a higher good than riches. (*c*) When used in a concrete sense πίστις means the *guarantee* which makes it possible to feel trust, that *which is reliable* (or the *assurance of reliability*). Here too we find at first the sacral and juristic usage. It stands for *plighting troth*, the *pledge of faithfulness, becoming bail* (Soph. *Oed. Col.* 1632, *Trach.* 1182 f.). From this point πίστις can on the one hand gain the meaning of *certainty, credibility* (e.g. Aristot. *Eth. Nic.* X.9, p 1179 a 17 f.), and on the other that of *evidence, proof* (e.g. Democr. Fr. 125). It denotes in

---

[1] So explicitly in Plato. Cf. especially *Rep.* VI.511e. For the Platonic concept of πίστις cf. J. Stengel, *Plato als Erzieher* (1928), p. 233: the word πίστις in the subject index.

[2] cf. on δόξα, TWNT, II, p. 237.

particular the reliability of persons, *loyalty* (e.g. Aesch. *Pers.* 443). It is mentioned especially as an attribute of friendship (e.g. Xenoph. *An.* I.6.3).

4. Πιστεύω (in use only from the seventh century) is derived from πιστός and means to *trust*, to *rely on*.[1] Treaties and oaths are objects of πιστεύειν (Xenoph. *An.* III.1.29, V.2.9), also laws (Aeschin. *Oratio in Ctesiphum,* 1); then means of power, such as military equipment (Polyb. 5.62.6) or in the abstract: the state of reliability (Demosth. *Or.* 44.3) or the possibility of it (Plat. *Rep.* X.603b); finally persons (e.g. Thuc. III.83. 2) and in this case πιστεύειν can receive the shade of meaning of to *obey* (e.g. Soph. *Oed. Tyr.* 625). The passive πιστεύεσθαι means to *be trusted* (e.g. Xenoph. *An.* VII.6.33). In so far as words can be the object of πιστεύειν (e.g. Hdt. II.118), it acquires the meaning of to *believe,* and can in this sense have a person as an object (in the dative, e.g. Hdt. II.120) or a thing (in the accusative, Aristot. *An. Pri.* II.23, p 68 b 13). But it can also be construed with περί (e.g. Hdt. IV.96) or with the accusative and infinitive (e.g. Hdt. VI.105), or with a clause with ὅτι (Plat. *Gorg.* 512e), and it can also be used absolutely, but in such a case an object is to be supplied (e.g. Soph. *Oed. Tyr.* 625). In the sense of to *believe,* it can also be used in the passive (Plat. *Leg.* I.636d; Aristot. *An.* III.3, p 428 b 4), and the dative personal object may in the passive construction become the subject (Xenoph. *An.* VII.7.25). In later times it often means to *entrust* (e.g. Plut. *Apophth.*: *Agis junior,* 2 [II.191e]) which is still rare in Attic Greek (e.g. Thuc. II.35.1); it is frequently so used in the passive (e.g. Polyb. 8.17.4).

5. The privative formation ἀπιστέω, derived from ἄπιστος, is apparently not attested with the meaning to *be untrustworthy, unreliable*; on the other hand it is found

[1] cf. E. Fraenkel, *Griech. Denominativa* (1906), p. 179.

with that of to *be suspicious, mistrustful, incredulous* (e.g.
Hom. *Od.* 13.339). In this sense it is applied particularly
to words (Eur. *Med.* 927) and can mean therefore *not to
believe* (Epict. II.22.23; Plot. *Enn.* V.8.11, p 246.2 ff.).
The passive can also be used in this way (Xenoph.
Hier. 4.1). The meaning to *be disobedient* has branched
off from this (e.g. Hdt. VI.108), particularly when laws
are the subject of πιστεύειν (Soph. *Ant.* 219, 381 f., 655 f.)

6. The noun belonging to it, ἀπιστία, means: (*a*) *un-
reliability, disloyalty* (Soph. *Oed. Col.* 611; Xenoph. *An.*
II. 5.21, III.2.3) and hence *untrustworthiness* (Hdt. I.193;
Plat. *Phaed.* 88d). (*b*) *Distrust, disbelief* (Theogn. 831).

7. Amongst additional formations with πιστ-, in view
of the NT, πιστόω must also be mentioned.[1] It means:
(*a*) to *make someone* πιστός, that is to say a person bound
to oneself by an oath, a treaty, bail, or similarly, and
therefore reliable (Soph. *Oed. Col.* 650; Thuc. IV.88).
In this sense it is also used in the passive (Hom. *Od.* 15.
436; Eur. *Iph. Aul.* 66). In the middle voice the meaning becomes to *give (mutual) pledges of fidelity* (Hom. *Il.*
6.238, 21.286; Polyb. 1.43.5, 18.22.6). (*b*) to *inspire
confidence in a person*. In this sense the passive is used: to
be rendered trustful, to feel confidence (Hom. *Od.* 21.217 f.;
Soph. *Oed. Col.* 1039).

8. We must observe that the formations with πιστ- did
not become technical terms of religious language in
classical Greek. It is true that faithfulness to one's word
is also a religious duty (Xenoph. *Ag.* 3.5) and loyalty
and piety are closely linked (Eur. *Hec.* 1234 f.). Moreover πίσυνος, which is synonymous with πιστός in the
sense of *relying on*, can have the deity as its object (Aesch.
Sept. c. Theb. 211 f.) and ἄπιστος = *unbelieving* can also
be directed towards a deity (Eur. *Iph. Taur.* 1475 f.).
But in no sense was πιστός used to denote the really

[1] cf. E. Fraenkel, op. cit. (p. 37, n. 1), p. 150.

religious relationship to God or the fundamental religious attitude of man.

Nor did πίστις become a technical term in religion; the most that can be said is that such a possibility was prepared for by the fact that πίστις in the sense of *reliance upon* can refer to a divine oracle (e.g. Soph. *Oed. Tyr.* 1445) and that in the sense of *conviction* can also have the existence of a deity as its object (Plat. *Leg.* XII.966d). Only the beginnings of a religious usage are to be found in the cases of πιστεύειν, ἀπιστεῖν and ἀπιστία. Πιστεύειν in the sense of to *trust* can be applied to the divine favour (τύχη, e.g. Thuc. V.104), and also to the deity (e.g. Aristoph. *Nu.* 437). When it means to *give credence to* the object can be both the works of man and divine oracles (e.g. Aesch. *Pers.* 800 f.), but also the deity itself (Soph. *Phil.* 1374). The same is true also for ἀπιστεῖν and ἀπιστία (e.g. Hdt. I. 158).

B. *Hellenistic usage*

1. *The development of a religious usage in philosophical discussion*

Whilst in the early Greek world it is customary to express the belief that there are gods by the word νομίζειν (Aesch. *Pers.* 497 f.), in later times πιστεύειν can also be said instead, in accordance with the fact that πιστεύειν may acquire the meaning to *believe* (cf. p. 37).

This linguistic usage is developed in the discussions against scepticism and atheism (cf. Plut. *Superst.* 11 [II.170 f.]). The belief that gods exist has its own proper certainty, but it is not at all self-evident and presupposes an obstacle to be overcome. The fact that divine control of the world is invisible must not be an

obstacle to believing in it.[1] Thus man must be educated
by knowledge to believe in the incorporeal, for the
instrument (or author) of faith cannot be sensual perception, but only the mind (cf. Plot. *Enn.* V.8.11, p 246.
2 ff.). The deity itself under certain circumstances
leads the unbeliever to belief.[2] This makes it clear that
πίστις is not only a theoretical conviction, but at the
same time piety. Similarly belief in God is also belief
in divine providence (cf. Plut. *Ser. Num. Pun.* 3 [II.
549b]), and the pious quality of such belief is emphasised by Plutarch (*Pyth. Or.* 18 [II.402c]). Porphyry describes how this belief determines the attitude
to life (*Marc.* 21 ff.). Belief in the invisible includes also
belief in the immortality of the soul (Plot. *Enn.* IV.7.10,
p 138.6 ff.), even the belief that one forms part of the
divine world oneself (Plot. *Enn.* IV.8.1, p 142.10 ff.)
and further the belief in a judgement after death.[3]
Hence it is intelligible that πίστις is reckoned by
Porphyry (*Marc.* 24) as one of the four elements
(στοιχεῖα).[4]

---

[1] Pseud.-Aristot. *Mund.* 6, p 399 b 21 f. But cf. already Heracl.
Fr. 86 (Diels, 7th ed., I.170.5 f.): 'the knowledge of the divine
is for the most part concealed from the understanding because
there is no belief in it' (so Diels, 2nd ed., I.74.34 ff.); cf. Plut.
De Coriolano 38 (I.232c), who refers to the statement of Heracl.,
when speaking of the πίστις in the wonderful quality of the power
(δύναμις) of God.

[2] Vett. Val. IX.1, p 331.12 f.: 'Life, the deity, comes to him
who has discerned law in the vicissitudes of life; it is denied to him
who has not discerned it.'

[3] cf. Scott I.366.6 ff.: 'the *incredibilitas humana* despises the
belief in a judgment after death, but the *incredibiles . . . post
delicta cogentur credere, non verbis, sed exemplis, nec minis, sed ipsa
passione poenarum* (Scott I.366.20 f.).

[4] Similarly in the *Orac. Chald.*, πίστις with truth (ἀλήθεια) and
love (ἔρως) forms a triad (W. Kroll, 'De Oraculis Chaldaicis',
Breslau Philologische Abh. VII.1 [1894], p. 26).

2. *The language of religious propaganda[1] and of Stoicism*

The use of πίστις as a technical term in religious language was encouraged further by the fact that it became the key word in the propaganda of the proselytising religions, not only Christianity. Every missionary sermon demands 'belief' in the deity it proclaims.

Thus Celsus says that some (the Christians) preach this saviour, others that one, but that they all say: *believe* (πίστευσον) *if you wish to be saved, or refuse* (Orig. *Cels.* VI.11). The Hermetic writings reflect this usage (e.g. *Corp. Herm.* 4.4). The mind as it follows the word of the sermon is raised to the truth and thus attains to belief.[2] Thus Lucius who has been instructed in the mysteries of Isis confesses *I now took part in the divine worship, full of that confidence* (*plena fiducia*) *which my knowledge of a kindred religion produced.* (Apul. *Met.* XI.28). This usage is also presupposed in the Litany of Isis (P. Oxy. XI.1380.152) in words which can only mean either 'who invoke thee as befits the relationship of belief (between God and man)' or 'according to the manner of believers'.[3] The Odes of Solomon show the same usage: 'Mercy is manifested for your deliverance. Believe and you will live and be delivered.'[4] In the sphere of belief in miracles and dogmas πιστεύειν etc.

[1] cf. Reitzenstein, *Hell. Myst.* pp. 234-6; O. Kitzig, *Die Bekehrung des Paulus* (1932), pp. 176-80.

[2] *Corp. Herm.* 9.10; unfortunately the text is not quite certain; cf. Scott I.185.25-186.4 and Reitzenstein, *Hell. Myst.* p. 235.

[3] cf. R. Reitzenstein, 'Die Formel Glaube, Liebe, Hoffnung bei Paulus', *NGG Philologischhist. Klasse* (1917), p. 132.

[4] Od. Sol. 34.6; cf. also 4.5, 8.11, 28.3, 29.6, 35.5, 13; and the 'believers' in 4.3, 15.10, 22.7. Naturally it is not possible to determine how far the mention of belief in Mandaean and Manichaean literature has its origin in the general religious history of Hellenism and how far Christian usage is at work here. Cf. H. Jonas, *Gnosis und spätantiker Geist*, I (²1954), p. 137 and the material collected in Wissmann, pp. 44 f.

is found in the Pythagorean legend[1]; and finally this terminology penetrated also into magic.[2] It must remain an open question whether the 'Virgin of Faith' who according to an Aramaean inscription is taken to wife by 'King Bel', is to be understood in this sense. 'The Virgin of Faith' seems to be a personification of the Mazdaean religion.[3] The title of the Gnostic work 'Pistis Sophia' is evidence for the mythological personification of Πίστις, but this may go back to Christian usage.[4]

In Stoicism too, πίστις has no religious significance in the sense of denoting the relationship of a man to the deity, so that the deity and his rule should be the object of πίστις. But the attitude of πίστις is certainly a religious attitude in so far as man, if he is πιστός or the like, expresses in it his relationship to God.

[1] Jamblichus, *Vit. Pyth.* 138, p 78.17 ff.; 148, p 83.18 ff.

[2] cf. Preis, *Zaub.* I.4.1012 ff.; XII.288 f.

[3] M. Lidzbarski, *Ephemeris*, I (1900), p. 69; Reitzenstein, *Hell. Myst.*, p. 235; H. Gressmann, 'Das religionsgeschichtliche Problem des Ursprungs der hell. Erlösungsreligion', ZKG, NF 3 (1922), p. 186.

[4] C. Schmidt, *Pistis Sophia* (1925), p. xxi; cf. the personification of Πίστις in the inscription of Aberkios (cf. F. J. Dölger *Ichthys* II (1922), pp. 482 f.); Ign. Sm. x.2 where Jesus Christ Himself is designated ἡ τελεία πίστις (or ἐλπίς).

III. FAITH IN JUDAISM

A. *The Old Testament heritage*

THE *he'^emin* of the OT (cf. pp. 10 ff.) is rendered in the
LXX almost without exception by πιστεύειν[1] and in fact
corresponds to the Greek πιστεύειν in so far as, like the
latter, it means *to trust* (in persons in I Sam. xxvii.12,
Mic. vii.5 etc.), *to put trust in* (words in Gen. xlv.26,
I Kings x.7, Prov. xiv.15 etc. cf. p. 37). Further
the meaning to put one's trust in God (Gen. xv.6,
Deut. i.32 etc.) and the fact that it is God's words which
are 'believed' (Ps. cvi. 12, 24) corresponds to the Greek
use of πιστεύειν (cf. pp. 38 f.). However what is
denoted by *he'^emin* and therewith the OT concept of
faith, has a richer content than that described in Greek
by πιστεύειν and the Greek concept of faith. Although
the shade of meaning 'to obey' can also be inherent in
the word πιστεύειν (cf. pp. 34, 37 f.), yet this element is
very much more prominent in 'to believe' in the OT
and is often the predominant one. When referring to
the relationship with God, *he'^emin* often has the meaning of 'to acknowledge' (Exod. xiv.31, Num. xx.12,
Isa. xliii.10) or 'to obey' (Deut. ix.23, Num. xiv.11,
II Kings xvii.14; similarly with reference to Moses, the
representative of God, in Exod. iv.1, 8 f.); hence God's
commandments also can be the object of *he'^emin* (cf.
p. 12).

In the OT to believe in God means also to acknowledge him to be God (cf. pp. 11 f.); this includes both
trust (cf. pp. 19 ff.) and hope (cf. pp. 27 f.) as well as
fear (cf. p. 14) and obedience (cf. p. 12). But these two
together form a unity, because trust is given a fundamen-

---

[1] See Additional Note, pp. 55 f.

43

tal sense (cf. p. 15) and embraces both the conquest of
fear as well as of self-confidence.[1] To believe is the
daring decision for God when a man renounces the
threatening world as well as his own strength (cf. p. 17).
It is therefore—and occasionally this is emphasised
(e.g. Gen. xv.6)—faith against appearances and 'as a
trustful decision for God it involves suppressed temptation'.[2] Such faith in God is not a general 'trust in
God', but is founded on what God has done in the past.[3]
It is therefore always closely related to the past and
thus is at the same time loyalty (cf. p. 14).

He who trusts (ma'^{a}$m\bar{\i}n = \pi\iota\sigma\tau\epsilon\dot{\upsilon}\omega\nu$) is at the same
time one who is loyal (ne'^{e}$m\bar{a}n = \pi\iota\sigma\tau\delta\varsigma$). By analogy
faith is closely related to the future (cf. p. 12); it is the
certainty that God will do what he has promised. Its
opposite is murmuring and doubting (cf. TWNT, I, pp.
729 ff., II, pp. 97 ff.) by which God is 'tempted'; it is
hoping expectantly (cf. pp. 28 f. and also p. 26, n. 1)
and being still. It is also closely related to the present,
as being obedience to God's commandments (cf. p. 12)
since by keeping them the nation must demonstrate its
loyalty to the covenant.

Faith of this kind applies essentially in the OT to the
history of the nation whose existence is founded on
God's action and whose obedience God demands.
Therefore actually the individual practises faith in so
far as he is a member of the nation; his faith is directed
towards the future of the nation.[4] Now it goes without

[1] This fundamental manner of understanding the concept has
of course not been developed in every case: cf. especially Isa.
vii.4-9, viii.5-15, xxviii.15 f., xxx.15-17 and the Psalms.

[2] cf. Schlatter, *Glaube*, pp. 10 f.

[3] Thus faith is not an attribute of a man's character, like $\pi\iota\sigma\tau\iota\varsigma$
in Stoicism.

[4] Abraham's faith too in Gen. xv.6 does not concern his personal fate, but the future of the nation whose ancestor he is. His
faith is a prototype.

saying that faith in God, corresponding to the completeness of God's claim on the nation, must determine its life in every respect and not only occasionally in particular circumstances. But—compared with the standard of the NT—it is also evident that the OT is not yet aware of faith as that attitude which dominates the life of a man absolutely, as can be seen for instance by the fact that the question of death is not brought within the range of the idea of faith. Where in the Psalms trust in God is voiced concerning the fate of an individual (cf. pp. 30 f.), one aspect only of this faith is meant, namely trust in God's help, especially in times of distress. This can already be seen from the fact that in these cases the word used is not *he'emīn* which associates faith with history, but *bṭḥ*, *qwh* and others.[1] Thus man's position is not conceived basically as one of insecurity in the presence of God, with the implication that a man can stand before God relying neither on his good deeds nor on his bad ones, but only on his 'faith', that is on a complete abandonment of himself, and that all his doings can have no value in God's sight except in so far as they spring from faith (Rom. xiv.23). In fact it is often the case that the claim to trust is founded on a man's piety[2] which is therefore not understood completely as faith.

Finally, in the OT, God's activity, to which man knows he is committed by his loyalty and on which he trustfully places his hope for the future, is understood to be an activity of this world, whether it takes place in the history of the nation or in the fate of the individual.

[1] It should be noticed that no noun connected with *he'emīn* has been found to correspond for example with *mibṭāḥ* or *tiqwāh* although *'emet* in the sense of loyalty can to a certain extent be considered as a substitute. Only in Aramaic was a noun formed from this with the meaning of loyalty and faith, cf. Schlatter, *Glaube*, pp. 559 f.

[2] e.g. Ps. xvi, xxxvii, lii, lxxi.

Therefore although faith, by its renunciation of both fear and self-reliance, implies a turning away from the world, yet it is not the radical attitude of casting off the world, like the NT πίστις; for with this faith the εἰρήνη πρὸς τὸν θεόν (Rom. v.1) is proof against the national history on this world's stage and against the fate of the individual in this life.

B. *The concept of faith in Judaism*[1]

The OT heritage was taken over as their own jointly by Palestinian as well as by Hellenistic Jewry. Consequently it is hardly possible to differentiate here between the two trends; only particular features within the general treatment may occasionally be brought out, and Philo must be treated separately.

1. *The Old Testament motifs*

The structure of the Jewish concept of faith (which needs to be presented here only according to its religious, and not its profane usage) exhibits the leading motifs of the OT throughout: faith is trusting (cf. pp. 19 ff.) just as much as believing; it includes loyalty (cf. p. 14) and obedience (cf. p. 12) just as much as hoping and expecting (cf. pp. 27 f.). Because these motifs have an underlying connexion, it often cannot be discerned which of them is predominant. Yet it is noticeable that in the rabbinic literature faith is understood onesidedly as obedience to the law, whilst in the Apocrypha and Pseudepigrapha the other motifs contained in the structure as a whole are more prominent.[2]

The idea of loyalty often stands out.[3] It applies to

---

[1] cf. Schlatter, *Glaube*, pp. 9-42; Bousset-Gressmann, pp. 190-201; Moore, II, pp. 237 f.; Wissmann, pp. 50-54; A. Meyer, *Das Rätsel des Jakobusbriefes* (1930), pp. 123-41.

[2] Str.-B. III, p. 188.

[3] Schlatter, *Glaube*, pp. 15 f. So also in the Qumran texts:

the 'covenants' of God (II Esdras iii.32). It must be preserved in affliction.[1] Faith will triumph[2]; *for he who believes will gain his life in truth* (Syr. Bar. liv.16). *Great in the sight of God is loyalty to faith.*[3] This quality is probably also meant when works and faith are combined (II Esdras ix.7, xiii.22). Abraham and other patriarchs are considered to be examples of such loyalty.[4] Loyalty has to prove itself particularly in temptation, as in the case of Abraham.[5] At the same time loyalty is obedience and so occasionally the law, the commandments, are named as objects of faith.[6] In the rabbinic literature too 'to believe in God' and 'to obey God' are synonymous.[7] Hand in hand with obedience we find trust. Keeping the law (*nsr* LXX πιστεύειν) and trusting God (*bṭḥ* LXX πεποιθέναι) appear as parallels.[8] Naturally there are many sayings in which faith is praised as trust in God[9] and men are exhorted to trust in God when in distress and in time

Manual of Discipline viii.3, x.25; *Hab. Comm.* viii.3. Here it is everywhere *'emūnā* whilst *'emet* seems to have throughout the meaning of 'truth'; and this appears perhaps also in the phrase *'āśā 'emet* (*to act truly*) i.5, viii.2.

[1] IV Macc. xv.24, xvi.22, xvii.2; Slav. En. lxii.1, lxvi.6; Ex. R. xv.7 (in Schlatter, *Glaube*, p. 17); Tg J I on Isa. xxviii.16 (in Meyer, op. cit. (p. 46, n. 1) p. 130; cf. Schlatter, *Glaube*, pp. 17 f.; Str.-B. III, pp. 192 f.

[2] II Esdras vii.34; other references in Str.-B. III, p. 193.

[3] Mekhilta Exod. xiv.31 and xv.1 (in Meyer op. cit. [p. 46, n. 1], p. 130).

[4] Sir. xliv.20; Jub. xix.9; I Macc. ii.52; IV Macc. xvi.22; Str.-B. III, pp. 199 ff.; Moore, II, pp. 237 f.

[5] Sir. ii.1 ff.; Judith viii.25 ff.; Ps. Sol. xvi.14 f.; cf. A. Sommer, *Der Begriff der Versuchung im AT und Judentum* (Diss. Breslau, 1935), pp. 12-15.

[6] Syr. Bar. liv.5, II Esdras vii.24; cf. Schlatter, *Glaube*, pp. 19 f.

[7] Str.-B. III, p. 191.

[8] Sir. xxii.24; cf. xi.21; Syr. Bar. xlviii.22; in the Greek text of Sir. xxxiii.3 the law actually takes the place of God.

[9] I Macc. ii.59; Jos. *Ant.* 3.309, 20.48; cf. Moore, I, pp. 136 f.

of trial.[1] Faith in divine providence is a specifically
Hellenistic phrase used for such trust in God (Jos. *Ant.*
4.60; *Ap.* 2.170). The antithesis of faith—both in the
sense of loyalty and of trust—is the doubt which tempts
God,[2] distrust.[3] On the other hand a characteristic of
faith is simplicity,[4] the single-minded aim of the heart.
This is demanded in the XII Testaments as the opposite
of double-mindedness,[5] which Rabbinic literature also
attacks.[6] Associated with this is the concept of the man
of little faith,[7] and also that of the hypocrite.[8] In so far
as trust in God is faith in his promise, it is at the same
time hope.[9] But in so far as it looks into the future in
general, it is in a more universal sense belief in retribution[10] and in so far as retribution is thought of as in
the hereafter such a faith becomes a party matter (cf.
G. F. Moore, *Judaism*, II (1927), pp. 279 ff.).

To hold that something is true, which is of the
essence of faith, when its object is originally God's word
and promises,[11] acquires in the controversies with other
religions and in propaganda a special meaning; belief

[1] Sir. ii.1 ff.; Jos. *Ant.* 2.333; cf. Meyer, op. cit. p. 46, n. 1),
131; Str.-B. III, pp. 191 f.

[2] Judith viii.12 ff., Wisd. of Sol. i.2; cf. Sommer, op. cit. (p. 47,
n. 5), pp. 11 f.

[3] Wisd. of Sol. i.2.

[4] Wisd. of Sol. i.1.

[5] Bousset-Gressmann, pp. 418 f.

[6] Schlatter, *Glaube*, pp. 18 f.; Str.-B. III, p. 751 on Jas. i.8;
Hauck, *Jakobusbrief* (1926), p. 49, n. 47.

[7] qᵉṭannē ’ᵃmānā, cf. Str.-B. I, pp. 438 f.; cf. especially Sota 48 b:
'He who has bread in his basket and says "What shall I eat to-
morrow?" belongs to the men of little faith', (cf. p. 62).

[8] Schlatter, *Glaube*, p. 19.

[9] Syr. Bar. xlii, lvii.2, lix.2, 10; II Esdras vi.5; cf. the linking of
believing and hoping in I Macc. ii.59, 61; Sir. ii.6, 8 f.

[10] Str.-B. III, pp. 190 f.

[11] Tobit xiv.4, Wisd. of Sol. xviii.6, Tg J I on Isa. vii.9 (the
words of the prophets).

in God becomes a confession of monotheism.[1] Naturally this meaning of faith is especially developed in Hellenistic Judaism (Sib. III.584 ff.). Thus we find in Philo (cf. pp. 52 ff.), sentences which seem to approximate to credal formulations (Philo. *Op. Mund.* 170-2, *Virt.* 216) and the first Mandate of Hermas also goes back to such a tradition.[2]

Since 'faith' is used so broadly to express the relationship of man to God and to his law, and consequently the attitude of the pious, it is easy to understand that words denoting faith can also be used absolutely. It is true that faith is usually qualified by the addition of its object (God, God's testimonies, and so forth).[3] But the absolute usage is also found. The pious can be described simply as the 'faithful',[4] and also as the 'believers' (II Esdras vii.131). The development of this usage evidently came about in order to contrast them firstly with the 'ungodly' amongst their own nation[5] and secondly with the heathen.[6] Analogously 'faith' is also employed absolutely.[7]

[1] Judith xiv.10; Eth. En. xliii.4, xlvi.4 f. etc.; cf. Str.-B. III, pp. 189 f.

[2] Herm. m.I.1. Cf. Dib. *Herm.* ad loc.; Windisch on Jas. ii.19; cf. Wissmann, pp. 49 f.

[3] Schlatter, *Glaube*, p. 20 A 1: 'It is instructive that the Targum is no longer able to accept the absolute usage of Isaiah, but supplies faith with an object in the words of the prophet.'

[4] Schlatter, *Glaube*, pp. 15 f.; Str.-B. III, p. 189; I Macc. ii.52; perhaps also Wisd. of Sol. iii.9 (cf. next note).

[5] Wisd. of Sol. iii.9 (if πιστοί here does not mean the 'pious'); II Esdras vii.131; Syr. Bar. xlii.2, liv.16, 21; Slav. En. li.2; rabbinic references in Str.-B. III, p. 189.

[6] Eth. En. xlvi.8; Sib. III. 69, 724, V.161, 426; cf. I Macc. ii. 59; Wisd. of Sol. xviii.13; cf. Str.-B. III, p. 189.

[7] Wisd. of Sol. iii.14 f.; Mekhilta Exod. xvi.19 (Schlatter, *Glaube*, p. 21); Tg J I on Isa. xxviii.16 (in Meyer, op. cit. [p. 46, n. 1], p. 130); Ass. Mos. iv.8; II Esdras vi.27, vii.34, ix.7; Eth. En. lviii.5, lxi.4, 11; Slav. En. lxii.1, lxvi.6; Syr. Bar. lix.10; Sib. III. 585; Test. L. viii.2. In the inscriptions in the Jewish catacomb on

To sum up it may be said that though the concept of faith in Judaism contains the same leading ideas as that of the OT, yet there is a great difference between them.[1]

2. How the faith of Judaism differs from that of the Old Testament

In consequence of the canonisation of tradition in the 'scripture', obedient loyalty acquires the character of obedience to the Law, i.e. it is no longer really loyalty toward the activity of God experienced in history whilst trusting in his future activity in the same sphere. History is, as it were, suspended and a real sense of being bound up with it is lacking. The significance of the past history is restricted to making the Jew conscious of the fact that he belongs to the called and chosen people. The present can no longer actively carry on history and its tradition, but is a medium for conveying only the canonised tradition. The text of the scriptures, accepted as belonging to a timeless present, is appropriated and interpreted by theological and legal study. Faith loses its character as a decision at a particular time in a historical situation, and 'therefore presents itself as something objective and persistent, as a form of consciousness, which having entered into the teaching

Monteverde 145: *quae vera fides* (N. Müller, *Die Inschriften der jüdischen Katakombe am Monteverde zu Rom* [1919], p. 134, or J. B. Frey, *Corpus Inscriptionum Judaicorum*, I [1936], no. 476; cf. also nos. 72 and 641).—The expression 'men of faith' is also found, cf. Str.-B. III, p. 189, in Heb. En. these 'men of faith' appear to be a circle in which apocalyptic mysteries are handed down. Cf. perhaps also the Qumran texts; cf. H. Bardtke, *Die Handschriften-funde am Toten Meer* (1952), p. 93 n. 4. Cf. also Wissmann, pp. 40-43.

[1] Schlatter, *Glaube*, p. 12: 'For the inner form of faith depends on what is presented to us in history as the act and gift of God. The divine gifts which Jewry in NT times knew that it possessed were the Bible and the Temple. From this knowledge sprang the differences between the attitude to belief of the Judaism contemporary with the NT and that of pre-exilic times.'

of the scriptures may be experienced in them'.[1] The
conception of the inspiration of the scriptures limits the
working of the spirit to the past[2] and limits the divine
activity to the historical events of the past. As a result
there arises a 'disparagement of the natural conditions
of life',[3] and faith, in so far as it nevertheless hopes that
God will act, is directed to one object only, namely
miracles.[4] In consequence, trust no longer applies to
their historical destiny, in which the nation and individuals are involved by what they do; but is essentially a matter of resigning oneself to suffering,[5] and a
belief in providence of a general nature, or the expectation of miracles. Hope looks beyond history to the
supernatural eschatological events and God's judgement is no longer thought of as being carried out in
historical happenings, but as eschatological action in a
court of law. In the same way the figure of the Messiah
as hoped for in the early days can be transformed under
the influence of the figure of the 'Son of Man' or even
be supplanted by it.[6] Salvation is no longer to be
bestowed upon the future generations of the nation,
but upon the faithful and the pious. Judgement will
become a universal judgement and faith with regard
to the future will become in the main belief in individual
retribution, itself lacking in confidence.[7]

Belief in retribution is at the same time belief in
merit. The faithful obedience to the law leads to
obedience to the letter and to counting as merit the

---

[1] Schlatter, *Glaube*, p. 20.   [2] Schlatter, *Glaube*, pp. 14 f.

[3] Schlatter, *Glaube*, pp. 22 f. The question whether it is com-
patible with faith to consult a doctor is an indication of this.

[4] Schlatter, *Glaube*, p. 25.

[5] This is particularly impressive in Akiba, cf. Schlatter, *Glaube*,
pp. 45-48.

[6] [cf. on this whole question S. Mowinckel, *He that cometh*, E.T.
by G. W. Anderson (1956), esp. Part II.]

[7] Schlatter, *Glaube*, pp. 32-35.

commandments which have been fulfilled. This presupposes that man is free in a way contrary to the freedom of genuine faith.[1] Man does not throw himself
completely on God's mercy and so God's mercy and
his condemnation to punishment diverge.[2] Mercy is
understood to be merely leniency which overlooks individual offences; the 'righteous' man is in no need of
mercy; only he who is 'converted' receives it[3]; the
righteous man relies on his own merit. By placing faith
beside works it is recognised that there is an obedience
of faith which is not simply satisfied by the righteousness of a man's works, but which means submission to
the divine will as a whole. But this insight loses its
value because faith itself is considered meritorious.[4]

3. *Philo's concept of faith*

Philo's description of faith places him within the
framework of Hellenistic Judaism, since faith means for
him primarily faith in the one God and trust in his
providence. Both are summed up in *Virt.* 216: 'And,
therefore, he is the first person (i.e. Abraham, cf. Gen.
xv.6) spoken of as believing in God, since he first
grasped a firm and unswerving conception of the truth
that there is one Cause above all, and that it provides
for the world and all that there is therein.' When
speaking of trust in God's help[5] and of his promises[6]

[1] Schlatter, *Glaube*, p. 26: 'By his act man substantiates God's
act.'

[2] Schlatter, *Glaube*, p. 40: 'Divine forgiveness . . . is not all of a
piece, and so cannot embrace the single personality and the
totality of its history and unite it with God.'

[3] Schlatter, *Glaube*, pp. 38 f.

[4] For the conception of the meritoriousness of faith see Schlatter,
Glaube, pp. 29-32. Meyer op. cit. (p. 46, n. 1), p. 132; Str.-B. III,
pp. 199-201.

[5] *Sacr. AC* 70; *Vit. Mos.* I.225, II.259.

[6] *Leg. All.* III.308; *Mut. Nom.* 166; *Abr.* 275.

Philo echoes the words of Judaism as a whole.[1] But the real meaning of faith consists for him in the fact that faith is turning away from the world of birth and death and turning towards the eternal God, by which man finds the security for which he is continually searching. Philo has therefore understood man's relation to God in terms of the Greek and Platonic tradition. Yet at the same time he holds fast to the meaning of *trust* as the basic significance of πίστις. He says for example: 'To trust God is a true teaching, but to trust our vain reasonings is a lie' (*Leg. All.* 229, and cf. 222 ff.); or: 'Now he who has sincerely believed in God has learned to disbelieve in all else, all that is created only to perish' (*Praem. Poen.* 28); or: 'But he to whom it is given to gaze and soar beyond not only material but all immaterial things, and to take God for his sole stay and support with a reasonableness whose resolution falters not, and a faith unswerving and securely founded, will be a truly happy and twice blessed man' (*Praem. Poen.* 30). The turning towards God is not indeed the response to God's word, that is to say, to his activity in history, but it is the result of contemplation of the world[2] and is an attitude of the mind ('dispositions', *Conf. Ling.* 31), a virtue, indeed the 'most perfect of virtues' (*Rer. Div. Her.* 96), the 'most sure and certain of the virtues' (*Virt.* 216), the 'queen of virtues' (*Abr.* 270). To attain to it is no small matter; it is a 'task for a great and celestial understanding' (*Rer. Div. Her.* 93), it is the prize, which Abraham struggled to acquire.[3] It is associated as closely as possible with the virtue of piety,[4] it is the 'blameless and fairest sacrifice' to God

---

[1] Philo also uses πίστις absolutely in *Poster. C.* 13, *Conf. Ling.* 31, *Migr. Abr.* 43 f., *Mut. Nom.* 182 etc.

[2] *Leg. All.* II.89.

[3] *Migr. Abr.* 44, *Praem. Poen.* 27.

[4] *Migr. Abr.* 132.

(*Cher.* 85); and thus it is at the same time 'the only truth and certain good'.

Πίστις is therefore basically the firmness of a man, that which cannot be shaken, which by abandoning self is founded on that which alone is firm, alone has real being. In so far as this means turning away from the transient and turning towards the eternal, Philo is following the Platonic tradition, but in so far as he denotes this conduct as πίστις he is following late Stoicism. He seems to be deviating from it when he introduces into its concept of πίστις, meaning *loyalty to oneself*, imperturbability, the OT and Jewish meaning of faith in the sense of *trust*. This was of course easily possible, for faith and loyalty have an inner unity in the OT and Judaism. In place of the ἐφ' ἡμῖν which according to Stoicism should determine man's purpose, Philo has put God who is considered all through to be the object of faith. But since man's relationship with the fellowship of his nation and with history has been severed and God is not seen in his historical activity, so faith is directed towards pure being, which however can only be described in the main negatively as the Other. Πίστις is the attitude of withdrawal from the world in a purely negative sense; no positive apprehension of the Other can be arrived at by πίστις, but only by ecstasy. Man does not stand in πίστις before God in order to receive from him. But it is the goal of piety towards which a man trains himself by his own strength.[1] Indeed, πίστις is not a relationship of man with God, but, as in Stoicism, it is a relationship of man with himself.

---

[1] cf. Schlatter, *Glaube*, p. 61: 'Thus here too the believer turns to look back on his behaviour as a believer and makes this the basis on which his participation with God is to rest.'

ADDITIONAL NOTE

LXX rendering of 'mn etc.

He'ᵉemīn is rendered in the LXX 45 times by πιστεύειν;
also 5 times by ἐμπιστεύειν, once each by καταπιστεύειν
and πεισθῆναι (cf. TWNT, VI, pp. 3 f.), and in variant
readings θέλειν. So too πιστεύειν, when it occurs, stands
almost invariably for *he'ᵉmīn*, once each for the *niph'al*
and *'aph'el* (in Aramaic) of *'mn*, once for *šm'* (= to *hear*;
this is in Jer. xxv.8, but clearly for the sake of variety;
in v. 7 *šm'* is rendered by ἀκούειν).

The other formations from the stem πιστ- are used
almost without exception for formations from the stem
'mn. Πιστός nearly always (29 times) represents the
niph'al of *'mn*, and πίστις stands 6 times for *'ᵉmet*, 20 times
for *'ᵉmūnā*, but conversely ἀλήθεια stands 87 times for
'ᵉmet and 22 times, especially in the Psalms, for *'ᵉmūnā*.
Besides, *'ᵉmet* is reproduced 12 times by ἀληθίνος, and
is rendered 6 times by δικαιοσύνη and 4 times by δίκαιος.
It should be noted that πιστεύειν is never used for *bṭh*
(cf. p. 26, n. 1).

It is noteworthy that πιστεύειν and πεποιθέναι never
represent the same Hebrew original. On the one hand
the *niph'al* and *hiph'il* of *'mn* are translated by πιστεύειν
with philological exactness. The derivatives of this
root in some cases have or receive in the LXX a quite
different meaning, but are in general likewise translated
by πιστεύειν, never by πεποιθέναι. Once only, in Prov.
xxvi.25, πεισθῆναι is used in the sense of 'letting oneself
be deceived'. On the other hand, πέποιθα certainly represents quite a number of Hebrew roots, even apart
from *bṭh*, and these are reproduced in the LXX in very
diverse ways. (In this respect *'mn* with its rendering in
Greek by one word only is a direct exception.) But for
none of the original Hebrew roots is πιστεύειν found as

a possible translation. This can hardly be accidental.

The LXX does not yet consider 'trust' and 'faith' as belonging together. Πέποιθα (=*bṭḥ*) is by this time a technical religious term. It is already used as such independently in the LXX, and is more frequent too in the later translators. On the other hand, πιστεύειν (='*mn*) is scarcely yet felt to be a religious concept. The later translators have in this respect an attitude no different from that of the LXX. There is a change only in so far as amongst the Hexaplaric translators, Aquila and Symmachus especially prefer πίστις for '*emūnā*. Other special renderings of the LXX also disappear. But there are philological reasons for this. The Hexaplaric translators, however, also keep to ἀλήθεια for '*emet* (Bertram).

Πιστεύειν and its compounds are construed throughout the LXX with the dative of the person (similarly in Josephus [cf. Schlatter, *Jos.* 28] and in Philo), or with the dative of the object (e.g. λόγῳ, ἀκοῇ and the like, perhaps also σημείοις Exod. iv.9). Besides this, it is found construed with ἐν in I Kingdoms (I Sam.) xxvii. 12, Mic. vii.5, Ps. lxxvii.11, II Chron. xx.20 (Dan. vi. 24); with ἐπί and the dative in Isa. xxviii.16 (probably the correct text); with ἐπί and the accusative in Wisd. of Sol. xii.1; with κατά and the genitive in Job iv.18, xv.15, xxiv.22. Naturally πιστεύειν can also govern a ὅτι clause, e.g. Exod. iv.5, Job. iv.16, Lam. iv. 12, Philo, *Migr. Abr.* 18, *Rer. Div. Her.* 101; or an accusative and infinitive: Jos. *Ap.* II.160. The noun πίστις is construed with the genitive: Jos. *Ap.* II.218; or with πρός: IV Macc. xv.24, xvi.22, Philo, *Rer. Div. Her.* 94, *Som.* I.68, *Abr.* 268, 270 f., 273, *Praem. Poen.* 27; or with περί: Jos. *Ap.* II.169.

IV. THE GROUP OF CONCEPTS ASSOCIATED WITH ΠΙ'ΣΤΙΣ IN THE NEW TESTAMENT

A. *Formal questions*

1. As regards the purely formal use of πιστεύω in the NT and in the other early Christian writings, there is only little that is peculiar as compared with Greek linguistic usage. As in Greek (cf. p. 37) πιστεύειν means to *rely on*, to *trust*,[1] or to *give credence to*.[2] It is construed with the dative of the person[3] or of the thing[4] and also with the accusative of the thing.[5] The Greek πιστεύειν περί is met with once only (John ix.18).[6] Naturally the absolute use is found also.[7] A ὅτι clause[8] and also an infinitive or an accusative and infinitive[9]

---

[1] A word in John iv.50; God in Acts xxvii.25, Barn. xvi.7, Herm. v.IV.2.6, m.XII.6.2 etc.; πνεύματι in Herm. m.XI.17.21.

[2] A word or the one who speaks it in Mark xiii.21, John iv.21.

[3] John iv.21, Acts xxvii.25, Ign. Rm. viii.2, Herm. m.I.2 etc. So too in Rom. iv.17 where the genitive is only the result of attraction. This must be distinguished from πιστεύειν with the dative meaning to *believe in* (cf. p. 58, n. 7).

[4] John iv.50 (λόγῳ), Acts xxiv.14 (τοῖς . . . γεγραμμένοις), II Clem. xi.1 (τῇ ἐπαγγελίᾳ), Herm., m.II.2 (τῇ καταλαλιᾷ).

[5] John xi.26, I Cor. xiii.7, Pol. viii.2.

[6] In Pol. vi.1 πιστεύειν κατά to *believe (something) against (somebody)* is found.

[7] Mark xiii.21, Luke xxii.67; I Cor. xi.18. Πιστεύειν, used absolutely in the religious sense, must be distinguished from this (cf. p. 72).

[8] Luke i.45; Acts ix.26, xxvii.25; John vi.69; Barn. vii.2; Herm. v.III.8.4, IV.2.4 etc. In these cases there is sometimes the shade of meaning *to consider possible*; see J. Jeremias, 'Beobachtungen zu nt.lichen Stellen an Hand des neugefundenen Griech. Hen. Textes', ZNW, 38 (1939), p. 120.

[9] Acts (viii.37), xv.11; Ign. Rm. x.2; cf. also Ign. Sm. iii.1. On Rom. xiv.2 (cf. below, p. 90).

can depend on πιστεύειν. The passive construction (to *be believed*) occurs as well.[1] Under the influence of the Semitic usage (cf. pp. 55 f.), πιστεύειν can also be used with ἐπί and the accusative[2] or dative[3] and also with ἐν.[4] But in particular the frequent expression πιστεύειν εἰς[5] in the sense of to *believe on*, found neither in Greek nor in the LXX,[6] is peculiar to the NT. This expression can scarcely be regarded as a development of πιστεύειν with the dative = to *trust*. Conversely the latter is often used following the analogy of πιστεύειν εἰς, that is to say in the sense of 'to *believe in*'.[7] On the contrary the fact that πιστεύειν εἰς and πιστεύειν ὅτι are equivalent shows that the phrase πιστεύειν εἰς is derived from the meaning of πιστεύειν, to *consider credible, true*.[8] Πιστεύειν εἰς Χριστὸν Ἰησοῦν (Gal. ii.16), εἰς αὐτόν and εἰς ἐμέ (often in John), and similar expressions, mean simply πιστεύειν ὅτι Ἰησοῦς ἀπέθανεν καὶ ἀνέστη (I Thess. iv.14, cf. Rom. x.9) or ὅτι Ἰησοῦς ἐστιν ὁ Χριστός (John xx.31) and the like. Especially in John πιστεύειν

---

[1] II Thess. i.10; I Tim. iii.16; Herm. m.III.3; Dg. xi.3, xii.8.

[2] Rom. iv.5, 24; Matt. xxvii.42; Acts ix.42, xi.17, xvi.31, xxii.19.

[3] I Tim. i.16. Cf. Rom. ix.33, I Pet. ii.6, following variant reading of Isa. xxviii.16.   [4] Mark i.15.

[5] cf. TWNT, II, p. 430. Moule, *Idiom Book*, p. 69, 80.

[6] Apart from Sir. xxxviii.31 where there is a mistranslation; cf. v. 31b and R. Smend, *Die Weisheit des Sir* (1906), p . 351; also Helbing, *Kasussyntax*, p. 201.

[7] Acts xvi.34 (τῷ θεῷ. D has ἐπὶ τὸν θεόν); xviii.8 (τῷ κυρίῳ. D has εἰς τὸν κύριον); Titus iii.8 (θεῷ).—In John also πιστεύειν εἰς and πιστεύειν with the dative alternate; but they do so in such a way that πιστεύειν with the dative has its original meaning: to *believe in someone* (with reference to what he says); thus v.38, 46 f., viii.45 f., x.37 f., xiv.11. The alternation (e.g. within the verses 29 f.) is not due to the change of meaning of πιστεύειν with the dative (this can only be assumed in John viii.31 and I John iii.23) but to the fact that for John *to believe the words of Jesus* is identical in substance with *to believe in Jesus* (cf. p. 73).

[8] The Jewish formula he'emīn le'šēm (A. Schlatter, *Der Evangelist Johannes* [²1948] on John i.12) can therefore hardly be a parallel.

εἰς and πιστεύειν ὅτι alternate constantly with the same meaning.[1] The same is proved by the passive phrase ἐπιστεύθη (sc. Ἰησοῦς Χριστός I Tim. iii.16) and the fact that πίστις εἰς is not the equivalent of πίστις with the dative, but of πίστις with the objective genitive (cf. below, p. 60). Thus πιστεύειν εἰς is to be understood as an abbreviation which became a formula in missionary parlance,[2] an abbreviation which is all the easier to understand since the term πίστις played a part in heathen as well as in Hellenistic Jewish propaganda (cf. pp. 41 f., 48 f.). In so far as πιστεύειν εἰς (especially in the aorist) means to be converted from the Jewish or heathen to the Christian faith (cf. pp. 68 f.), πιστεύειν εἰς is to be understood on the analogy of ἐπιστρέφειν ἐπί or πρός with the accusative; this can be seen, for example in the juxtaposition of I Thess. i.8 (ἡ πίστις ὑμῶν ἡ πρὸς τὸν θεόν) and i.9 (πῶς ἐπεστρέψατε πρὸς τὸν θεόν). Πιστεύειν used absolutely often alternates with πιστεύειν εἰς and has the same meaning.[3]

Πιστεύειν signifying to entrust is also found not infrequently (Luke xvi.11, John ii.24); the passive is used in the same way.[4] This is not a specifically Christian usage, not even if Christ is the one who is the confidant (Ign. Phld. ix.1).

2. The noun πίστις has, as in Greek (cf. pp. 35 ff.) the

[1] cf. also Acts viii.37 (E) where πιστεύειν, used absolutely, which elsewhere alternates with πιστεύειν εἰς, stands parallel with the accusative and infinitive.

[2] Ign. Mg. x.3 is perfectly clear: πιστεῦσαι (= to become a believer) εἰς Ἰουδαϊσμόν . . . εἰς Χριστιανισμόν.

[3] On the other hand πιστεύειν used absolutely means to believe with the sense of to trust, to have confidence in Mark v.36, ix.23 f., xi.23 f.; this also occurs in Ps. cxv (cxvi).1 to which Paul alludes in II Cor. iv.13, whilst giving ἐπίστευσα a new meaning in accordance with the sense of the Christian term.

[4] Rom. iii.2, I Cor. ix.17, Gal. ii.7, I Thess. ii.4, I Tim. i.11, Titus i.3.

twofold meaning of *loyalty* and *trust*. Yet it is seldom used in the former sense.[1] It is found with the meaning of trust only in religious usage. Here it is mostly used absolutely, but can also be construed with εἰς,[2] with ἐπί and the accusative (Heb. vi.1), with πρός and the accusative (I Thess. i.8, Philem. 5). Nor has the construction with ἐν[3] a different meaning; and the objective genitive can also be employed instead of using prepositions to complete it.[4]

3. Πιστός too has both the Greek meanings (cf. pp. 34 f.) of *loyal* and *trusting*. It is often used in the profane sense of *faithful*[5]. So there is no question of a religious meaning for faithfulness when it is practised in the service of God (I Cor. iv.2, 17, vii.25); on the other hand it might be so used when describing loyalty to the faith (Rev. ii.10, xvii.14?) or when the μάρτυς (*witness*) is described as πιστός (Rev. ii.13).[6] But no religious usage is

[1] Of God's fidelity in Rom. iii.3; loyalty amongst fellowmen in Matt. xxiii.23, Gal. v.22, Titus ii.10; fidelity towards Christ in I Tim. v.12 (here πίστις almost means an oath; see Pr-Bauer); probably also in the traditional saying used in Luke xxii.32 (see Bultmann, *Die Geschichte der synoptischen Tradition* (³1957), p. 288), although the evangelist understands it as faith.—In Acts xvii.31 we find πίστιν παρέχειν in the Greek sense of to *give bail, submit evidence*; see M. Dibelius, *Aufsätze zur Apostelgeschichte* (1951), p. 54.

[2] Acts xx.21, xxiv.24, xxvi.8; Col. ii.5; I Pet. i.21(?).

[3] Gal. iii.26(?), Col. i.4, Eph. i.15, I Tim. iii.13, II Tim. iii.15; not Rom. iii.25 (cf. TWNT III.322).

[4] Mark xi.22; Acts iii.16, xix.20(D); Rom. iii.22, 26; Gal. ii.16, iii.22; Phil. i.27, iii.9; Col. ii.12; Eph. iii.12; II Thess. ii.13; Rev. xiv.12; I Clem. iii.4, xxvii.3; Ign. Eph. xvi.2, xx.1; Barn. vi.7; Herm. m.XI.9. There is no justification for the suggestion made by G. Schläger, 'Bemerkungen zu πίστις Ἰησοῦ Χριστοῦ', ZNW, 7 (1906), 356-8 to strike out the genitives Ἰησοῦ Χριστοῦ and Ἰησοῦ in Rom. iii.22, 26; Gal. ii.16, iii.22.

[5] Matt. xxiv.25, xxv.21, 23; Luke xvi.10 f.; I Tim. iii.11; II Tim. ii.2; cf. III John 5: πιστὸν ποιεῖν to *behave loyally*.

[6] Here Antipas is described as a 'faithful witness' who was not deflected from his witnessing even by death. It may be noted that

intended when the words of the Christian message are called πιστός, *trustworthy*, as in the formula πιστὸς ὁ λόγος (καὶ πάσης ἀποδοχῆς ἄξιος),[1] or when it is said of Christian prophecy: οἱ λόγοι πιστοὶ καὶ ἀληθινοί εἰσιν (Rev. xxi.5, xxii.6). There is just as little of a religious meaning when God himself or Christ is designated as πιστός.[2] Πιστός, *trusting*, is not employed in a profane, but only in a religious sense, and indeed with a Christian meaning and therefore denotes *believing, full of faith* (on this see pp. 81 f.).

4. Πιστόω is found in the NT only in the passive in I Tim. iii.16 meaning to *be made a believer*; similarly in I Clem. xlii.3. On the other hand in I Clem. xv.4 (from Ps. lxxvii [lxxviii].37) it has the meaning of *being faithful to*.

5. Amongst the privative formations ἄπιστος is found in Luke xii.46 perhaps denoting *unfaithful* (as contrasted with *faithful* in v. 42). Yet it is more probable that Luke intends the word to mean *unbelieving, not a Christian*.[3] It is often found with this sense (cf. p. 82). With the more general meaning of *unbelieving* it occurs in Mark ix.19 and parallels (*without trust, without confidence*) and in John xx.27 (with regard to the news of the resurrection, cf. v. 25). Ἄπιστος is used in Acts xxvi.8 to mean *incredible*.

6. Ἀπιστέω in Rom. iii.3, II Tim. ii.13 means to *be*

in Rev. i.5, iii.14, Jesus Christ is described as 'faithful witness'. Cf. TWNT, II, pp. 499 f.

[1] I Tim. i.15, iii.1, iv.9; II Tim. ii.11; Titus iii.8; cf. Titus i.9; see M. Dibelius, *Die Pastoralbriefe* ([3]1955) on I Tim. i.15. The formula is probably to be regarded as a fixed kerygmatic expression, cf. TWNT, II, p. 54.

[2] I Cor. x.13; II Cor. i.18; I Clem. xxvii.1, lx.1; II Clem. xi.6; Ign. Tr. xiii.3, etc. of God; II Tim. ii.13; Heb. ii.17, iii.2 of Christ.

[3] The passage comes from Q, the text of which may have been preserved in Matt. xxiv.51 with its μετὰ τῶν ὑποκριτῶν whilst Luke has altered it to μετὰ τῶν ἀπίστων.

faithless; in Luke xxiv.11, 41, Acts xxviii.24 (the opposite, of πείθεσθαι) to *disbelieve* (words); thus also in the spurious ending of Mark in xvi.11; whilst it appears here in xvi.16 in the technical sense of *refusing to believe* the Christian gospel.

7. 'Απιστία means *faithlessness* in Rom. iii.3 and Heb. iii.12. Heb. iii.19 (cf. ἀπειθεῖν in v. 18) shows how closely related to this is the meaning *disobedience*. For the general sense of *unbelief*, as lack of faith or trust see Mark vi.6 and parallels, ix.24, Matt. xvii.20 (variant reading); Rom. iv.20. For unbelief with regard to words see Mark xvi.14, to the Christian kerygma see Rom. xi.20, 23, I Tim. i.13.

8. 'Ολιγόπιστος (cf. p. 48, n. 7) lacking in Greek and derived from Judaism, is found only in the synoptists: Matt. vi.30 and parallels, viii.26, xiv.31, xvi.8. The noun ὀλιγοπιστία is in Matt. xvii.20 (אB).

B.   *The common Christian usage*

1.   *The persistence of the Old Testament and Jewish tradition*

In primitive Christianity πίστις became the predominant designation of the relationship of man to God. This is due in part to the fact that, already in the OT and in Judaism, 'faith' had become a special expression for the religious attitude (cf. pp. 11 f., 49 f.), and moreover that early Christianity, like Judaism, was a missionary religion. Faith means turning towards the God disclosed by the preaching. Thus in the common Christian usage the heritage of the OT and of Judaism is to a large extent brought out in what is meant by πίστις (πιστεύειν, πιστός).

(*a*) Πιστεύω often means to put faith in the words of God. Therefore faith applies to the 'scriptures' (John ii.22); to what is written in the law and the prophets (Acts xxiv.14); to what the prophets said (Luke xxiv.25)

or simply to the prophets (Acts xxvi.27); to Moses or
his writings (John v.46 f.); and similarly to what God
is saying at present, for example by an angel (Luke i.20,
45, Acts xxvii.25). John the Baptist can also be described in this sense as the one who is to be 'believed'
(Mark xi.31, Matt. xxi.32); and the Johannine gospel
(and this gospel alone!) says similarly that Jesus and his
word are believed or ought to be believed[1]; for he is indeed sent by God (v.38) and speaks the words of God
(iii.34 *et passim*). In fact, for John this means nothing
else than 'to believe in Jesus' (cf. p. 73 and p. 58, n. 7).
But it is characteristic of John that these two coincide.[2]

(*b*) It is brought out particularly in Heb. xi that,
just as in the OT, to *believe* the words is to *obey* them
(cf. p. 47). Here the πίστις of the OT personages has
in some cases the more or less avowed sense of obedience.[3] How obvious it is for πιστεύειν to include the
meaning of to *obey* is evident from the fact that the
acceptance of the Christian preaching is expressed by
πιστεύειν as well as by πείθεσθαι and that unbelief can
be denoted not only by ἀπιστεῖν but equally well by
ἀπειθεῖν.[4] It was chiefly Paul who emphasised that the
nature of faith is that of obedience. For him πίστις is
also ὑπακοή, as can be seen by comparing Rom. i.8,
I Thess. i.8 with Rom. xv.18, xvi.19, or II Cor. x.5 f.
with x.15. Faith means to him *to give heed* (ὑπακούειν)
to the gospel (Rom. x.16); to reject faith means not to submit to the righteousness offered to faith in the gospel

[1] John ii.22, v.46 f., viii.45 f. etc.
[2] The unbelieving attitude towards (crucial) words can be
expressed by ἀπιστεῖν (Luke xxiv.11, 41, Acts xxviii.24 [the
opposite of πείθεσθαι], Mark xvi.11), or by ἀπιστία (Mark xvi.14).
[3] e.g. Heb. xi.4-6, 8, also 27 f., 30 f., 33. Correspondingly
ἀπιστία = *disobedience* in Heb. iii.19 (cf. ἀπειθεῖν v. 18).
[4] In Rom. ii.8 the antithetic formula stresses that the proper
relationship to God is one of obedience (cf. also Gal. v.7). On the
usage of πείθεσθαι and ἀπειθεῖν cf. TWNT, VI, pp. 4, 11.

(Rom. x.3). He can call the acceptance of the gospel in faith *obedience in acknowledging the gospel of Christ* (II Cor. ix.13). He joins them together in ὑπακοὴ πίστεως (Rom. i.5).[1] For the theological interpretation of faith in these passages see pp. 87 f.

(*c*) Further, the meaning of 'trust', which in the OT and Judaism (cf. p. 47) is linked with 'faith', is not lacking in the NT, and it is especially prominent where the OT and Jewish influence is strong. Trust in God is mentioned relatively seldom (cf. TWNT, VI, p. 6). But it is natural for the πίστις of the OT personages in Heb. xi to be *trust* just as much as *obedience*; the paraphrase in v. 11: (Sarah) *considered him faithful* (πιστόν) *who had promised*, agrees with this. In fact πίστις in v. 11 is on the one hand trust that God will carry out his promise (cf. p. 48)[2] and on the other trust in his power to work miracles, as in vv. 17-19 and vv. 29 f. It is in this sense that the synoptists speak of faith in Jesus' miraculous powers.[3] In the Christian mission, this is replaced by faith in the wonder-working name (ὄνομα) of Jesus (Acts iii.16)[4] or in the power of the apostles to effect miracles (Acts xiv.9). In general 'faith' in the synoptists denotes trust in the miraculous help of God,[5]

---

[1] The phrase εἰς ὑπακοὴν πίστεως in Rom. xvi.26 and the words ὑπηκούσατε etc. in Rom. vi.17 agree with Pauline usage; but it may be that neither passage is really Paul's (cf. R. Bultmann, 'Glossen in R.', ThLZ, 72 [1947], p. 202).

[2] Similarly in xi.7, 8 ff., 13, 17, etc.; also in II Clem. xi.1; Herm. s.I.7, m.XII.6.2; correspondingly faith in God's future reward Herm. s.II.5; cf. v.III.8.4, 6.5.

[3] Πιστεύειν in Mark v.36; Matt. viii.8, 13, ix.28; in Mark ii.5, v.34, x.52; Matt. viii.10 and parallels; ix.29, xv.28; like a formula in Luke xvii.19.

[4] iii.6 reveals how the healing takes place, and subsequently in v. 16 it is said that *his name has made him strong*. The name is associated with the power (cf. TWNT, V, p. 276, Allmen, VB, pp. 278 ff., J. Pederson, *Israel*, I-II (1926), pp. 245-59).

[5] Mark iv.40, ix.23 f.

indeed in one's own power to perform miracles,[1] (so also in Paul in I Cor. xii.9, xiii.2). That such πίστις is basically faith in prayer is already intimated in Mark xi.22 by the fact that it is described as πίστις θεοῦ[2] and this is made clear by the saying added in Mark xi.24 in which πίστις explicitly means faith in prayer. The confident faith in prayer which does not doubt is described elsewhere too as πίστις.[3] In Paul the meaning of πίστις as trust is in general less prominent (but cf. p. 60); yet it is present when Paul is speaking of Abraham's faith as trust in God's power to perform miracles (Rom. iv.17-20). It is probable that the phrase *that he might be the father* in Rom. iv.11 is not intended to be a consecutive clause but to indicate the content of Abraham's faith; in that case the πίστις is the trust that God's promise will be fulfilled; similarly also possibly the phrase *that he might become the father* in Rom. iv.18. In Rom. ix.33, x.11 too, where Paul, alluding to Isa. xxviii.16 speaks of πιστεύειν ἐπ' αὐτῷ (i.e. God), πιστεύειν is intended to mean trust.[4] Ἀπιστία

---

[1] Mark xi.22 f. and parallels; Matt. xvii.20, Luke xvii.6.

[2] The ἔχετε πίστιν θεοῦ is an introductory addition of Mark (see Bultmann, *Die Geschichte der synoptischen Tradition* ([3]1937), p. 95), which is not found in the Q variants in Matt. xvii.20, Luke xvii.6, and which Matt. xxi.21 also avoids in the parallel to Mark. Πίστις θεοῦ is found only here with this meaning (Rom. iii.3 God's faithfulness); this is in line not with the OT and Jewish usage, but with missionary terminology (θεοῦ is missing in some MSS); cf. Lohmeyer, *Mark* ad loc.

[3] Jas. i.6, v.15; Herm. m.IX.6-12, cf. v.IV.2.6.

[4] cf. the even more colourless phrases such as 'to serve . . . in the assurance born of a good faith' in I Clem. xxvi.1 as a description of piety; Herm. m.I.2: 'believe him therefore and fear him' cf. Dg. x.i. In I Clem. xxxv.2 'faith with assurance' is reckoned amongst the blessings of salvation; similarly it appears in Herm. m.VI.1.1-2.10 as a virtue beside fear and self-control. In what follows πίστις is described as faith in the righteous or in the angel of righteousness. In Herm. s.IX.15.2 f. Πίστις appears as the first

is used several times with a corresponding meaning. In Rom. iv.20 it denotes lack of faith in God's power to work miracles, in Mark vi.6, ix.24 in that of Jesus, in Matt. xvii.20 (so in D, the Latin versions and Sinaitic Syriac) in one's own. Ἄπιστος has the same meaning in Mark ix.19. Ὀλιγόπιστος, taken over from Judaism (cf. p. 48, n. 7), has a similar sense.[1] We find ἀπιστία linked with double-mindedness in II Clem. xix.2 meaning lack of faith, i.e. of trust in general.

(d) There is a very close connexion between trust in God and hope (cf. p. 48 and p. 26, n. 1). This is emphasised in Rom. iv.18 by the words *In hope he believed against hope* and is evident also in the description of πίστις in Heb. xi. After all faith in God's promise is itself hope at the same time; and this meaning predominates in Heb. xi.[2] It is just for this reason that the OT personages can be examples for Christians whose faith is indeed also directed towards the future promised by God. Both of them know that they are *strangers and exiles on the earth* (v. 13)—the more so because the future promised to the faithful of the OT is really the same as that promised to the Christian[3] and neither has yet experienced the fulfilment.[4] The paradox of such hopeful trust is as strongly emphasised in Heb. xi as in Rom. iv.19. It is directed towards what is invisible (v. 7) or rather towards the one who is invisible (v. 27). For the sake of this paradox Heb. xi has, it is true, also accepted the Hellenistic (and Philo's) idea: πίστις is directed towards the invisible because this is not only the

of the virtuous virgins corresponding to Ἀπιστία as the first of the vices.

[1] Matt. vi.30 and its parallel speaks of the feebleness of trust in God, whilst in Matt. viii.26, xiv.31, xvi.8 lack of trust in Jesus' power to work miracles may be meant. In Matt. xvii.20 ℵ and B read ὀλιγοπιστία to denote the disciples' weak faith with regard to their own power to work miracles.   [2] cf. Käsemann, pp. 19-27.

[3] vv. 7, 10, 14-16, 26.   [4] vv. 13, 39 f.

promised future, but also the heavenly reality which cannot be perceived by the senses, but can only be believed in faith: *By faith we understand that the world was created by the word of God so that what is seen was made out of things which do not appear* (v. 3). And the preceding definition in v. 1 sums up both aspects: *Now faith is the assurance* (ὑπόστασις, cf. p. 26, n. 1) *of things hoped for, the conviction of things not seen.*[1] If this construction is put on faith, then it follows on the one hand that Heb. xi, which in other respects is couched in terms of the language of the OT, can understand faith in accordance with missionary terminology also: *For whoever would draw near to God must believe that he is and that he rewards them who seek him* (v. 6; cf. vi.1). On the other hand it causes special emphasis to be placed on that aspect of faith which turns away from this world and looks toward the heavenly world (vv. 7, 15 f., 24-26; cf. xii.2[2]). The element of hope in faith is also preserved where, in the specifically Christian usage (cf. p. 69), πίστις means faith in Christ. This is done in such a way that hope is named beside faith, but expressly distinguished from it. The less the Christian πίστις εἰς . . . as such is hope, the more hope (ἐλπίς), especially in Paul, retains its own element of faithful trust derived from the OT (cf. p. 26, n. 1). Πίστις and ἐλπίς appear side by side (and linked with ἀγάπη) in I Thess. i.3, I Cor. xiii.13, or in other combinations.[3] The fundamental connexion is emphasised in I Pet. i.21 in the words *so that your faith and hope are in God* (cf. p. 26, n. 1).

(*e*) The OT meaning of *loyalty* (cf. pp. 46 f.) is still discernible in πίστις. This is evident in the conclusion drawn from the remembrance of the witnesses to faith

---

[1] Πίστις can acquire this shade of meaning in Paul's writings too: II Cor. v.7.

[2] Paul draws the same conclusion in II Cor. v.6 ff.

[3] Col. i.4 f., 23, Heb. vi.11 (variant reading); cf. Barn. iv.8.

in Heb. xii.1: *let us run with perseverance the race that is set before us,* corresponding to what leads up to ch. xi: *for you have need of perseverance* (x.36). Hope and perseverance naturally belong together (cf. p. 26, n. 1). In the same way πίστις and perseverance are associated in I Thess. i.4[1]; similarly πίστις and patience in Heb. vi.12; also ἀγάπη, πίστις, service and perseverance in Rev. ii.19. The πίστις of the leaders who are held up as examples for imitation in Heb. xiii.7, is also to be understood essentially as loyalty; similarly πίστις has the same meaning when it is said in II Tim. iv.7: *I have kept the faith*[2] or when in Rev. ii.13 the church in Pergamum is praised: *you hold fast my name and you did not deny my faith.* Conversely ἀπιστία in Heb. iii.12 and ἀπιστεῖν in II Tim. ii.13 mean the *unfaithfulness* of Christians. In Heb. xi.17 it is said that πίστις holds firm in temptation and in Jas. i.2 f. that it produces steadfastness. In I Peter also the meaning of πίστις as loyalty is brought out, for it is to stand firm when tested.[3] When Paul is thinking of the 'faith' of Israel, the element of loyalty comes into play for him too. Thus in Rom. iii.3 he speaks of ἀπιστεῖν and of the ἀπιστία = the *faithlessness* of Israel. But where he enjoins loyalty to faith, he urges *to stand firm in the faith* (I Cor. xvi.13),[4] that is to say, πίστις as such does not mean loyalty, rather it is the *faith* to which loyalty is due.

2. *The specifically Christian usage*

(a) The specifically Christian sense of πίστις must be distinguished from all these meanings. It is indicated most clearly by the formula πίστις εἰς (cf. pp. 58, 60). Here πίστις is understood as the acceptance of the

---

[1] Also in Rev. xiii.10 (cf. xiv.12).
[2] For τὴν πίστιν τηρεῖν = to *keep faith* see Pr.-Bauer[4] s.v.
[3] I Pet. i.7; cf. also i.5, 9, v.9.
[4] cf. *stand firm in the Lord* Phil. iv.1, I Thess. iii.8.

Christian kerygma and consequently of the saving faith which recognises and appropriates God's work of salvation brought about by Christ. Naturally πίστις here too implies the sense of *giving credence*; and the elements of obedience, trust, hope and loyalty can also be included in the meaning—in the same way as conversely, where one of these senses is the primary one, the reference to Christ can be comprised in it.[1] But the primary meaning in the specifically Christian usage is the acceptance of the kerygma of Christ.[2] This usage is accounted for by its being in the first place missionary terminology (cf. pp. 48 f., 59). At first, 'belief in Christ' is used with the same meaning as 'belief in God', namely with regard to those who do not yet know the only God and do not yet believe in Him, but must first 'believe' in Him, namely in the sense of recognising His existence in order that they may then be able to 'believe' in Him in the sense of the OT conception of faith. Heb. xi.6 employs πιστεύειν expressly in the former sense (cf. above, pp. 66 f.). In fact the early Christian missionaries preached belief in Christ at the same time as belief in the only God whom the heathen are to confess, having rejected 'idols'. Thus the conversion of the Thessalonians is described in I Thess. i.8 as their πίστις πρὸς τὸν θεόν; and this expression is explained in v. 9: *how you turned to God from*

---

[1] Perhaps the clearest example is in Rev. xiv.12 where to πίστις =*loyalty* there is attached the objective genitive Ἰησοῦ which denotes the real subject of the kerygma.

[2] Rom. x.14-17 describes in detail how πίστις is the acceptance of the kerygma.—The kerygma is the object of faith in I Cor. i.21, ii.4 f., xv.11, 14; Herm. s.VIII.3. 2; so is the *gospel* (εὐαγγέλιον) in I Cor. xv.2; Phil. i.27(?); Eph. i.13; Acts viii.12, xv.7; Mark i.15; cf. Dg. xi.6;—the *testimony* (μαρτύριον) in II Thess. i.10, I John v.10; cf. John i.7;—*obedience* (ἀκοή) in Rom. x.16, John xii.38; cf. Herm. s.IX.17.4;—λόγος in Acts iv.4, xiii.48; Eph. i.13; Barn. ix.3; cf. xi.11 and cf. Barn. xvi.9.

idols (cf. p. 59). According to Heb. vi.1, πίστις ἐπὶ θεόν belongs to the rudiments of Christianity beside *repentance from dead works*.[1] In the OT and in Judaism (quite apart from propaganda) 'belief' is demanded as the appropriate attitude towards the God who has made himself known long ago and whose existence is not doubted. On the other hand, the early Christian kerygma brings the message that there is one God and together with it the message concerning Jesus Christ, His son, and of what God has done through Him and will continue to do. The acceptance of this kerygma is called πιστεύειν. It is therefore clear that in the specifically Christian πίστις, the element of trustful hope becomes less prominent. The πίστις εἰς ... looks first and foremost at what God has done, not at what he is going to do.[2]

(*b*) In Rom. x.9 (cf. p. 58) Paul indicates the content of the Christian faith in one sentence in which he is consciously expressing, not a conception peculiar to himself, but that which is taken for granted by every Christian preacher: *if you confess* (ὁμολογεῖν) *with your lips that Jesus is Lord and believe* (πιστεύειν) *in your heart that God raised him from the dead, you will be saved.* Since in the synonymous parallelism ὁμολογεῖν and πιστεύειν have the same meaning,[3] it is clear that the Christian faith consists in recognising Jesus as Lord and at the same time accepting ('believing to be true') the miracle of the resurrection. It is obvious, and it is confirmed by other statements, that these tenets form a unity in themselves, and that therefore the resurrection is not

[1] cf. the manner in which in Acts xvii.22-31 the theological and Christological preaching is combined. Cf. also Herm. m.I.1; cf. p. 49, n. 2.

[2] See J. Weiss, *Das Urchristentum* (1917), p. 323; Wissmann, pp. 71 f.; Mundle, pp. 73-114.

[3] Belief and confession are also closely linked by Paul in II Cor. iv.13 (cf. TWNT, V, p. 209).

merely a remarkable occurrence, but is the fact of salvation on the strength of which Jesus became Lord. Naturally because they have this close internal connexion with each other, now the one statement, now the other, can be made alone, or the saving event may be described in other terms, or in more detail; but it is always the whole which is meant. *So we preach and so you believed* says Paul in I Cor. xv.11 with reference to the gospel (v. 1), to which it appertains *as of first importance* (ἐν πρώτοις v. 3) that Christ died for our sins, was buried and was raised on the third day and declared Himself to be the risen one. According to Rom. iv.24 Christians believe in *him who raised from the dead Jesus our Lord* (similarly Col. ii.12); according to I Thess. iv.14 *we believe that Jesus died and rose again.*[1] If the picture outlined in Phil. ii.6-11 of Christ's humiliation and exaltation is not explicitly denoted as the object of πίστις, yet it is to be understood as such. *To confess that Jesus Christ is Lord*—in so far as it is carried out by those on earth—is nothing else than a confession of πίστις (cf. Rom. x.9). The kerygmatic parts of the speeches in the Acts[2] describe the contents of πίστις, even if it is not always stated in so many words (as in xiii.39). For kerygma and belief of course belong together (cf. p. 69, n. 2; cf. I Tim. iii.16). Moreover it makes no difference whether in the place of the title of Kyrios[3] other titles are used to denote the honour due to Jesus, naming Him as the object of πιστεύειν; as for example in John xx.31: *in order that you may believe that Jesus is the Christ, the son of God*[4] or whether in the ὅτι-clause the work of salvation is described by means of

---

[1] cf. I Pet. i.21; Pol. ii.1.
[2] Acts ii.22-24, iii.13-15, x.37-41, xiii.26-37.
[3] cf. *Lord* in this series, esp. pp. 97 ff.
[4] cf. also John xi.27, vi.69, further I John v.1, 5, Acts viii.37 (so E and other MSS).

other concepts, as for example *that I came from the Father* (John xvi.27, 30), *that thou didst send me* (John xi.42, xvii.8, 21) or by the still more specifically Johannine: *that I am in the Father and the Father in me* (John xiv.10 f.) or by the simple *that I am* (John viii.24, xiii.19).[1] The salvation wrought by God in Christ can be designated as the object of faith in more general terms as the *love which God has for us* (I John iv.16) or by its significance: *But if we have died with Christ, we believe that we shall also live with him* (Rom. vi.8).[2] An epitomising expression for this saving faith is the formula πιστεύειν (πίστις) εἰς. . . .[3] In the place of the construction with prepositions the objective genitive can be used with πίστις.[4] In this sense πίστις and πιστεύειν can also be used absolutely, and this is so frequent in the writings of Paul, in the 'Deutero'-Pauline literature, in the Acts, in

[1] In the succeeding period the motive behind the wording was often to contradict a false doctrine, as e.g. Ign. Sm. iii.1.

[2] 'Faith in a divine spirit' in Herm. m.XI.9 probably means the belief that the divine spirit exists, or rather that it is bestowed within the congregation.

[3] Πιστεύειν εἰς: εἰς τὸν Ἰησοῦν in Acts xix.4, John xii.11; εἰς Χριστὸν Ἰησοῦν in Gal. ii.16; cf. I Pet. i.8; εἰς τὸν κύριον in Acts xiv.23; Herm. m.IV.3.3; cf. Rom. x.14; εἰς τὸν υἱόν John iii.36; cf. John iii.16, 18; εἰς τὸν υἱὸν τοῦ θεοῦ in I John v.10; εἰς τὸν υἱὸν τοῦ ἀνθρώπου in John ix.35; εἰς αὐτόν in Acts x.43; John ii.11, iv.39, vii.31, viii.30, etc; εἰς ἐμέ in John vi.35, xiv.1, xvi.9, xvii.20; Matt. xviii.6; εἰς τὸ φῶς in John xii.36; εἰς τὸ ὄνομα in John i.12, ii.23 (αὐτοῦ); in John iii.18 (τοῦ μονογενοῦς υἱοῦ τοῦ θεοῦ); in I John v.13 (τοῦ υἱοῦ τοῦ θεοῦ); εἰς ὃν ἀπέστειλεν ἐκεῖνος in John vi.29. Πίστις εἰς: εἰς τὸν κύριον ἡμῶν Ἰησοῦν in Acts xx.21; εἰς Χριστὸν Ἰησοῦν in Acts xxiv.24; εἰς Χριστόν in Col. ii.5; πρὸς τὸν κύριον Ἰησοῦν in Philem. 5; εἰς ἐμέ in Acts xxvi.18.

[4] Πίστις with objective genitive: Ἰησοῦ Χριστοῦ in Rom. iii.22; Gal. ii.16, iii.22; Ἰησοῦ in Rom. iii.26; Rev. xiv.12; Χριστοῦ in Phil. iii.9; τοῦ κυρίου ἡμῶν Ἰησοῦ Χριστοῦ in James ii.1, cf. Eph. iii. 12; τοῦ κυρίου in Herm. v.IV.1.8; see VI.1.2, 3.6; τοῦ υἱοῦ τοῦ θεοῦ in Gal. ii.20; Herm. s.IX.16.5; τοῦ ὀνόματος αὐτοῦ in Acts iii.16; μου in Rev. ii.13.

John's writings and later, that examples are superfluous. Mark and Luke have also been influenced by the usage.[1]

(c) The question therefore arises whether this epitomising phrase πίστις (πιστεύειν) εἰς . . . which came into being for linguistic reasons in the first instance, can acquire at the same time a meaning of its own, i.e. whether it can be used to denote a personal relationship to Christ as well; thus—since of course πιστεύειν εἰς Χριστὸν Ἰησοῦν is the gateway to salvation—'faith in Christ' would have essentially the same significance as the relationship with God.

Now it is worth observing that the relationship with God is practically never denoted in the NT by πιστεύειν εἰς.[2] Conversely the usual form of words in the LXX describing the relationship with God, πιστεύειν with the dative and πιστεύειν ἐπί with the dative (cf. p. 58), are practically never applied to the relationship with Christ. Πιστεύειν with the dative, which in Rom. iv.3 (17), Gal. iii.6, Titus iii.8, Acts xvi.34 (D: ἐπὶ τὸν θεόν) describes the relationship with God,[3] is indeed found frequently in John to denote the relationship with Jesus, but here it does not mean to *believe* (in Jesus), but to *give credence to* Jesus or his words. It is true that for John this is actually identical with πιστεύειν εἰς (αὐτόν) but must not be confused with it linguistically

[1] Πίστις in Luke xviii.8; πιστεύειν in Mark ix.42, Luke viii.12 f.; similarly in the spurious ending in Mark xvi.16 f.

[2] There are only two possible cases: (a) I Pet. i.21 (cf. p. 67). If this meant: *so that your faith and your hope are directed towards God*, then the εἰς would be caused, not by πίστις, but by ἐλπίς (similarly in I Clem. xii.7) in accordance with the linguistic usage attested since the LXX (see II Cor. i.10, Acts xxiv.15, John v.45. Cf. p. 26, n. 1. (b) John xiv.1: πιστεύετε ἐν τὸν θεόν, καὶ εἰς ἐμὲ πιστεύετε. A unique case; the wording is chosen to express the oneness of Jesus with God.

[3] In addition Acts xvi.15 (D): πιστὸς τῷ θεῷ. Also in John v.24; I John v.10 πιστεύειν with the dative; but here in the particular meaning of *giving credence* (to God).

(cf. pp. 58 f.). Apart from these cases πιστεύειν with the dative is found only seldom applied to Jesus, and only once in the NT is a personal relationship with Christ expressed by it: II Tim. i.12 οἶδα γὰρ ᾧ πεπίστευκα, where the sense of 'trusting' is combined with that of 'believing in'; similarly also in Ign. Tr. ix.2. On the other hand in Matt. xxvii.42 (D), Acts xviii.8 (cf. xvi. 15); I John iii.23, as this passage in particular shows clearly it must be understood on the analogy of πιστεύειν εἰς (cf. p. 59). Πιστεύειν ἐπί with the dative in Rom. ix. 33, x.11; I Pet. ii.6; I Clem. xxxiv.4, quoting Isa. xxviii.15, denotes the relationship with God and is used for the relationship with Jesus only in I Tim. i.16, where the addition of εἰς ζωὴν αἰώνιον shows that the sense of hopeful trust predominates.[1] On the other hand the formula πιστεύειν ἐπί with the accusative, still rare in the LXX, is found several times and shows that the relationship with God and with Christ is the same.[2] For there is no doubt that it is not an epitomising formula, but denotes a turning towards the person of the Lord, just as πίστις ἐπὶ θεόν (Heb. vi.1; cf. Acts xvi.34 (D)) and πίστις πρὸς τὸν θεόν (I Thess. i.8; cf. p. 60) denote turning to God from heathenism.[3] In the same way τὴν πίστιν ἣν ἔχεις πρὸς τὸν Κύριον Ἰησοῦν in Philem. 5 shows that πιστεύειν can be

---

[1] The occasional πιστεύειν ἐν in Mark i.15, John iii.15 (?), and also πίστις ἐν in Gal. iii.26(?), Col. i.4(?), Eph. i.15, I Tim. iii.13, II Tim. iii.15; I Clem. xxii.1 must no doubt be understood not as a return to the LXX phrase, but as a linguistic variation on πιστεύειν (πίστις) εἰς.

[2] Acts ix.42, xi.17, xvi.31, xxii.19; Matt. xxvii.42 (D: αὐτῷ; 𝕳: ἐπ' αὐτῷ).

[3] The case is different in Rom. iv.24 (altered in Col. ii.12, I Pet. i.21) where *to them who believe in* (ἐπὶ + acc.) *him who raised from the dead Jesus our Lord* is construed obviously on the analogy of ἐλπίζειν ἐπί and has the same meaning (cf. Barn. xi.8). Similarly Rom. iv.5 (cf. iv.18).

used to denote a personal relationship with Christ.

But the crucial point is this: faith in Christ, as being the acceptance of the kerygma about Him, does not merely affirm the existence of a hitherto unknown divine personage, a 'foreign divinity' (Acts xvii.18). For the figure of Jesus Christ cannot be separated from his 'myth', i.e. from the history of the events of his life, death and resurrection. But this history is salvation history, i.e. the man who by his 'faith' affirms the kerygma, acknowledges thereby that this history took place for him[1]; and since Jesus Christ became Lord by means of His history,[2] the acceptance of the kerygma includes the acknowledgement of Jesus Christ as Lord, and indeed this finds expression in the phrase πίστις εἰς τὸν κύριον ἡμῶν ᾿Ιησοῦν and similar ones. In that case πιστεύειν εἰς Χριστὸν ᾿Ιησοῦν means in actual fact a personal relationship with Christ, analogous to that with God and yet differing from it. If the OT relationship with God is called 'faith in God', then faith of this kind is already different from the πίστις εἰς Χριστὸν ᾿Ιησοῦν owing to the fact that the OT faith—as being obedience and loyalty—is directed towards the God whose existence is already always taken for granted. But faith in Jesus Christ, in its original and proper sense, is not obedience to the Lord who has always been known. On the contrary it is by faith that the existence of this Lord is first perceived and acknowledged. Faith lays hold of the conviction that for the believer this Lord, Jesus Christ, exists. For this Lord first meets him only in the kerygma, and he believes on the strength

---

[1] What is said in the NT by ὑπέρ and περί and similarly constructed formulae, is expressed later in phrases such as πιστεύειν εἰς τὸν θάνατον αὐτοῦ in Ign. Tr. ii.1; εἰς τὸ αἷμα Χριστοῦ in Ign. Sm. vi.1; cf. Barn. vii.2 (Barn. xi.8, cf. p. 74, n. 3).

[2] Phil. ii.9-11, Acts ii.36 (cf. Acts v.31 where He is made 'saviour').

of the kerygma, and in the future he can always only believe on the strength of this message. This never becomes a mere instructive piece of information, which might be dispensed with once it had become known, but always remains the foundation of the faith. For God instituted the word of reconciliation together with the Christ event (II Cor. v.18 f.). Therefore faith in the kerygma and in the person mediated by it are inseparable, and faith always remains a 'bold venture' in the sense that it is based on the kerygma.

So now individual passages show that the phrase πιστεύειν εἰς Χριστὸν Ἰησοῦν, which was originally a set form of words, can really express a personal relationship. Firstly Rom. x.9 proves clearly that to believe in Jesus Christ means to acknowledge him as Lord; and when according to Rom. x.14 πιστεύειν εἰς αὐτόν leads men to call upon him, then this πιστεύειν brings about a personal relationship with him, because it results in baptism. That faith passes into fellowship with him is shown by Rom. vi.8, Gal. ii.20, and in a special manner by Phil. i.29: *For it has been granted to you that for the sake of Christ you should not only believe in him* (τὸ εἰς αὐτὸν πιστεύειν) *but also suffer for his sake*, or by I Pet. i.8: (at the revelation of Jesus Christ) *whom not having seen you love, in whom* (εἰς ὅν), *though now you see him not, yet believing* (πιστεύοντες), *you rejoice* . . . , or by Acts xiv.2: *they committed them to the Lord in whom they believed*. To these must be added those few cases in which the relationship with Christ is expressed by πιστεύειν with the dative in the sense of *trust* (cf. p. 74)[1] and by πιστεύειν ἐπί (cf. p. 74) or by πίστις πρός (Philem. 5).[2]

---

[1] In later writings cf. Ign. Phld. viii.1 (cf. Pol. vii.3); Dg. ix.6.

[2] It is possible that Philem. 5 is even speaking of a love directed towards the Lord Jesus. But it is probable that an inversion has taken place (Lohmeyer, *Philemon*, ad loc.), so that πίστις felt for Christ and love for the saints are meant.

(d) The saving faith, which is denoted by πίστις and πιστεύειν—it may be absolutely or with a qualification —can be regarded from the point of view either of its origin or of its continuing existence. When repentance and πίστις are preached (Acts xx.21, cf. Heb. vi.1), the hearers are urged to repent and to become believers. Πίστις is understood as the acceptance of the Christian message, e.g. in Rom. i.5, iii.25, x.17; I Cor. xv.14, 17, and probably also in I Thess. i.8 (that you became believers); Rom. i.8, xi.20 (you stand fast only through faith) and in all the passages where Paul is speaking of being justified or of the justification ἐκ πίστεως as in Rom. iii.28, v.1; Gal. iii.24; Phil. iii.9 and elsewhere. Naturally it is used in this way also in the period after Paul.[1] Corresponding to this, ἀπιστία is the rejection of the Christian kerygma (Rom. xi.20, 23).

In other passages πίστις means being a believer, ranked amongst the believers. This is especially clear when the 'lifetime of faith' is mentioned,[2] and also probably in I Cor. ii.5; II Cor. i.24, xiii.5; Gal. ii.20; I Thess. iii.2, 5 ff.; in addition to Paul in Eph. vi.16, I Tim. iii.13, Jas. ii.1, 5 and elsewhere.[3] But it is often uncertain whether it would not be better to understand it as confidence, for πίστις is frequently used to denote not so much the fact of being a believer, but rather the emotional state, the state of activity, of being a believer. This is the case when mention is made of the measure of faith (Rom. xii.3),[4] of the weakness of faith (Rom.

---

[1] Col. i.4; Eph. i.15; II Thess. iii.2; Acts xiii.8, xiv.27, xx.21, xxvi.18; Heb. iv.2; Herm. v.I.3.4.

[2] Did. xvi.2, Barn. iv.9; cf. Herm. v.III.5.4: 'they are young in the faith'.

[3] Ἀπιστία is used in I Tim. i.13 in the sense corresponding to this; so also in Ign. Eph. viii.2, unless this is not to be considered as a still more hackneyed usage, so that πίστις and ἀπιστία mean simply Christianity and heathenism.

[4] Cf. v. 6, which speaks of the proportion (ἀναλογία) of faith with

xiv.1)[1] or of its strength,[2] of the increase of faith (II Cor. x.15),[3] of steadfastness in the faith,[4] its abundance[5] or its superabundance (II Cor. viii.7), of the practice of it (I Thess. i.3: *remembering your words of faith*, cf. Philem. 6) or of its unity,[6] and in all those passages in which πίστις and ἀγάπη[7] are linked.[8]

(e) In all these cases it is self-evident that πίστις is the *fides qua creditur* (of course as applied to its object). But as the usage developed it came also to mean the *fides quae creditur*. When Paul can call the message requiring faith (*fides qua creditur*) the ῥῆμα τῆς πίστεως (Rom. x.8) or when he denotes it as the ἀκοὴ πίστεως (*the preaching which requires faith* or . . . *which opens up the possibility of faith* in Gal. iii.2, 5), it is natural for him to summarise it as εὐαγγελίζεσθαι τὴν πίστιν (*to preach the faith*, Gal. i.23). In this way the message itself can also be called

reference to the gift of prophecy, a gift which is particularly dangerous and in need of examination (cf. I Cor. xii.10, xiv.29) because it can be practised without πίστις (cf. TWNT, I, pp. 350 f.)

[1] cf. Herm. s.IX.26.8, and conversely Herm. m.V.2.3.

[2] cf. Col. ii.7: βεβαιούμενοι τῇ πίστει; cf. also Herm. v.III.5.5, m.XII.6.1, v.III.12.3; I Clem. i.2; Acts xvi.5; Col. ii.5; Ign. Eph. x.2.

[3] Phil. i.25: εἰς τὴν ὑμῶν προκοπὴν καὶ χαρὰν τῆς πίστεως, cf. Pol. iii.2.

[4] Col. i.23: εἴ γε ἐπιμένετε τῇ πίστει, Acts xiv.22; Herm. s. VIII.9.1; Did. xvi.5; cf. Ign. Sm. i.1.

[5] Πλήρης πίστεως in Acts vi.5, xi.24; cf. Herm. m.V.2.1, XII.5.4; Ign. Sm. introduction.

[6] Eph. iv.13: *until we all attain to the unity of the faith* (εἰς τὴν ἑνότητα τῆς πίστεως) *and of the knowledge of the Son of God*; cf. Ign. Eph. xiii.1, xx.2; Herm. s.IX.17.4, similarly IX.18.4.

[7] II Thess. i.3; Eph. iii.17, vi.23; I Tim. i.14, ii.15, iv.12; Ign. Sm. introduction; Herm. s.IX.17.4; 18.4.

[8] In addition cf. perhaps Rom. i.12, xiv.22 f.; II Cor. iv.13. We can however scarcely understand ἐκ πίστεως εἰς πίστιν in Rom. i.17 as meaning: *from becoming believers to having confidence*. Cf. also the phrase *from glory to glory* in II Cor. iii.18, and on this TWNT, II, pp. 254 f.

πίστις. Besides, Paul can use πίστις in the sense of a standard or a principle, since it is the attitude which God requires of men and as such is the way of salvation offered by God, as when he contrasts νόμος and πίστις as being the two paths to salvation (Rom. iii.31, iv.14) and speaks of the 'coming' of πίστις[1] as of an independent entity (Gal. iii.23, 25). Consequently he can form the combination νόμος πίστεως (Rom. iii.23).[2] Πίστις is also understood as a principle in Rom. iv.16, Gal. iii.12, I Cor. xiii.13. Therefore Paul can already use πίστις quite simply in the sense of 'Christianity', which again can mean being a Christian (i.e. Christian behaviour) or the Christian message, teaching, principles. Thus for example when he speaks of οἰκεῖοι τῆς πίστεως = 'fellow-Christians' (lit. those belonging to the household of faith, Gal. vi.10) or of πίστις as the object of εὐαγγελίζε-σθαι (to preach) as well as of πορθεῖν (to destroy, Gal. i.21) and perhaps also when he says: *if prophecy, according to the proportion of faith* (Rom. xii.6).

Apart from Paul's epistles, πίστις is found meaning the preaching of the faith in Acts vi.7: *were obedient to the faith*; and as a principle in Eph. iv.5: *one Lord, one faith, one baptism*.[3] Πίστις as the *fides quae creditur* is meant when the *mystery of the faith* is mentioned (I Tim. iii.9; iii.16 tells what this is). Hence πίστις and *good doctrine* can be linked together (I Tim. iv.6); to succumb to false doctrine is called *departing from the faith* (I Tim. iv.1) or to *make shipwreck* or to *miss the mark as regards the faith* (I Tim. i.19, vi.21).[4] The right doctrine handed down by the Church is also πίστις in Jude iii.20, II Pet. i.1. Set phrases containing the word πίστις meaning

[1] The *coming of faith* marks for Paul a vital stage in the experience of salvation, i.e. the coming of the time characterised by faith in place of the time characterised by law (Rom. vii.9), cf. TWNT, II, p. 672.

[2] cf. *Law* to be published in this series.   [3] cf. also I Clem. lviii.2; Ign. Sm. x. 2.   [4] cf. I Tim. i.6 and II Tim. ii.18.

Christianity take the place of the adjective 'Christian' which had not yet come into use: *in a common faith* (Titus i.4); *according to the faith of God's elect* (Titus i.1); *in the faith* (I Tim. i.2, 4, Titus iii.15) or *in faith and truth* (I Tim. ii.7); *in the faith of Jesus Christ* (Ign. Mg. i.1).

(*f*) The meaning of πιστεύειν has developed and become differentiated in a similar manner. Certainly in most cases πιστεύειν means to *accept the message*,[1] especially when it is used in the aorist,[2] but also in the perfect.[3] The same sense is given by the participles of the aorist[4] and of the perfect[5] and of course by the imperative,[6] and πιστεύειν often has this meaning in clauses introduced by ἵνα.[7] The present tense now and then also has the meaning of *laying hold of faith (wishing to believe).*[8] The occasional linking of πιστεύειν with *repent*[9] and with *be baptised*[10] proves that πιστεύειν can

[1] cf. the synonymity of to *receive the word* with πιστεύειν in I Thess. i.6; Acts viii.13 f., xvii.11 f.; Luke viii.3. Corresponding with this ἀπιστεῖν means to reject the kerygma in Mark xvi.16; Ign. Eph. xviii.1.

[2] Rom. x.14, 16, xiii.11; I Cor. iii.5, xv.2, 11; II Cor. iv.13; Gal. ii.16; Acts iv.16, viii.13, ix.42, xviii.8 etc.; John iv.39, 41, vii.31, 48, xvii.8 etc.; Herm. v.III.6.1, s.IX.22.3; II Clem. xv.3; Pol. viii.2; Barn. xvi.7 (aorist infinitive).

[3] Acts xiv.23; II Tim. i.12; John iii.18, vi.69, xi.27; I John iv.16, v.10.

[4] Eph. i.13; Acts xi.17, 21, xix.2; Heb. iv.3; John vii.39; Mark xvi.16; Herm. m.IV.3.3, s.VIII.3.2, IX.13.5; Ign. Phld. v.2; II Clem. ii.3.

[5] Titus iii.8; Acts xvi.34, xviii.27, xix.18, xxi.25; Herm. v.III. 6.4, 7.1.

[6] Mark i.15; Acts xvi.31; John x.37 f., xii.36, xiv.1, 11; Barn. iii.6 (future).

[7] John i.7, ix.36, xi.42, xvii.21, xix.35, xx.31; I John iii.23.

[8] John i.50, iii.12, iv.42, vi.64 (?), x.26, xiv.10, xvi.30 f. In a different sense in Rom. x.9; I Tim. i.16; Acts xv.7; John iii.12, v.44.

[9] Mark i.15; Kerygma Petri (ed. Klostermann in *Kleine Texte*, 3 [1933]), iii.15; Herm. s.IX.22.3.

[10] Acts viii.12, xvi.31-33, xviii.8 (cf. ii.41, xi.18; Heb. vi.1 f.); Mark xvi.16.

denote that action of laying hold of the belief which is the basis of Christianity.[1] More rarely πιστεύειν means to *be a believer*, to *hold the faith*; yet probably the present must frequently be understood in this sense.[2] The timeless present of a proposition such as Rom. x.10: *for with the heart man believes unto righteousness* is somewhat different; here πιστεύειν can mean both *accepting a belief* and *being a believer*. The frequent use of the present participle in Paul and John has the same meaning.[3] That the sense has become less precise is shown especially in the use of the participle. The present participle is, it is true, still in some passages a genuine participle (*those who are the believing ones in me*), particularly when a qualification is added (εἰς . . . , ἐπί . . .),[4] or when the words 'we (you), the believing ones' are used.[5] But in other passages the phrase οἱπιστεύοντες stands simply for the term 'the Christians[6]'; the aorist[7] and the perfect[8] participles can be used in the same way.

When this point is reached, the meaning of the participle of πιστεύειν is merged with that of πιστός. Πιστός too is sometimes qualified by an object, so that the

[1] cf. also 'those that should believe' I Clem. xlii.4; Herm. m. IV.3.3, s.IX.30.3.

[2] Rom. vi.8; I Thess. iv.14; Acts xv.11; Luke viii.13; John xvi.9; Ign. Mg. ix.1 (2); II Clem. xvii.3, xx.2.

[3] Rom. iv.24; I Cor. i.21; Gal. iii.22; John i.12, iii.18, 36, vi. 35, 47, vii.38, xi.25 etc.; I John v.5, 13 (variant reading). Also I Pet. ii.6 (quoting Isa. xxviii.16); Herm. s.VIII.3.3. Often with πᾶς: Rom. i.16, iii.22, x.4; John iii.15 f.; I John v.1; Acts x.43, xiii.39.

[4] Acts xxii.19, Matt. xviii.6, John i.12.

[5] Eph. i.19; I Pet. i.8, ii.7, i.21 (so ℵ C 𝕳). Probably also Acts v.14.

[6] Acts xix.18 (D), II Thess. i.10 (variant reading), Mark ix.42.

[7] Acts ii.44 (?), iv.32 (?); II Thess. i.10; Herm. s.IX.27.11 etc. There is a curious phrase in Ign. Mg. x.3: 'in Christianity wherein every tongue believed'.

[8] Acts xxi.20, 25.

word acquires the verbal force of 'believing'.[1] Although
this is still retained in the phrase *do not be faithless*
(ἄπιστος) *but believing* (πιστός) in John xx.27,[2] yet it has
usually been lost. The adjective πιστός means *Christian*,[3]
the noun *the Christian*.[4] Corresponding to this is the use
of ἄπιστος (cf. p. 61), which still has the force of a verb
in John xx.27, but is mainly used in the technical sense
of *not Christian*.[5]

3. *The relationship of Christian 'faith' to that of the Old
   Testament*

The manner in which Christians in general understood their faith in the NT and in primitive Christianity
may be summed up as follows. When 'faith' is mentioned, it sometimes has the traditional meaning as in
the OT and Judaism (cf. pp. 62 ff.), sometimes a quite
fresh meaning (cf. pp. 68 ff.), although these two aspects

[1] Acts xvi.15; τῷ κυρίῳ (D: θεῷ); I Pet. i.21 (variant reading:
πιστεύοντες) εἰς θεόν. On the other hand in the case of πιστός
(Col. i.2; Eph. i.1) the ἐν Χριστῷ ('Ιησοῦ) is not a statement of the
object but means 'those who are in Christ (Jesus)'; πιστός is therefore here used absolutely.

[2] Perhaps also in I Tim. iv.3; but in Rev. xvii.14 πιστός probably means *loyal*. Πιστός seems to have the force of a verb in the
list of Christian 'virtues' in I Clem. xlviii.5 and in the combination
πιστοὶ καὶ ἀγαθά in Herm. s.VIII.7.4, 10.1 or in the phrase 'for
though one be a man of faith' in Herm. m.VI.2.7 and in 'faithful
and strong men' in Herm. m.IX.9.

[3] I Cor. vii.14 (variant reading), I Tim. vi.2, Titus i.6, Acts
xvi.1, Ign. Rm. iii.2, Mg. v.2, Herm. s.VIII.9.1. Cf. πιστὸς ἐν
κυρίῳ =*Christian* in Herm. m.IV.1. 4.

[4] II Cor. vi.15; I Tim. iv.10, 12, v.16; Acts x.45. Cf. Ign. Sm.
i.2. For πιστός in inscriptions see E. Peterson, *Εἷς Θεός* (1926),
pp. 32-34, 309. Cf. Tertullian, *De cultu feminarum*, II.4 and 5
(CSEL, 69, 78 f.): *fidelis* =*Christianus*.

[5] I Cor. vi.6, vii.12-15, x.27, xiv.22-24; II Cor. iv.4, vi.14 f.;
I Tim. v.8; Titus i.15; Rev. xxi.8; Ign. Mg. v.2; II Clem. xvii.5;
Mart. Pol. xvi.1; Dg. xi.2.—In Ign. Tr. x.1; Sm. ii.1, v.3 it
appears particularly as the quality of the teachers of false doctrines.

need not exclude one another (cf. p. 69). Their relationship will be made clearer if we consider the relationship between the specifically Christian idea of faith and that of the OT in general. In so far as πίστις (πιστεύειν) in the NT stands for belief in God's word (cf. pp. 62 f.), there is no difference in comparison with the OT and Judaism (cf. pp. 48 f.); and the specifically Christian πιστεύειν εἰς . . . (cf. p. 58) also includes this belief, since it is of course always at the same time belief in the preaching which brings the word of God. But this word of God has acquired a different quality (cf. p. 70). It is not associated with God's activity in the sense that it claims loyalty by reason of this activity or that it promises activity by God in the future. It is bound up with what God does in the sense that this is first revealed in this word.

In the OT the godly man believes (in loyalty and obedience) in God by reason of what He does; he does not 'believe' the actions themselves because they are plain to see in the national history.[1] In the NT it is precisely that which God does which is to be 'believed'; for that part of it which is exposed to view is the life of Jesus who lived on earth in the form of a servant and ended His life on the cross. That the 'foolishness' of the cross is divine 'wisdom', that the crucified is also He who rose again, who is exalted, who is the Lord, that thus, what was done to Him is a divine act of salvation —all this is not plain to see, but is only made plain by the words of the preaching. Consequently it may even be said that what God did is His word, so that John—

---

[1] In Ps. lxxii.32 too where God's wonders are mentioned as the subject of *heʾemîn*, it is not a question of belief 'in' God's deeds, but of loyalty towards God on account of his wonders. Cf. Exod. iv.8 f. which speaks of *heʾemîn in the voice of the sign* and then, in abbreviated form, *in the signs*, on the strength of which the people are to put faith in Moses.

drawing this conclusion—can call Jesus the logos, the 'word'. For this reason to *believe in the word of God* becomes πιστεύειν εἰς Χριστόν.

This already conveys the fact that when the NT requires faith, it involves no return to the position of the prophets (and the Psalms) of the OT. Faith is not the trust in God's fidelity to the covenant which has proved itself reliable and will continue to be so. For God's activity in which πίστις puts its trust does not demonstrate its nature in the fate of the nation as a whole or in that of the individual, but in God's eschatological action—for this describes what He effected in Christ—which brings all history to an end.[1] In so far as πίστις in this sphere means trust (cf. p. 64), it is trust in God's power to work miracles, which can awaken life out of death, and which will awaken us too, as it awakened Christ.[2] In so far as it is hope (cf. p. 66), it looks forward to the completion of the work of salvation begun in Christ, which is brought to an end, not in the glorious conclusion of a national history, but in the fulness of the Church. In so far as hopeful trust in a more general sense can spring up on the basis of the Christian πίστις—trust in Christ as in God—it is the hopeful trust that in the situation created by Christ between the moments 'no longer' and 'not yet', the Lord, i.e. God, will not let him who trusts in Him be put to shame.[3]

---

[1] With regard to this it is significant to note which are the blessings of salvation apprehended in faith; they are the eschatological gifts: forgiveness of sins (Col. i.14; Eph. i.7; Luke xxiv.47; Acts ii.38, v.31, x.43, xiii.38, xxvi.18 etc.); righteousness (Rom. i.17, x.10; Phil. iii.9; Acts xiii.39; II Clem. xxxii.4 etc.); salvation in the eschatological sense (Rom. i.16, x.10; I Cor. i.21; II Tim. iii.15; Luke viii.12; Acts xv.11, xvi.31 etc.); life (or eternal life) (Rom. i.17; Gal. iii.11; John xx.31; Barn. i.6, xi.11 etc.); spirit (Gal. iii.14, v.5 etc.).

[2] Rom. vi.8, viii.11; I Cor. vi.14; II Cor. iv.14.

[3] Rom. ix.33, x.11; I Pet. ii.6.

It is the faith that if we have died with Christ, we shall also live with Him (Rom. vi.8), that God will preserve him who believes until 'that day' (II Tim. i.12), for eternal life (I Tim. i.16). It is the hopeful trust which expresses itself in the sentences beginning with: πιστὸς (*faithful*) ὁ θεός[1] or ὁ κύριος (II Thess. iii.3, II Tim. ii.13), all declaring that God, or the Lord, will keep safe him who believes (Phil. i.6, ii.13). In so far as faith itself is loyalty (cf. pp. 67 f.), it is not loyalty in view of the mercy shown by God in the national history, but confidence in the act of salvation in Christ, the only 'name' which can bring salvation (Acts iv.12). It is a matter of remaining loyal, of 'standing firm' in the faith[2] in all temptations, above all in persecution. The obedience of πίστις (cf. p. 63) is not obedience under God's commandments which require law and justice for the national life, but the 'obedience of faith' to the one way of salvation opened up in Christ. It is of course also a turning away from sin—since salvation includes the forgiveness of sin.[3]

In every case πίστις is seen to be the act in virtue of which man separates himself from the world and turns round completely towards God in response to God's eschatological deed in Christ. It is the act on which the new eschatological existence of the Christian is founded and it is the attitude which goes with it.[4] Πίστις, being the attitude which constitutes a man's existence, has complete control of his life. So the absolute use of πίστις and πιστεύειν, not known in the OT (except in Isa. vii.9?, xxviii.16) and beginning to

[1] I Cor. i.9, x.13; I Thess. v.24; Heb. x.23.

[2] I Cor. xvi.13; II Cor. xiii.5; cf. Gal. v.i; Col. iv.12; Eph. vi.11 ff.

[3] cf. the combination of πίστις and μετάνοια (repentance), cf. p. 80, n. 9).

[4] cf. the combination of πιστεύειν and βαπτισθῆναι (being baptised), cf. p. 80, n. 10).

be developed in Judaism (cf. p. 49), becomes prevalent. Not until this point does 'faith' become simply the designation of the religion, and the 'believers' or 'those who have faith' are the Christians. As this action and attitude of faith, which is decisive for man, is directed towards Christ, it might seem as if the Christian faith pushed the relationship with God into the background. However the belief of those who place their faith in Christ is directed precisely to what God did in Christ. And the mere fact that the NT does not use πιστεύειν εἰς Χριστόν as an alternative to πιστεύειν εἰς τὸν θεόν indicates that God and Christ do not stand before the believer as two separate objects of faith—either side by side or the one subordinate to the other. On the contrary, in Christ, God himself meets him; and God meets him only in Christ. In Christ dwells the whole fulness of the deity (Col. i.19, ii.9). To put it another way, Christ is God's eschatological deed, beside which there is no room for any other deed claiming or promoting faith. Whilst the godly man in the OT is expecting further activity by God because of what he has already experienced, the godly man of the NT is still expecting only that the salvation already wrought by God will disclose itself fully. Christ is God's last deed, including the future in its scope.[1]

C. Πίστις and πιστεύω in Paul[2]

1. Paul and the common Christian concept of faith

(a) The common Christian usage, as it has already been described, making use of references to Pauline passages too (cf. pp. 62-82), is fundamental for that of

[1] The consciousness of this is clearly expressed e.g. in Heb. i.1 f.

[2] For the literature on this chapter see pp. xii f. and further the wealth of literature on Paul. Cf. e.g. Michaelis 116-38; Lohmeyer 62-156; Mittring 146.

Paul. For Paul too, who placed the concept of πίστις in
the centre of his theology, it is not a spiritual attitude of
man, but in the first place the acceptance of the kerygma,[1] i.e. submission to the way of salvation determined
by God and made accessible in Christ. Thus for Paul
too πίστις is always faith in. . . .[2] Πίστις and ὁμολογία
therefore belong together, as stated explicitly in Rom.
x.9 (cf. p. 70). In the ὁμολογία, the believer turns himself away from himself and confesses Jesus Christ as his
Lord, and this involves at the same time a confession
that he owes all that he is and has to what God has
done in Christ. So Paul gives no more of a description
than do the other NT writers of 'the psychological process involved in the development of faith'.[3] Thus for example in Gal. iii.23-26 it is the story of salvation which is
sketched, not (in the manner of Philo) the dawn of faith
in the individual; faith is exhibited by Paul as a historical,
not as a psychological possibility. According to Paul
the salvation effected in history is made real for the
individual not in religious experience, but in the
baptism performed on him (Gal. iii.27-29) and πίστις
appropriates it. Thus it does not stand at the end of
the road to God, as in Philo (cf. p. 53), but at the
beginning. Even if πίστις is the devout acceptance of
what the kerygma preaches, yet it is not restricted to a
fides historica, because by confessing God's deed it
acknowledges that it is valid for each individual.
Πίστις, in that it is ὁμολογία, is at the same time ὑπακοή

[1] Rom. x.17: cf. p. 69, n. 2.
[2] On πίστις with the objective genitive cf. p. 60; on the interpretation in Paul see A. Deismann, *Paulus* ([2]1925), 126 f.; O.
Schmitz, *Die Christusgemeinschaft des Paulus im Lichte seines Genitiv-
gebrauchs* (1924); A. Wikenhauser, *Die Christusmystik des heiligen
Paulus* (1928), *passim*; cf. Wissmann, pp. 68-75; Mundle, pp. 75-94
on πιστεύειν with εἰς cf. p. 58; with clauses introduced by ὅτι
cf. p. 58.
[3] Schlatter, *Glaube*, p. 260.

(cf. p. 63), that is to say the actual recognition of the saving way of grace ordained by God. For ὑπακοή is the acceptance of the divine grace, because this grace is offered to man in the paradoxical form of the cross of Christ; i.e. because the divine act of grace means the judgement brought about by the cross on man with his sins as well as with his striving for righteousness or wisdom. So faith is the obedient acceptance of the divine verdict on the understanding of himself which man has had up to that point.

Thus the knowledge imparted by the kerygma and appropriated by faith includes both the knowledge concerning God's deed in Christ and also a new under-standing by man of himself. Πίστις is the peculiar manner in which the divine χάρις is understood, and that means at the same time to know oneself to be under χάρις. Paul speaks of the knowledge of the be-liever in a double sense: first the knowledge of salvation communicated by the kerygma[1] and then the new knowledge of himself which comes to the man who believes.[2] The element of trust is also included in this knowledge of oneself through God's saving act. It is true that in Paul πίστις has only rarely the immediate meaning of trust (cf. p. 64) since it is in the first place ὁμολογία and ὑπακοή. But the use of πεποιθέναι (cf. TWNT, VI, pp. 6 f.) shows that trust (like hope, cf. p. 66) is part of faith. This element is distinguished from πίστις by the concept of παρρησία.[3]

(b) If πίστις is both ὁμολογία and ὑπακοή, then it is intelligible that not only the act of becoming a believer, but also the state of being a believer can be denoted by

[1] Rom. vi.8 f., II Cor. iv.13 f., cf. Rom. x.14-17.

[2] Rom. v.3, xiv.14; II Cor. i.7, v.6; Phil. i.19.

[3] This is a boldness or frankness towards God (e.g. Eph. iii.12) and towards men (e.g. Eph. vi.19 f.), including the idea of bold-ness in the gospel. Cf. TWNT, V, p. 881.

πίστις (πιστεύειν). For this purpose Paul can form the phrases πίστιν ἔχειν (Rom. xiv.22, Philem. 5), εἶναι ἐν τῇ πίστει (II Cor. xiii.5), ἑστάναι ἐν τῇ πίστει (I Cor. xvi.13, II Cor. i.24). The meaning of this last phrase is made clear by the parallel statements ἑστάναι ἐν κυρίῳ (I Thess. iii.8), in χάρις (Rom. v.2),[1] in the εὐαγγέλιον (I Cor. xv.1), namely that to be a believer signifies to belong to the Lord and to the grace made accessible by Him and declared in the gospel.

At the same time the contexts in which εἶναι and ἑστάναι ἐν τῇ πίστει are found, show that to be a believer is not a static condition, but that it takes place amidst the vicissitudes of each man's life, that it is has constantly to hold its own against the danger of falling (πίπτειν, cf. TWNT, VI, pp. 164 ff.).[2] Thus πίστις has not done all that it is required of it when the kerygma has been accepted, as though it were merely the declaration made on admission to a new religion. It has to maintain itself continuously as the controlling attitude to life in the face of temptations. This is evident e.g. from Rom. xi.20: σὺ δέ τῇ πίστει ἕστηκας which does not mean: *you stand in the faith*, but *you have won your position through faith*—which in this context denotes through faith alone, not by your own deserts— a clear allusion to the fact that to be a Christian is to be constantly relating oneself to God's act of salvation. Therefore although this appears to contradict the interpretation of πίστις as a single decisive action in turning to God's grace, yet degrees and possibilities of πίστις for individuals are mentioned. There are *deficiencies in faith* (I Thess. iii.10); there is growth in faith (II Cor. x.15); there is fulness of faith[3]; there is weak-

---

[1] cf. Gal. v.4: τῆς χάριτος ἐξεπέσατε.
[2] I Cor. x.12, Rom. xiv.4, Gal. v.4.
[3] Paul uses for this the words πληροφορηθῆναι (Rom. iv.21, xiv.5) or πληροφορία (I Thess. 1.5). By these he means being fully con-

ness of faith (Rom. xiv.1). If to be *weak in faith* in Rom. xiv.1 f. means the same as being weak with regard to the conscience in I Cor. viii.7-12, it becomes evident that a Christian practises his faith by knowing what he has to do on each occasion. Hence the curious phrase ὃς μὲν πιστεύει φαγεῖν πάντα (Rom. xiv.2) and hence in particular the formulation of the principle: πᾶν δὲ ὃ οὐκ ἐκ πίστεως ἁμαρτία ἐστίν (Rom. xiv.23). Although all believers stand in one and the same πίστις, their decisions about what to do and what not to do may diverge, because their πιστεύειν has to be worked out in the conduct of each one. The principle is: *Let each be fully convinced in his own mind* (Rom. xiv.5); for the faith that each man has towards God is always expressed in his own life: *The faith that you have, keep between yourself and God* (Rom. xiv.22). Thinking must be guided *according to the measure of faith which God has apportioned to each* (Rom. xii.3). In this matter it is a question not only of degrees and stages of πίστις, but also of the variations brought about by the different gifts and circumstances of individuals, as the connexion between Rom. xii.6 (*having gifts differing according to the grace that was given to us*) and Rom. xii.3 (cf. above) shows. So Paul can speak of an ἔργον πίστεως (I Thess. i.3) and he indicates the whole sphere in which πίστις must work itself out in the life of each one by the words: *faith working through love* (πίστις δι' ἀγάπης ἐνεργουμένη, Gal. v.6).[1]

Even in statements such as these by Paul, the fundamental content of the Christian faith displays itself vinced and having firm confidence, which are qualities inherent in faith.

[1] cf. the rest of the passages where πίστις is combined with ἀγάπη (I Cor. xiii.13; I Thess. i.3, iii.6, v.8; Philem. 5) and with ὑπομονή (I Thess. i.3). In the list of virtues in Gal. v.22 πίστις can hardly mean 'the Christian faith', but only loyalty of men to one another.

more and more fully and clearly. But Paul has displayed it to its fullest extent by contrasting it to the exclusion of all else with the ἔργα νόμου, and by his thorough development of its quality of ὑπακοή.

2. *The Pauline concept of faith contrasted with Judaism*

(*a*) Faith and works. The novelty and the completely different quality of the relationship to God, which is presented by regarding πίστις as the acceptance of God's saving act and as involving continual reference to it, is expressed by Paul when he consistently and firmly attaches the blessings of salvation exclusively to πίστις. Whilst these are termed—as in Judaism— δικαιοσύνη, there follows for Paul that which is a paradox in Judaism, namely that δικαιοσύνη is bestowed as a gift to πίστις, that it is therefore not awarded to man by virtue of his works.[1] Man can only stand before God by virtue of his πίστις and never by virtue of his works.[2] The whole epistle to the Galatians is an attack on the misunderstanding which is still possible that πίστις would have to be supplemented by the performing of some kind of works of the law. By this it becomes perfectly clear that πίστις is the complete surrender of a man to God, and indeed a surrender which a man cannot in any way decide to make of his own accord—for in that case he would remain in the domain of ἔργα—but which can only be a surrender to God's grace, and thus only a response to God's act (cf. p. 85). But it is at the same time equally clear that this surrender is a motion of the will, and in fact a basic decision of the will, by which a man hands himself over completely. It is an act in which the whole man is himself involved, whilst in the case of the ἔργον he always stands

---

[1] cf. *Righteousness* in this series, pp. 46 ff.

[2] Rom. iii.20-22, 25, 28, iv.2, 5 f., ix.30-32, x.4-6; Gal. ii.16, iii.6 ff.; Phil. iii.9 etc.

beside what he accomplishes. Paul expresses the active
quality of πίστις on the one hand by understanding it
as ὑπακοή (cf. pp. 87 f.), on the other quite unconsciously
by never calling it inspired, as e.g. Augustine does.[1]
The believer has the spirit bestowed upon him, but
πίστις is not a gift of the spirit.[2] Faith is the behaviour
of the man who is 'crucified with Christ', who no longer
lives as himself, but as one in whom Christ lives (Gal.
ii.19 f.). If the paradox that πίστις, being a motion of
the will, is a negation of the will itself, is not understood,
the antithesis πίστις—ἔργα νόμου is easily misunderstood,
as though πίστις were after all again thought to be a
good work, an achievement[3]. In that case Paul's
rejection of works would be interpreted as applying
only to the works of the Mosaic law, whilst 'a certain
measure of independent human activity' is always
assumed when faith is an act of obedience.[4] But in
actual fact there is no assumption of a certain measure
of independent activity in faith. It is an act in the
highest sense, and at the same time the opposite of
every 'work', every achievement, because the act of
faith consists simply in the denying of all that a man
does to establish his existence. Paul does not think of
the rejection of ἔργα in any kind of restricted sense, but
as a matter of principle, and this is shown by the fact

[1] cf. H. Jonas, *Augustin und das paulinische Freiheitsproblem* (1930),
pp. 54-62.

[2] The case is somewhat different when πίστις is mentioned in
the thanksgivings in the introductions to the epistles (Rom. i.8,
I Thess. i.3, Philem. 5; so also in Col. i.4). For Paul can certainly consider it a gift (of God) that a community has come to
believe in Christ (Phil. i.29). But when in I Cor. i.4-7 he names
what the spirit has given to the community, it is characteristic
that πίστις is lacking.

[3] cf. the discussion of this antithesis in TWNT, II, pp. 647 ff.
Cf. also *Law* to be published in this series, and Allmen, VB, pp.
224 ff.

[4] Mundle, p. 101.

that beside the antithesis πίστις—ἔργα there stands the other one χάρις—ἔργα with the same meaning,[1] and that Paul quite consciously contrasts χάρις with working which can claim a reward, and frames the antithesis κατὰ χάριν (as of grace)—κατὰ ὀφείλημα (as a due, Rom. iv.4 f.). It is clear too that when Paul demands of a believer that he should fulfil the law in a new sense, namely in ἀγάπη (Rom. xiii.8-10, Gal. v.14), the ἔργα νόμου are not rejected in view of what they contain (i.e. as the law of Moses), but in view of the manner in which they are carried out. Finally Paul sets out perfectly clearly the motive for rejecting works: the road of the ἔργα νόμου is the wrong road to salvation because man wishes to use it as a basis for his boasting, his claim on God.[2] Since by destroying human boasting, both the Jewish righteousness of works as well as the pagan wisdom are equally affected, it becomes clear that when Paul rejects ἔργα he is rejecting a definite—and in fact *the* characteristic—human attitude, namely man's attitude of being self-confident before God, or of trying to become so. Therefore πίστις appears to be genuine ὑπακοή, which is the basic attitude demanded by God and made possible by God's act of grace in Christ, as contrasted not only with the specifically Jewish, but also with the specifically pagan attitude, that of the natural man in general, who imagines that he can hold his own before God by his own strength.

(b) It is clear that, if πίστις is an attitude like this, it is not something a man achieves as occasion offers and amongst other things, but that it is a fundamental attitude to life, determining his conduct in every detail (cf. p. 89). It has also been made clear that to become a believer and to be a believer belong inseparably together (cf. pp. 88 f.), since the surrender of human

[1] Rom. iv.16, vi.14, xi.5 f.; Gal. ii.21.
[2] Rom. iii.27, iv.1 f.; cf. on 'boasting' TWNT, III, pp. 648 ff.

security by the act of becoming a believer must be carried through by the continual subjugation of the natural man. And in so far as πίστις, being genuine ὑπακοή, is the surrender of the natural man, it is the eschatological attitude made possible by God's eschatological deed. It is the attitude of the 'new' man. This eschatological quality of πίστις is indicated by the fact that the phrase ἐν πίστει stands as a parallel beside the phrases ἐν κυρίῳ and ἐν χάριτι (cf. p. 89). Now it is just these phrases which designate the eschatological existence: he who is ἐν Χριστῷ is a new creature (II Cor. v.17); the period of χάρις has taken the place of that of νόμος (Rom. vi.14, etc); the 'coming' of πίστις is the eschatological time (Gal. iii.23 ff.).

3. The Pauline concept of faith contrasted with Gnosticism[1]

(a) Paul has not developed the meaning of faith as contrasted with Gnosticism as fully as he has the contrast with Judaism; yet his statements are sufficiently clear. As an eschatological attitude πίστις must not be misunderstood as though it were already itself eschatological fulfilment. It is not as in Philo a disposition of the soul, not the reward, the prize of the contest itself (cf. p. 53). Its meaning is rather that the man who is justified through faith (Phil. iii.9) is constantly striving for fulfilment, pressing on to the prize (Phil. iii.12-14). In πίστις it is not the finality of the eschatological existence, as in γνῶσις as understood by the Gnostics, which is conceived as real. Πίστις does not escape from the temporary nature of historical existence, but it embodies the eschatological existence in this life on earth.[2] For as on the one hand it is always referring back to what God has done in Christ (Rom. x.9), so on the other it directs

---

[1] cf. Gnosis in this series.
[2] H. Jonas, Der Begriff der Gnosis (Dissertation, 1930), pp. 43 f.

its gaze to the future, to what God will do (Rom. vi.8: *we believe that we shall also live with him*). This reference to the past and the future form one whole (I Thess. iv.14), just because God's action in the past is His eschatological action which determines and controls all the future. The knowledge about the new life imparted together with the faith is concerned with the future (II Cor. iv.13 f., Rom. vi.8 f.; cf. p. 88). Thus beside πίστις stands ἔλπις (cf. p. 66). And if πίστις, regarded as reliance on God's grace, will not be brought to an end even in the eschatological fulfilment, but will 'abide' (I Cor. xiii.13), yet this present life in πίστις is after all a temporary one in so far as sight is still lacking: *for we walk by faith, not by sight* (II Cor. v.7). Our salvation has become through πίστις not a possession at our disposal, but a sure hope (Rom. viii. 24 f. Gal. v.5, cf. p. 26, n. 1).

(*b*) This corresponds with the fact that πίστις is man's awareness that he is under divine grace (cf. p. 88). For this χάρις is not a divine δύναμις in the Gnostic sense which is poured into a man and transforms his nature, destroying his historical being. It is on the contrary understood strictly as the grace of the God who is the judge. It therefore always meets a man as the grace of forgiveness, in which is included the condemnation of sin and the subjection of a man to the demanding will of God, who desires that good should be done. Thus it never allows a man to escape from the concrete circumstances of his historical life. Therefore as ἔλπις belongs to πίστις so also, as part of its nature, does φόβος. This is indeed not the fear which lies hidden behind all the eagerness of the natural man to win his salvation through his own strength, for the believer has after all not received a *spirit of servitude again unto fear* but a *spirit of adoption* (Rom. viii.15). But he is not removed from God's imperative; and the φόβος befitting him is nothing else than the knowledge that he does not stand on his own feet, the anxiety not to fall away from χάρις whether in thoughtlessness or in the pride of his presumed security. Hence the paradoxical reason *God is at work in you, both to will and to work,* given for the admonition: *with fear and trembling work out your own salvation* (Phil. ii.12 f.). Hence the admonition to the Gentile Christians: *They* (the Jews) *were broken off because of their unbelief, but you stand fast only in faith. Do not become proud, but fear* (Rom. xi.20). How this fear becomes one with the boldness and confidence of faith is shown in II Cor. v.11: the phrase *knowing therefore the fear of the Lord* corresponds to *having therefore such hope, we make use of all boldness* in iii.12 and to *such boldness we have* in iii.4. Φόβος denotes the knowledge of the believer that he is in the sight of God (κατέναντι θεοῦ, ii.17 or ἐνώπιον τοῦ θεοῦ, iv.2). Hence the admonitions to stand firm in the faith,[1] for the believer is exposed to temptation[2] and must constantly examine himself.[3]

(*c*) If πίστις, as the Christian state of existence, signifies in contrast to Judaism the 'no longer', in contrast to Gnosticism it denotes the 'not yet'. For Christian existence in πίστις is the paradoxical existence within the historical life on earth, an existence in the 'no longer' and the 'not yet' at the same time, as it is described most clearly in Phil. iii.12-14. 'No longer', for the decision of faith has cast aside the past of self-confidence and self-praise (Phil. iii.4-8). But as this decision takes place under God's grace and does not take a man out of his historical life on earth, it must be carried through by continually working it out afresh and the 'forgotten' past is ever present in the state of having been van-

---

[1] I Cor. xvi.13; cf. I Cor. x.12; Gal. v. i; Phil. i.27, iv.1.

[2] I Cor. vii.5, Gal. vi.1, I Thess. iii.5.

[3] I Cor. xi.28, II Cor. xiii.5, Gal. vi.3 f.

quished. To this extent remembrance (but not re-
morse) is a part of faith, which 'forgets', not by putting
out of the mind, but by no longer allowing oneself to be
caught. 'Not yet', to the extent that the surrender of
the old existence is just the surrender of the self-
security which supposes that it can control its own
existence, i.e. to the extent that this surrender excludes
the possibility of receiving in exchange a new possession
at one's own disposal. What has happened is not the
exchange of an old possession, formerly at one's own
disposal, for a fresh one under one's own control from
now onwards. On the contrary the change from the
former to the present state means to renounce every
desire to possess in utter devotion to the grace of God.
'Not yet': having regard to man of whom in his
historical life on earth it cannot be said that he 'has
apprehended'; but 'nevertheless already' in so far as for
him it is true that he 'has been apprehended by Christ
Jesus'.

D. Πιστεύω in John

1. Πιστεύω as acceptance of the message

With the exception of I John v.4 where ἡ πίστις ἡμῶν
describes the power which overcomes the world (κόσμος),[1]
the noun πίστις does not occur in the gospel or the
epistles of John. On the other hand the verb πιστεύειν
is found very often, and particularly in the common
Christian sense of the acceptance of the Christian
message concerning Jesus. The content of the message
can be given in different ways by a ὅτι-clause (cf. p. 57);
instead of this, shortened expressions with πιστεύειν εἰς
appear in several variations (cf. p. 72, n. 3). Πιστεύειν

---

[1] cf. on this TWNT, III, pp. 867 ff. and esp. p. 895, mentioning
in particular I John v.4 f.

used absolutely is frequently found with the same meaning.[1]

2. Πιστεύω εἰς and πιστεύω with the dative

It is peculiar to John that instead of πιστεύειν εἰς, πιστεύειν with the dative can also occur (cf. p. 58, n. 7), and in fact without the linguistic difference involving a difference of meaning; that is to say, for John 'to give credence to the preaching of Jesus' (who tells the truth, viii.40, 45), or to His word (ii.22), His words (v.47) and 'to believe in Jesus who is being preached', mean the same thing.[2] This corresponds to the fact that John has united the preacher with what is being preached, a union not yet achieved in the synoptic presentation. In doing so John certainly does not intend to 'correct' the presentation of the synoptists. On the contrary it might rather be said that he wishes to correct the kerygma. For he wants to demonstrate that in the kerygma He who is being preached is Himself encountered and speaks. What the kerygma preaches as something that has happened—God's action—itself possesses the nature of the word. Therefore John can designate Jesus himself as the 'Logos' (i.1) and thereby he gives complete expression to the idea that God's word and action are a unity. In the word God's action is encountered and God's action is His word (cf. pp. 83 f.). Ἀκούειν can be synonymous with πιστεύειν.[3] 'To be-

---

[1] Thus e.g. πιστεύειν εἰς αὐτόν, πιστεύειν used absolutely and πιστεύειν εἰς τὸ ὄνομα . . . alternate with each other in iii.18; cf. the alternation of πιστεύειν εἰς and πιστεύειν used absolutely in iv.39, 41, of πιστεύειν used absolutely and πιστεύειν ὅτι in xi.40, 42, xvi.30 f., of πιστεύειν εἰς and πιστεύειν ὅτι in xi.25-27.

[2] cf. the alternation of πιστεύειν εἰς αὐτόν and πιστεύειν αὐτῷ in viii.30 f. In the same way receive him (i.12, v.43) is found beside receive the words (xii.48, xvii.8).

[3] John v.25, vi.60, viii.43, 47, xviii.37.

lieve in Him' is equivalent to 'to come to Him',[1] 'to receive Him' (i.12, v.43), 'to love Him'.[2]

3. *Faith and Salvation*

Believing procures salvation, when this belief is directed to the word preached by Jesus and proclaiming Him and is thus directed to Jesus Himself. This fact is expressed in the continually repeated and varied sayings that the believer has (eternal) life,[3] that he has passed from death to life (v.24, cf. viii.24), that he is not condemned (iii.18) and so forth.[4] It goes without saying that the meaning is: this faith alone procures salvation. It is true that John has not brought this out like Paul by the antithesis $\pi i\sigma\tau\iota\varsigma - \check{\epsilon}\rho\gamma\alpha$ (cf. pp. 91 ff.). For the 'Jews' whom Jesus is attacking in the Johannine gospel[5] are of a completely different type from the Jews (and Judaisers) against whom Paul speaks.[6] The motive for the Johannine sayings concerning $\pi i\sigma\tau\iota\varsigma$ is not, like that of the Pauline ones, the question of the way of salvation. John is fighting for the right conception of salvation itself. And for him the characteristic name for this is not, as for Paul, $\delta\iota\kappa\alpha\iota\sigma\sigma\acute{\nu}\nu\eta$, but simply $\zeta\omega\acute{\eta}$.[7] Now if this is so, there appears to be agreement between the Christian preaching and the 'world' to which it is addressed, in so far as all the world desires 'life' as its salvation. But it is just the purpose of the Johannine preaching to show that this agreement is only apparent. What all the world calls 'life' is no life at all, but only the semblance of life. The world

---

[1] v.40, vi.35, 37, 44 f., 65, vii.37.

[2] viii.42, xiv.15, 21, 23 f., 28, xvi.27.

[3] iii.15 f., 36, vi.40, 47, xx.31; I John v.13.

[4] vi.35, xi.25 f., xii.36, 46; I John v.1, 5.

[5] cf. on this TWNT, III, pp. 378 ff.

[6] cf. TWNT, III, pp. 382 ff.

[7] A translation of the articles on $\zeta\omega\acute{\eta}$ and $\theta\acute{\alpha}\nu\alpha\tau\sigma\varsigma$ (*Life* and *Death*) is to appear shortly in this series.

has its being, not in error, but in lying (viii.44, 55),
and because Jesus speaks the truth, it does not believe
Him (viii.46). The world does not dispute the demand
for faith, as do the Jews of Paul, but would be prepared
at once to believe that Jesus is the Son of God, if only
He would supply evidence of His authenticity,[1] if He
whose language it does not understand (viii.43) would
only express what He says in such a way that it understands it (x.24), that is to say, if He would accept its
criteria concerning what is true. But what He says is
for the world only a παροιμία, a *figure* (x.6, xvi.25, 29)
and only becomes a plain saying[2] to him who believes
(xvi.25, 29). He cannot say it in the way in which they
understand it, for in that case it would be something
different.

4. *Faith as renunciation of the world*

It becomes evident from all this that the world has
no idea what salvation, 'life', really is. Hence the Jews
search the scriptures, thinking that they will find life
in them (v.39),[3] and do not wish to come to Jesus in
order to have life. They would have to turn themselves
from lying to the truth. They would have to sweep
away all the standards and opinions by which they had
lived up till then, to abandon all their former certainties.
It is just this, the renunciation of the world, i.e. a man's
renunciation of himself, which is the basic meaning of
faith. It is a man's self-surrender, his turning to the
invisible (xx.29), to that over which he has no control.
The antithesis makes this perfectly clear. Men cannot believe because they 'receive glory from one
another' (v.44), because by mutually acknowledging
each other's position they gain their security, they con-

---

[1] vi.30; cf. the demand for a proof of authenticity in ii.18.
[2] Expressed in x.24 by παρρησία.
[3] Ἐρευνᾶτε is indicative, not imperative.

solidate their 'world' and shut it off at the top against God, because they do not desire the glory of God. Thus ch. vi makes it clear that the crowds cannot believe in Jesus as the bread of life, because they demand the kind of bread which secures for them their physical earthly existence. Thus v.1-16, ix.1-34 illustrate the fact that the 'Jews' do not tolerate the disturbance of their mode of life safeguarded by legal correctness. Thus v.17 ff. and ch. xi require that a man should abandon the ideas of life and death which are familiar and authoritative for him, in order to be receptive to that life which Jesus gives and which appears where the world only sees death. It is demanded that the world should give up the conception of a 'Son of Man', a Saviour, who when he comes will remain for ever (xii.34), which naturally means that it should abandon the conception that a time of salvation brought about by God's action will be a permanent condition of affairs on earth.

That believing is a basic renunciation of the world is demonstrated by a series of statements which say that the act of believing itself is not an activity of this world, but a happening rooted in the beyond, an act or gift of God Himself.[1] It is necessary to be 'of God', 'of the truth', to be able to hear His voice (viii.47, xviii.37). It is necessary to belong to 'His own' to be able to believe (x.26). Understood as mere dogma, such sayings would simply state that only he can believe for whom it is determined—which would certainly be ill in keeping with the call sent out to all the world to make a decision for faith and with the reproach of evil intentions (cf. pp. 99 f.). In fact those sayings state that the process of believing must be understood not as a happening of this world, but only as a miracle, and thus they describe faith itself as the act of removal out of

[1] vi.37, 44, 65; cf. Bultmann, *Johannes* on vi.45.

this world. Jesus has chosen His own out of the world so that they are no longer ἐκ τοῦ κόσμου i.e. that they no longer belong to the world (xv.19, xvii.14, cf. κόσμος in TWNT, IV, pp. 895 f., Allmen, VB, pp. 470 f.).

Furthermore that this is the nature of faith is demonstrated by the fact that its object is set forth as something incredible to the intelligence of the world. There is agreement between Jesus and the world that 'faith' is concerned with God, in other words, with the divine world. But the scandal which causes the world to lose confidence in itself or to decide definitely for the darkness is the fact that the Son of God appears as a man: *the word became flesh* in i.14.[1] For neither is faith by any means a dualistic philosophy of life, which makes a man whose security has perhaps become precarious renounce the world in order to raise himself up to a world beyond by speculation or devout meditation and feelings. The 'removal out of this world', which takes place by believing is not an act which a man can perform freely for himself, and for the achievement of which the word of Jesus would only provide 'the occasion'. Such an act would include the assumption that the divine world was at a man's disposal for him to lay hold of; and this assumption would itself demolish what it is intended to prove. On the contrary the removal out of this world is thought of as fundamental, because God is thought of as one who acts in freedom. Removal out of the world only becomes a possibility for man through God's revelation. His revelation is the eschatological event which brings the

---

[1] It is typical that in John it is not Jesus' cross which is the real scandal, as it is in Paul, that is to say, not the fact that His righteousness is open to question, but the scandal is His human nature as such, that is to say, that His divine quality is not demonstrable. In John the cross appears rather as the end of His human nature, as His being glorified.

world to an end, since it signifies judgement for the world,[1] so that the verdict issues in life or death according to a man's faith. It is only now, since *the light came into the world* (iii.19) that the possibility of belief and unbelief exists in the decisive sense.[2]   Thus only now through the coming of the revealer has removal out of the world become possible. But it is just the revelation which is the scandal; the invisible becomes visible to an extent such as by the world's standards it neither could nor should become. God's son came in the flesh,[3] a man whose parents and home are known (vi.42, vii.27, 41), who does not conform to what the messianic teaching, i.e. the world's conceptions of God's revelation, requires (vii.27, 41 f.), who breaks the law, declares himself equal with God (v.17-19). He will build a new temple in three days (ii.20), will be greater than Abraham (viii.58), His word is said to preserve from death. Who does He claim to be (viii.53)? He refuses to produce His authority or admits it only in a paradoxical sense (ii.19, viii.28). The fact is that only by faith can the truth of His word be discerned.[4] Nor do His *signs* provide unequivocal authorisation complying with the demand of the world. They are misunderstood (vi.26) and their chief effect is to cause a scandal and finally to bring Him to the cross.[5]

All this shows that the removal out of the world must not be understood as flight from the world, but as the reversal, the shattering, of the world's criteria and appraisals; that it would be a misconception to suppose that the believer must be taken out of the world (xvii.

---

[1] iii.16-21 (cf. on this Bultmann, *Johannes*, pp. 111 f.), v.21-27, ix.39, xii.31.

[2] cf. R. Bultmann, *Glauben und Verstehen*, I (²1954), pp. 134-52.

[3] i.14 and, obviously against Gnosticism, I John iv.2, II John 7.

[4] iii.33; cf. for this Bultmann, *Johannes*, ad loc.; also on v.31-37.

[5] cf. Bultmann, *Johannes*, pp. 152 f., 161 and on vi.30.

15). On the contrary his rejection of the world means
that he has renounced evil (xvii.15). For 'world' is
for John not a natural entity, not, as in Gnosticism, a
region which encircles a man with the compulsion of
fate and is alien to his being, but a historical entity
which is formed by those who turn themselves away
from the light, from God. Each one has himself a share
in its importance and power through his own conduct.[1]
For this world the revelation is a scandal, because it calls
this world in question; it is the judgement of the world
(iii.19, xii.31). And faith is the act of removal out of
this world by overcoming the scandal, that is to say, by
abandoning all reliance on one's own power. Expressed
positively, it is the acceptance of the revelation encountered in the word.

5. *The relationship of the Johannine concept of faith to that
of Paul*

The inner agreement with Paul is evident, in so far
as for Paul too faith is the surrender of reliance on one's
own power, of the righteousness attained by one's own
strength, of boasting (cf. p. 93). Faith is for John as for
Paul not a good work, nor is lack of faith an evil one.
Faith and unbelief alike are indeed decisions and to
that extent they are action in the true sense.[2] The
agreement between John and Paul consists also in the
fact that faith has the quality of obedience. This is
clear because 'to keep the word' or 'the commandments'
can be used as synonyms for πιστεύειν. These phrases,
which mean obedience to command,[3] are used by John
with a different meaning, partly for the obedient accep-

---

[1] cf. Bultmann, *Johannes*, pp. 33 f.

[2] cf. Bultmann, *Johannes*, pp. 112-15 and on vi.28 f.

[3] Thus I Sam. xv.11 (LXX); Ecclus. xxix.1; Jos. *Ant.* 8.120;
Matt. xix.17; cf. I Cor. vii.19.

tance of the word,[1] partly for the loyalty of this obedience.[2]

6. *The anti-gnostic character of the Johannine concept of faith*

But it is just as evident that John's attack is not directed against the peculiarly Jewish aspiration for righteousness for oneself, but against the world in general, of which the Jews are only a particular case. They are not prevented from believing because they rely on the law of Moses and their works, but because they are ἐκ τοῦ κόσμου.[3] Thus the Jews serve as representatives of 'the world' in general, as is shown clearly e.g. by the transition in ch. iii from an attack on the Jews to an attack on the world.[4] In so far as John is alluding to a particular expression of worldliness, it is to Gnosticism, which is attempting to establish itself again within Christianity itself.

When πιστεύειν is grasped as an act of complete removal out of the world (cf. p. 101), it can be understood to be a withdrawal from the world in the wrong sense. Whilst negatively it means to renounce the world, yet it must at the same time be positively to lay hold of the world above. Actually it may be said, and it is said again and again, that faith has life (iii.15 f., etc.), that the believer has already passed from death to life (v.24; I John iii.14), that he will never die (xi.26). Therefore in believing, the eschaton has already been reached and thereby the whole future of the world in time has been outstripped. The eschaton has become the present.

This is a terminology such as is known in Gnosticism

---

[1] xv.20 and probably also viii.51 f., xvii.6.

[2] Thus xiv.23 f., xiv.15, 21 (cf. Rev. xii.17, xiv.12). Similarly xii.47. Of Jesus' obedience to His vocation, viii.55. For an extension of the meaning of these phrases cf. pp. 109 f.

[3] viii.23, xv.19, xvii.14, 16, xviii.36; cf. viii.44, 47.

[4] cf. Bultmann, *Johannes*, pp. 103 f.

also, and its manner of expressing its concepts has largely influenced John's language. But it would not only be wrong to interpret this terminology by its meaning in Gnosticism. Its special purpose is to make a distinction from Gnosticism, and the evangelist takes over the latter's questionings in order to place them under the light of Jesus' revelation. In fact, John's concept of faith has an anti-gnostic bias, to be seen in his explanation of the peculiar relationship of the 'already' to the 'not yet' of faith. The 'already' or the 'no longer' which is comprised in faith, is obvious in so far as faith is the complete renunciation of the world and has life 'already'. But the believer has life 'only' in faith; he does not have it as a possession, as a quality belonging to his nature. He does not—as he would in the Gnostic sense—partake of the divine nature. John does not know that final phenomenon of Gnosticism, ecstasy, in which what belongs to the other world (in a peculiar self-contradiction) is to be made into a reality in this world.[1] To behold the glory of the Son is granted only by seeing Him who became flesh (i.14), and emphasis is placed on the reality of the incarnation in contrast to Gnosticism (I John iv.2, II John 7). To see the glory directly is reserved for a future existence beyond this world (xvii.24). So long as the believers are in the world, they must not imagine themselves to be removed from life in this world (xv.15). On the contrary they are exposed to the continual attacks of the world, as was Jesus Himself during his life in the flesh (xv.18 ff.). Now this means that faith cannot dissociate itself from its connexion with the word. It possesses what it 'already' possesses, in fact 'only' as faith in the word—and just this is how faith is removal out of this world in the full sense. For

---

[1] cf. H. Jonas, op. cit. (p. 94, n. 2), p. 21; H. Jonas, *Gnosis und spätantiker Geist*, I ([2]1954), pp. 199-203.

God's revelation is present in the world 'only' as the word which challenges the world. Therefore faith is temporary by nature, and this is obvious too from the fact that the revealer Himself can certainly be said to know, but not to believe (cf. p. 108).

7. Believing and Knowing[1]

The act of believing therefore does not transfer a man into a state of being removed out of the world, but it is the act of removal out of the world which must be accomplished constantly anew, so that the whole of life is dominated by it through and through. This is shown clearly by the admonitions to *continue*.[2] Believing must become a *continuing in his word* (viii.31); whether or not believers belong to Him and continue in Him, depends on His words continuing in them.[3] To those who continue is promised also the knowledge of the truth (viii.32); and indeed the changing aspects of πιστεύειν are elucidated by its relationship to γινώσκειν. John cannot contrast πιστεύειν with γινώσκειν in the same way as Paul contrasts πίστις with ἔργα νόμου (cf. pp. 91 ff.), for γινώσκειν is not a way of salvation analogous to ἔργα νόμου and hence in competition with πιστεύειν.[4] Its relationship to πιστεύειν is more complicated. There is no distinction between the objects of πιστεύειν and γινώσκειν. Both believing and knowing are concerned with the fact that the Father sent

[1] cf. *Gnosis* in this series, cf. esp. 49 f.

[2] John particularly stresses the immutable and indestructible nature of the Christian experience of divine immanence. God is in Christ (xiv.10); the believers are in Christ and Christ in the believers (xv.4-7 etc.); cf. TWNT, IV, p. 580. cf. Allmen, VB, pp. 102 f.

[3] xv.4-7. Fidelity in belief can also be called *keeping the word* or *the commandments*.

[4] No doubt John intentionally avoids the noun γνῶσις in the gospel as in the epistles.

Jesus[1]; that he who believes (xvi.27-30), like him who knows (vii.17), is aware that Jesus, or alternatively His teaching, comes from the Father. If knowing reaches the truth (viii.32), so equally does believing in Him (xiv.1) who indeed is the truth (xiv.6). That He is the Christ is accepted as the object of faith in xi.27 and xx.31; in vi.69 as that of πιστεύειν and γινώσκειν combined. Since πιστεύειν not infrequently denotes the act of first turning to Jesus,[2] it is natural in those passages in which both verbs are used together in the order πιστεύειν—γινώσκειν, to understand πιστεύειν just as that first turning, and γινώσκειν as the knowledge growing out of it to which faith moves on.[3] But the reverse order is also possible (xvi.30, xvii.8; I John iv.16), and in these cases πιστεύειν appears to be the attitude arising out of γινώσκειν. That both can be used shows that we may not distinguish πιστεύειν and γινώσκειν merely as the initial and final stages, not to mention the fact that we would have to differentiate between two types of Christians, the 'pistics' and the 'gnostics', as happens in Christian Gnosticism. On the contrary it becomes evident, in opposition to Gnosticism, that knowledge can never soar beyond faith and leave it behind. All knowledge that starts with faith continues in faith; but all faith should also become knowledge. As all knowledge must always be imbued with faith, so faith comes to be its true self by knowledge. Furthermore, if it is realised that the relationship of the Father to the Son is never spoken of as faith, but only as knowledge, it is clear that this association of faith and knowledge describes human faith which must develop into knowledge, yet without ever reaching a final state

[1] Believing: xi.42, xvii.8, 21; knowing: xvii.3.

[2] cf. p. 80 and cf. the admonitions to continue, p. 107.

[3] vi.69, viii.31 f.; cf. x.38. Thus *to continue in him* can pick up again *to know him* in v.4.

of pure gnosis. Only when human existence comes to an end as an earthly human one will the faith which knows or the knowledge which believes be replaced by sight which will then no longer be directed to the glory of the Son veiled in flesh, but will behold this glory directly (xvii.24).

8. *Faith and Love*

The believer cannot realise the possibility of his being removed out of the world whilst he is within the world, in such a way as to make it actual to himself as a condition. For he is in fact only in faith a man who overcomes the world (I John v.4). But it is possible for his removal out of the world to be demonstrated, namely by his conduct. This is generally called keeping the commandments or alternatively the word[1] given by Jesus.[2] These phrases can describe the obedience and the loyalty of faith (cf. p. 104), and equally the conduct resulting from faith (xv.10; I John ii.3 f., iii.22, v.2). The double meaning of the phrases indicates the inner unity of faith and action, just as in I John iii.23 f. the substance of God's commandment is stated as the twofold one of believing and loving. The unity of believing and acting accords with the substance of the commandments, in so far as the action which they require is nothing else than love (xiii.34, xv.12; I John ii.7 f., iv. 21).[3] For since faith knows Jesus as the revealer of the divine love (iii.16), to believe is itself to receive His love, and by this receiving of love, loving feelings spring up in the believer. The love for one another is founded on the love Jesus shows to His own.[4] To *love*

[1] The meaning is the same, as is shown in particular by the change in I John ii.3-5.

[2] i.e. His *new* commandment, which is love; cf. John xiii.34, cf. TWNT, II, p. 550.   [3] cf. *Love* in this series, esp. pp. 61 ff.

[4] xiii.34; the καθώς means 'by reason of that which' as frequently in John.

one another (xv.11-17) corresponds to remaining in Him, or in His love (xv.1-10). Similarly I John develops in all kinds of variations the theme that we are under an obligation to love our brother because we have received the love of God, given to us by the sending of His Son.[1] Such love possesses the nature of demonstration, for: *in this shall all men know that you are my disciples, if you have love for one another* (xiii.35).

[1] I John ii.5, 9-11, iii.10 f., 13-17, 23 f.; especially iv.7-21, v.1-3.

INDEX OF REFERENCES

GENERAL INDEX

II

SPIRIT OF GOD

BY

EDUARD SCHWEIZER

AND OTHERS

Translated
from the German
by A. E. Harvey

TRANSLATOR'S PREFACE

THE article on πνεῦμα is one of the longest in Kittel's *Wörterbuch*, and in order to bring it within the range of this series, it has been necessary to omit some of the material. The principle I have followed is to include only those parts which are directly relevant to the concept of the Spirit of God (hence the title of this book). Thus, the long contribution by Hermann Kleinknecht on the word πνεῦμα in Greek literature, and also that by Werner Bieder on πνεῦμα in the Septuagint and Hellenistic Judaism, have been omitted altogether, since they throw light more on the history of the word than on the development of the concept. This translation therefore begins with the section by Friedrich Baumgärtel on the Old Testament (omitting only the purely lexicographical material); this is followed by a part of Erik Sjöberg's section on Rabbinic Judaism; and the remainder represents the important contribution of Eduard Schweizer, culminating in his exhaustive treatment of πνεῦμα in the New Testament. Here, the only omissions are a few notes and references to the work of German scholars. I hope that this principle of selection will not have frustrated the intention of the authors; its justification is that it makes it possible to present to the English reader their important and stimulating discussion of the Spirit of God.

The compression and exhaustiveness required by the *Wörterbuch* make the original German not always easy to read. I have done my best to make this translation as lucid as possible for the reader. Detailed discussions of particular passages are printed (as in the German) in smaller type, and may be passed over at a first reading.

Untranslated quotations in Greek and Hebrew are avoided
in the main text, and (on the assumption that readers of
German will not be using this book anyway) all references
to untranslated German works have been omitted, except
for a few standard commentaries and works of reference.
Even so, I am aware that much of the book is far from easy
reading; but further simplification would have distorted
the original, and I can only hope that the reader will
persevere through all complexities of the subject and
inelegancies of translation, and will gain for himself, as I
have, a richer understanding of the Holy Spirit.

A. E. HARVEY

CONTENTS

BIBLIOGRAPHY

GENERAL

E. DE W. BURTON, *Spirit, Soul and Flesh. . . in Greek writings and translated works from the earliest period to 180 A.D.* (1918).

LINDSAY DEWAR, *The Holy Spirit and Modern Thought* (1959).

C. H. DODD, *The Interpretation of the Fourth Gospel* (1953), 213–27.

H. B. SWETE, Article, *Holy Spirit*, in Hastings' *Dictionary of the Bible.*

OLD TESTAMENT

N. H. SNAITH, *The Distinctive Ideas of the Old Testament* (1944), ch. vii.

J. PEDERSEN, *Israel* I/II (1926), 102–106.

TH. C. VRIEZEN, *Outline of O. T. Theology*, E.T. 249–51.

JUDAISM ETC.

J. ABELSON, *The Immanence of God in Rabbinical Literature* (1912), 174–277.

L. BLAU, Article, *Holy Spirit*, in the *Jewish Encyclopaedia*, VI 447–50.

W. D. DAVIES, *Paul and the Dead Sea Scrolls: Flesh and Spirit*, in *The Scrolls and the New Testament*, ed. K. Stendahl (1958), 171–82.

G. F. MOORE, *Judaism* (1927 ff.), I 237, 247, 371–2, 401–13, 421–2, 445–59, 485–9; II 287–322, 353, 384, 389–90. (cited: Moore).

G. F. MOORE, *Intermediaries in Jewish Theology*, H.Th.R. 15 (1922), 41–85.

NEW TESTAMENT

C. K. BARRETT, *The Holy Spirit and the Gospel Tradition* (1947) (cited: Gospel Tradition).

C. K. BARRETT, *The Holy Spirit in the Fourth Gospel*, J.T.S. N.S. 1 (1950) 1–15.

E. W. BULLINGER, *The Spirit and his Gifts* (1953).

R. BULTMANN, *Theology of the New Testament*, E.T. I 153–64, 203–10, 333–9 (cited: *T.N.T.*).

E. DE W. BURTON, *Commentary on Galatians* (I.C.C.) 486–92.

H. E. DANA, *The Holy Spirit in Acts* (1943).

J. E. FISON, *The Blessing of the Holy Spirit* (1950).

F. J. FOAKES-JACKSON and K. LAKE, *The Beginnings of Christianity* (1920–1923) (cited: Jackson-Lake).

W. F. HOWARD, *Christianity according to St. John* (1943).

G. W. H. LAMPE, *The Seal of the Spirit* (1951).

G. W. H. LAMPE, *The Holy Spirit in the Writings of St. Luke*, in: *Studies in the Gospels*, ed. D. E. Nineham (1955).

E. SCHWEIZER, *The Spirit of Power*, Interpretation 6 (1952) 259-78.

E. F. SCOTT, *The Spirit in the New Testament* (1923).

H. B. SWETE, *The Holy Spirit in the New Testament* (1909).

ABBREVIATIONS

Bl.-Debr.	F. Blass, *Grammatik des Neutestamentlichen Griechisch*, bearbeitet von A. Debrunner
Bousset-Gressmann	W. Bousset, *Die Religion des Judentums im späthellenistischen Zeitalter*, herausgegeben von H. Gressmann (1926)
C.H.	Corpus Hermeticum
Exp.	The Expositor
Exp.T.	The Expository Times
H.Th.R.	The Harvard Theological Review
I.C.C.	International Critical Commentary
J.B.L.	Journal of Biblical Literature
J.Q.R.	Jewish Quarterly Review
J.T.S.	Journal of Theological Studies (N.S.: New Series)
N.T.St.	New Testament Studies
Rev. Bib.	Revue Biblique
R.H.Ph.R.	Revue d'Histoire et de Philosophie religieuses
R.H.R.	Revue de l'Histoire des Religions
Str.-B.	H. L. Strack and P. Billerbeck, *Kommentar zum N.T. aus Talmud und Midrasch.*
Z.N.W.	Zeitschrift für Neutestamentliche Wissenschaft
LXX	Septuagint
E.T.	English Translation
[ ]	enclose additional notes by the Translator

THE OLD TESTAMENT

"THE Egyptians are men (אדם) and not God (אל), and their horses are flesh (בשר) and not spirit (רוח)" says Isaiah (xxxi. 3). "Flesh" is earthly fragility and weakness —its bearer is "man"; "spirit" is absolute power and majesty—its bearer is "God". Thus gains expression the dynamic element which is contained in the Spirit of God (רוח יהוה), and which is perceptible in the working of this Spirit: the Spirit of God turns the desert into a paradise, and makes it an abode of justice and righteousness (Isa. xxxii. 15 ff.).

But the concept is not only dynamic, it is also ethical (cf. Isa. xxx. 1: where plans are carried out, which are not of the Spirit of God, there sin is heaped up). The Spirit of God is a creative, transforming power (cf. Ps. li. 12–13), and its purpose is to create a sphere of religion and morals. In this sense, the Spirit of God rests upon the Messiah as the "spirit of counsel and might" and as the "spirit of knowledge and the fear of the Lord" (Isa. xi. 2); and in this sense it is at work through the Servant of God (Isa. xlii. 1 ff.). Israel's destiny is fulfilled through the Spirit of God, which transforms hearts of stone into hearts of flesh, and changes the nation into a community devoted to God (Ezek. xxxvi. 26–7).[1]

Yet it would not be true to say that according to the prophets the Spirit of God will only give free rein to its life-giving power in the New Age. The transformation of the nation into a true People of God comes to pass the moment the nation is judged; and the prophets see this

---

[1] Cf. also Isa. iv. 2 ff.; xliv. 3; Zech. xii. 10.

judgment as something already being carried out—the
present already anticipates the future. Isa. xxxi. 3—
and similarly xxx. 1 ff.—implies both promise and judgment at the same time: for the prophets, each is equally
a present manifestation of the operation of the Spirit of
God.

Up to this point the principle is clear, especially in the
major prophets: the Spirit of God is power, power with a
moral emphasis. It is active power, that is to say, it is
the personal activity of God's will, achieving a moral and
religious object. It impinges on Israel as the power of
history; for the transformation to the new state of affairs,
the creation of the "New Spirit",[1] takes place by means of
the judgment of God fulfilled in historical events; and this
transformation means the end, and at the same time the
consummation, of the history of Israel. Thus any poly-
theistic sense of a divine power immanent in the world is
ruled out; and the acknowledgment of any such power
is regarded as an escape from the active, personal power of
God's will, from his absolute *majestas*, and therefore as a rebellion of the will against God, as sin. At the same time,
the idea that divine powers can be regularly present in
man is also ruled out. This is the opposite of Egyptian and
Babylonian religion, where the king is the incarnation of
divine power. In Israel there is no God-man. Man is
subject to this power, but he is not identified with it, he
is "flesh" and not "spirit". Moreover, the Spirit of God,
as the operation of God's will, may be perceptible, but it is
inscrutable. You cannot say when it operates or how it
operates. Both the terminology and the content of the
prophetic message are always indefinite; its diversity,
even inconsistency, cannot be removed by any attempt at
harmonization. The dynamic element of the Spirit of
God is or will be perceptible, but its logic is a mystery.
It is the untrammelled, incalculable operation of God's
will. The when and the how of God's "plan" remains a

[1] Ezek. xi. 19; xviii. 31; xxxvi. 26; Ps. li. 12.

secret; but the reality of his activity and power is indisputable.

The second characteristic of the Spirit of God is brought out by the priestly writer in the sentence, "The Spirit of God moved over the water" (Gen. i. 2). Here, as before, the Spirit of God is grasped as a dynamic and creative principle. But it is not a matter only, or even principally, of the activity of God's will completing the creation of the universe (cf. Ps. xxxiii. 6); it is much more the fact that this dynamic force is responsible for all that is alive, for all physical life. The Spirit of God is the active principle which proceeds from God and gives life to the physical world (Gen. ii. 7[1]). It is implicitly connected with the phrase, "and God spake", דבר יהוה. God creates "by the breath of his mouth" (ברוח פיו Ps. xxxiii. 6, parallel to "by the word of God", בדבר יהוה). But by the activity of his Spirit, God also sustains his creation: if God should take back his Spirit (רוח), his breath (נשמה), to himself, all flesh would perish (Job xxxiv. 14; cf. Ps. civ. 29-30). "The Spirit of God has created me, and the breath of the Almighty gives me life" (Job xxxiii. 4).

In this connection the same definition holds good, of the Spirit of God as the creative, active, personal power of God. This excludes any belief in divine powers, in the sense of an understanding of the universe and the natural order based on pantheism, myth and mysticism. No immanent, divine forces of nature exist. By contrast with the neighbouring religions, nature has no power in it, no God in it.

Here, too, God's creative power is a free gift. But here, too, it is inscrutable, even uncanny. There are limits to the gift of the Spirit (Gen. vi. 3). There is no way of discovering when God may take back his "breath". The divine activity is discoverable and perceptible, but inscrutable.

All this is fundamental.

---

[1] Compare Gen. ii. 7 נשמת חיים with Gen. vi. 17 רוח חיים.

However, there is an example of Israel experiencing the activity of the Spirit of God in history in another way, and this time we miss the previous emphasis on an ethical and religious factor.[1] At a time when there is still no territorial kingdom, God raises up charismatic leaders for the people, and enables them, with his Spirit, to act for a national or political cause. Othniel (Judges iii. 10), Gideon (vi. 34), Jephtha (xi. 29) and Saul (I Sam. xi. 6) are examples. David, too, has the Spirit of God come upon him when he is anointed by Samuel (I Sam. xvi. 13). Here again, the Spirit is logically inscrutable, incalculable; it gives a share of itself as and to whom it will. Men who up to now have been completely unnoticed suddenly come forward as leaders under the working of the Spirit.

The sudden and uncanny side of the Spirit's activity receives special emphasis in the description of ecstatic experiences. The subject of an ecstatic experience is called "a man of the Spirit" (איש הרוח Hos. ix. 7). The Spirit of God comes mightily on Saul (צלח על), so that he falls into ecstasy (I Sam. x. 6, 10). Samson's giant strength breaks forth suddenly in ecstatic excitement, and is the effect of the Spirit of God (Judges xiv. 6, 19; xv. 14 —where the expression is again צלח על). A theoretical analysis of the working of the Spirit may be found in Num. xi. 24 ff. (E): God takes some of the Spirit which is in Moses, and apportions it to the seventy elders, who fall into an ecstasy. The ecstasy then spreads infectiously. The reference is also to ecstatic experience in those passages in which the Spirit of God causes prophetic utterance,[2] or snatches a man away (Ezek. iii. 14). Here again the Spirit of God is manifested as the unpredictable and irresistible working of God's power, often even with a touch of the demonic about it. The activity of the Spirit

---

[1] Nevertheless this factor is still present in Israel's national consciousness; for the "Holy War" is an institution with its roots in cult. Cf. G. v. Rad, *Der Heilige Krieg im alten Israel* (1951), 29–33.

[2] Gen. xli. 38; II Sam. xxiii. 2; I Kings xxii. 24; Num. xxiv. 2; Isa. lxi. 1; Ezek. xi. 5; Joel iii. 1–2; II Chron. xxiv. 20.

of God can be easily traced and perceived, but the logic of why, when and for how long it comes, is inscrutable.

These last observations bring us into the sphere of the phenomena of comparative religion; for the neighbouring religions are also aware of the operation of God's power. Ecstatic experience can hardly have had its origin in Israel, or even in the other Semitic religions: Indo-Germanic religions present a much more likely field.

It is not by chance that Hebrew expresses "spirit" and "wind" by the same concept רוח. The wind is powerful, with a power that cannot be withstood; moreover it is mysterious: "the wind blows where it wills, and you hear the sound of it, but you do not know whence it comes or whither it goes" (John iii. 8). To this extent, any mysterious, unpredictable power is one with the wind. The divine stirrings are a *breathing* (רוח) of God, and they are recognized in neighbouring religions as divine powers and forces that bring salvation or destruction. Israel with its spirit-faith has its roots deep in its surroundings.

The major prophets took the spirit-concept out of these surroundings, and transformed the divine spirit from something religiously and ethically neutral into the concept of the purposeful and deliberate operation of God's personal power. The Spirit of God is the concept (however much it resists logical analysis) for the activity of the one and only God in history and creation. In fact, it can serve as a direct expression for God's inner being and for his present reality.[1]

"Is God's Spirit too short?" (הקצר רוח יהוה, Mic. ii. 7) was once the threat uttered against Micah by his opponents. Now that judgment had been passed on the people, faith held fast to the belief that the Spirit of God is not "too short", that (despite all appearances) God in his Spirit is present as Lord of history. God keeps to his promise, the promise out of which his Spirit has

---

[1] Cf. Ps. cxxxix. 7, where רוח יהוה is used in parallel to פני יהוה.

fashioned history and will lead it to its destined end. The Spirit of God, as God's mighty and irresistible saving activity, becomes a source of help and strength: "My Spirit is in the midst of you, be not afraid!" (Hag. ii. 5), "Not by might nor by power, but by my Spirit shall it happen" (Zech. iv. 6), the Spirit of God gathers all God's people together (Zech. vi. 1 ff.). The Spirit of God is the seal of God's faithfulness to his covenant (Isa. lix. 21).

One further strand remains to be indicated in the concept of the Spirit of God in Israel. If the Old Testament has taken the power out of all cosmic and earthly dominions and powers, it has anchored the demonic firmly in the Almighty power, that is to say, in the Spirit of God. The Spirit of God can become active as an Evil Spirit (רוח רעה Judges ix. 23; I Sam. xvi. 14 ff.; xviii. 10). This Evil Spirit is found eventually opposed to God and is hypostatized: in I Kings xxii. 19 ff. "the Spirit" comes forward from the host standing around God and offers himself to be a lying spirit in the mouth of the prophets. In an exactly similar situation, the book of Job (i. 6 ff.) uses the concept "Satan" for the incarnation of this Evil Spirit of God.[1]

---

[1] "Satan" becomes the heading under which this strand of Israel's spirit-theology must be followed up. See the article διάβολος in Kittel.

BETWEEN THE OLD AND NEW TESTAMENTS[1]

THE Jews were confronted inescapably by the Old Testament message that God and his Spirit are extraneous to man. Being seized of God is an effect of grace, not of nature. So much was implied in the proposition that the soul of man proceeds from the Spirit of God. But at this point a problem arose which was to be a source of trouble for generations. As soon as the soul became, no longer just the life-force, but the personally responsible Self which even survives death, the following questions became burning issues: if the soul is a part of God's Spirit, must it not be saved automatically? Or is there another human self to be distinguished from it, which can either absorb or expel, either keep pure or defile, this part of the Spirit of God? Or must this part of the Spirit of God be understood as the possibility of free decision? How can the actual working of the Spirit of God be distinguished from this? How is life after death to be conceived of?

These questions are wrestled with in Judaism, in Gnosticism and in the New Testament.

A. RABBINIC JUDAISM

In Rabbinic thought, "the Spirit" is essentially the prophetic Spirit which speaks in the Old Testament.[2] All the writings in the Old Testament are inspired by the Spirit,[3] and the question whether a particular writing

---

[1] This heading is convenient, if inexact: many of the writings referred to are later than the N.T., but are nevertheless valuable for elucidating pre-N.T. ideas.

[2] Gen. xli. 38; II Sam. xxiii. 2; I Kings xxii. 24 (cf. II Chron. xviii. 23); Num. xxiv. 2; Isa. lxi. 1; Ezek. xi. 5; Joel iii. 1–2; II Chron. xxiv. 20.

[3] Cant. R. i. 1, §5–10; Lev. R. xv. 2 on xiii. 2 (Str.-B. II, 134 f.; IV, 444). Cf. IV Ezra xiv. 21; Apoc. Jos. i. 41.

should be taken into the Canon is identical with the question whether it was written in the Holy Spirit.[1]   Consequently, a saying from the Old Testament can be quoted either as a saying of the Torah or as a saying of the Holy Spirit.[2]   However, the fact that the Holy Scriptures as a whole are inspired by the Holy Spirit does not prevent certain passages being read as the utterances of different speakers, of whom the Holy Spirit may be one.   One sentence in the text may be understood as a statement made by Israel (or other persons or groups), and another as a reply made by the Holy Spirit.   For example, in Deut. xxi, verse 7 is taken as spoken by the elders in the city concerned, 8α by the priests and 8β by the Holy Spirit.   In Judges v, verse 28β is spoken by Sisera's mother, 29 by his wife and daughter, and 31α by the Holy Spirit.[3]   It is also possible to put two different texts together, taking one as a statement by Israel, the other as the subsequent reply of the Holy Spirit.   In this case the texts concerned are ones which exalt God on the one hand and Israel on the other.   For instance, in Deut. vi. 4 ("Hear, O Israel . . . .") Israel confesses Yahweh to be the one true God; the answer of the Holy Spirit is in II Sam. vii. 3, where it calls Israel a people unique on earth.[4] In statements like these, the Holy Spirit is God's representative and expresses his reaction to what has been said and done, though without being identified with him.[5]

Another factor in Rabbinic thought is the relation between the Holy Spirit and a God-fearing life.   From this

---

[1] T. Yad. ii. 14 (Str.-B. II, 135); B. Meg. 7a.

[2] It must not be concluded from this that the Torah was identified with the Holy Spirit, as J. Abelson does (*The Immanence of God in Rabbinical Literature*, 225).

[3] T. Sota, ix. 2–3, 9; J. Sota, ix. 7 (23d/24a).   See H. Parzen, J.Q.R. 20 (1929/30), 56–60.

[4] M. Ex. xv. 2 (ed. Horowitz and Rabin (1931), 126); Sifre Deut. 335 on xxxiii. 26 (ed. M. Friedmann (1864), 148a).   Cf. Str.-B. II, 136.

[5] Nevertheless it is also possible for a passage of Scripture to be interpreted in such a way that certain words in it are spoken by the Holy Spirit to God himself.   Examples of this appear in the very few passages in Rabbinic Literature where the Spirit appears as an Advocate before God: Lev. R. vi. 1 on v. i; Deut. R. iii. 11 on ix. 1.

angle, the gift of the Spirit is thought of principally as a reward for a life of obedience. In the first instance, the possession of the Spirit is represented as a consequence of a just life, not as a cause of it; but naturally, once it is given to a man, it inspires him still more to holiness of life. Where the Holy Spirit is, there there are devout and just men; and where there are just men, there the Holy Spirit is bestowed. At the edge of the Red Sea the Israelites had faith: therefore the Holy Spirit rested upon them. From this R. Nehemiah draws the general conclusion: "Whoever submits to a command in faith is worthy that the Holy Spirit should rest upon him."[1] "Whoever studies [the Torah] with intent to perform it earns the gift of the Holy Spirit", says R. Aha.[2] "Whoever sacrifices himself for Israel will receive the reward of honour, greatness and the Holy Spirit."[3]

When the devout man sins, the Holy Spirit departs from him[4]; the same happens when he approaches a place which is under the power of sin.[5] The Spirit cannot be effectual in unclean surroundings; and so (according to a widespread opinion) it is restricted to the land of Israel: outside Palestine there is no divine inspiration.[6] It is true that in the beginning the heathen could also receive the Holy Spirit, and therefore prophets rose up among them.[7] But after Balaam had misused his prophetic gift,

---

[1] M. Ex. xv. 1 (Horovitz, 114). Cf. Str.–B. II, 135.

[2] Lev. R. xxxv. vii. on xxvi. 3 (Str.–B. II, 134).

[3] Num. R. xv. 20 on xi. 16 (Str.–B. II, 133 f.). Compare with all this the celebrated sequence of R. Phineas b. Jair: "Zeal (in obedience to the Law) leads to bodily purity, which leads to ritual purity, which leads to temperance, which leads to holiness, which leads to humility, which leads to penitence, which leads to piety, which leads to the Holy Spirit, which leads to the Resurrection, which comes by means of the prophet Elijah, of blessed memory." Str.–B. I, 194. Cf. A. Büchler, *Types of Jewish Palestinian Piety*, 42–67.

[4] Gen. R. lx. 3 on xxii. 14 (ed. J. Theodor (1903), 644).

[5] E.g. from Esther, as she approached the palace of the heathen king, Yalkuṭ Shim'oni, Esth. v. 2, cf. Abelson, *op. cit.* 270. Cf. also Gen. R. lxv on xxvi. 34 (Theodor, 715); R. Joshua b. Levi: the Holy Ghost departed from Isaac on account of Esau.

[6] M. Ex. xii. 1 (Horovitz, 3). Cf. Str.–B. I, 643; Parzen, *op. cit.* 53.

[7] Str.–B. II, 130.

the Holy Spirit was taken away from the heathen and reserved for Israel.[1]

Apart from this, strength and health in body and soul are necessary conditions for possessing the Spirit. "The Holy Spirit rests only on a joyful heart."[2] When Jacob, on the news of Joseph's death, gave himself up to his grief, the Holy Spirit left him.[3] To receive the Holy Spirit you must rejoice at God's command[4]—and with that we are back in the world of ethical religion.

Who then was regarded as having the gift of the Spirit? The answer may be given under three heads: the past, the future and the present.

(a) *The past:* In Jewish thought, the great figures of the Old Testament period were regarded as inspired by the Holy Spirit. Naturally this goes mainly for the prophets (Ecclus. xlviii. 12, 24), but there are also other Old Testament figures who speak under prophetic inspiration. Rebecca blessed Jacob "after the Spirit of truth had entered into her mouth" (Jub. xxv. 14). Isaac blessed Levi and Judah by the Spirit of divination (Jub. xxxi. 12). Joseph had the Spirit of God in him in the form of power to live a moral life: "merciful and compassionate, he never bore a grudge" (Test. Sim. iv. 4). The Rabbis took this conception of the patriarchs a stage further. In their view, all those in the Old Testament who feared God, spoke and acted under the influence of the Holy Spirit. All the devout and the righteous of earlier generations were initiated into the secrets of God through their prophetic gifts.[5] Naturally the great figures in the history

---

[1] Tanḥ. בלק 231a; Num. R. xx. 1 on xxii. 2 (Str.-B. II, 130). According to other authorities this happened after Israel had received the Torah (Str.-B. II, 130) or after the completion of the Tent of Meeting (Cant. R. ii. 3, R. Isaac).

[2] J. Sukka, v. 1 (55a, 63), cf. Str.-B. I, 643.

[3] Gen. R. xli. 6 on xlii. 1 (Theodor, 1121); Tg. J.1. Gen. xlv. 27. Similarly in his last days Jacob forfeited his prophetic gift owing to his age and physical weakness, Gen. R. xcvii on xlviii. 10 (Theodor, 1243).

[4] B. Pes. 117a (Str.-B. III, 312).

[5] Gen. R. xlvii on xlix. 27 (Theodor, 1224); Tanḥ. ויחי 58a (ed. S. Buber (1885), §13, 110a); cf. Str.-B. II, 131-2.

of salvation possessed the Spirit to an exceptional degree. Moses was a prophet, as the Old Testament proved. David and Solomon, as authors of Old Testament scriptures, must have possessed the Holy Spirit.[1] Only if he possessed the Spirit could a priest successfully give oracles by Urim and Thummim.[2] The patriarchs possessed it as a matter of course; but their wives also were subject to visions and utterances due to the Holy Spirit.[3]

(b) *The future:* It follows from Isa. xi. 2 that in the Last Age the Messiah will possess the Spirit of God. This continues to be the Jewish conception, and is documented as much by the apocrypha and pseudepigrapha as by Rabbinic writings. "The Lord made him mighty in the Holy Spirit", ὁ θεὸς κατειργάσατο αὐτὸν δυνατὸν ἐν πνεύματι ἁγίῳ, says Ps. Sol. xvii. 37 of the Messianic King, cf. Ps. Sol. xviii. 7. Eth. Enoch xlix. 3 has this expansion of Isa. xi. 2: on the chosen one, the Son of Man, "rests the Spirit of wisdom, and the Spirit which gives insight, and the Spirit of counsel and power, and the Spirit of just men departed", and again (lxii. 2) "the Spirit of righteousness is poured out upon him". The same is said of the Messiah in Test. Levi xviii. 7 and Test. Judah xxiv. 2. Tg. Isa. xlii. 1–4 interprets the Servant (עבד) as the Messiah and makes God say of him: "I will make my Holy Spirit rest upon him" (the same in Tg. Isa. xi. 2). The Targum reflects the general Rabbinic view which is based on Isa. xi. 2.

On the other hand, the Messiah himself is never identified with the Spirit of God—not even in R. Simeon b. Lakish's commentary on Gen. i. 2 (Gen. R. ii. 4; Theodor,

---

[1] Str.-B. II, 132.
[2] B. Yoma, 73b; Str.-B. II, 132.
[3] Isaac: Gen. R. lxxv. 8 on xxxii. 4 (Theodor, 886); Jacob: lxxxiv. 19 on xxxvii. 33 (Theodor, 1024) and xcviii. 7 on xlii. 11 (Theodor, 1127); Joseph: xciii. 12 on xlv. 14 (Theodor, 1170); Sarah: xlv. 2 on xvi. 2 (Theodor, 449); Rachel: lxxii. 6 on xxx. 31 (Theodor, 845). Cf. also B. Meg. 14a for the seven prophetesses in Israel: Sarah, Miriam, Deborah, Hannah, Abigail (cf. Eccl. R. iii. 21), Huldah and Esther. Both Tamar (Gen. R. lxxxv. 9 on xxxviii. 18, Theodor, 1042) and Rahab (Sifre Deut. xxii on i. 24 Friedmann, 69b) prophesied and had visions in the Spirit.

16–17), where he finds the four heathen kingdoms alluded to in the words which describe the original chaos, and the Spirit of the Messiah in the Spirit which moved upon the waters.   Here it would be as wrong to identify the Messiah with the Spirit of God as it would be to identify the four heathen kingdoms with the original chaos.[1]

In the Last Age, too, the ransomed righteous will receive the Spirit of God.   Moral renewal is expected as the result of a change in the spirit and heart of man.   Some authorities (e.g. Jub. i. 23; IV Ezra vi. 26) say that this will be effected by God himself, others that it will be through the Spirit poured out upon the righteous.   ''The Spirit of salvation'', ''the Spirit of grace'', will be given them by God himself (Test. Jud. xxiv. 3) or by his Messiah (Test. Levi xviii. 11).   It is true that in the apocrypha and pseudepigrapha the connection between the final renewal and the gift of the Spirit is not often found,[2] but this makes the Rabbinic sources all the clearer.   In them, the pivotal texts from Scripture dealing with future expectations are Ezek. xxxvi. 26–7 and xxxvii. 14.   These are the authority for expecting the resurrection to take place through the Spirit of God.[3]   Ezek. xxxvi. 26–7 is also the basis for the hope that in the age to come God will destroy the evil instinct—he will take away the heart of stone—and will put his Spirit within the Israelites.[4]   This

[1] By his interpretation the Rabbi has no intention of describing the events which accompanied the creation of the world, but is eliciting, by the usual Rabbinic technique of exposition, the deeper meaning of the text, which is to be found behind the literal meaning.   This same passage also contains the message of the enemies of Israel and of the Messiah who will come to redeem it when it turns to God (which is the meaning of the ''moving upon the waters'': for according to Lam. ii. 19 the waters contain an allusion to repentance).   Cf. Str.-B. II, 350.   Nevertheless, it is wrong to speak as if the Rabbi were interpreting *allegorically*: the Rabbinic view is that this is a question of the real meaning of the text, and not of arbitrary fantasies.

[2] There are no other passages besides those mentioned.   The statement that God will give ''Spirit and Life'' to the devout (II Macc. vii. 23; xiv. 46; Sib. IV, 46, 189) does not refer to the Spirit of God, but to the newly bestowed life-force of men.

[3] For the Spirit as the power effecting resurrection see above, p. 19, n. 3.

[4] Pesikṭ. 165a; Tanḥ., קדושים, 170b; שלח לך, 216a (Str.-B. III, 240).

leads on the one hand to the Spirit being understood as giving *moral* inspiration, as a power converting the wills of men. But at the same time there are other texts which place in the foreground the *inspirational* power of the Spirit: in the Last Age, all the Israelites will be prophets. For this, Joel iii. 1–2 is the decisive passage of Scripture.[1]

(c) *The present:* In the apocrypha and pseudepigrapha, although it is recognized that the great period of prophetic revelation has passed, it is unhesitatingly regarded as a possibility that even now the Spirit may still be granted to men.[2] On the other hand, the Rabbis state explicitly that after the last prophets (Haggai, Zechariah and Malachi) the Holy Spirit has departed from Israel.[3] They even think it possible that the Spirit has never been present in the Second Temple.[4] There can no longer be any revelation inspired by the Spirit which could be put on a level with the Old Testament.

That this was no mere piece of theological speculation but a factor in practical living can be seen from statements that this or that Rabbi would have been worthy of possessing the Holy Spirit, but did not receive it because the present generation is unworthy of it.[5] R. Akiba laments that the Spirit is no longer given even though things are done which ought properly to lead to the gift of it.[6] In fact, however, the view that the Holy Spirit is no longer to be had was not always consistently maintained by the Rabbis.

[1] Str.-B. II, 134, 615–6; IV, 915. The same in Sib. III, 582.
[2] E.g. Wisd. ix. 17; vii. 7; Ecclus. xxxix. 6.
[3] T. Sota, xiii. 2. Cf. Str.-B. I, 127.
[4] B. Joma, xxi. b; J. Taan, ii. 1 (65a, 59). Cf. Str.-B. II, 133. Eccles. R. xii. 7 end: after the destruction of the First Temple the Holy Spirit departed from Israel (Str.-B. II, 133).
[5] This is said of Hillel and of Samuel the Little. T. Sota, xiii. 3–4. Cf. Str.-B. I, 129. According to T. Sota, xiii. 4, Samuel the Little did in fact prophesy in the hour of death, and possess some measure of inspiration by the Holy Spirit (Str.-B. II, 133).
[6] B. Sanh. 656. The same occurs in Sifre Deut. clxxiii on xviii. 11 (Friedmann, 107b) as a saying of R. Eleazar b. Azariah.

The conception of the Spirit as the agent of the divine creation is to be found in the apocrypha and pseudepigrapha (Judith xvi. 14; Wisdom i. 7; xii. 1; Syr. Baruch xxi. 4), and the belief that the Spirit was instrumental in the Creation must also have been current in Palestinian Judaism, and could be derived from the Old Testament. But there are very few instances of it, and this function of the Spirit definitely recedes in importance compared with the conception of the Spirit as the bearer of prophetic revelation and as an endowment of the devout. In early Rabbinic literature the "cosmic" function of the Spirit does not appear to be mentioned at all.[1]

> In Gen. i. 2 רוח is normally understood as "wind".[2] R. Simeon b. Lakish, on the basis of Ps. cxxxix. 5, takes it to mean Adam's Spirit, which was the first of God's creations, while his body (according to Gen. i. 26) was the last.[3] Tg.J. I and II Gen. i. 2 paraphrase "the Spirit of God" by "the Spirit of the mercy of JHWH", and so discern in this passage the thought that God has created the world *with mercy*.[4]

A striking development in Judaism is the way in which the Spirit becomes an independent person. In Rabbinic literature the Spirit is often spoken of in personal categories. There are a mass of instances of the Holy Spirit speaking, crying out, warning, lamenting, weeping, rejoicing, consoling and so on.[5] Indeed the Spirit can even be represented as speaking to God.[6] For this reason it has often been maintained that in Judaism the Spirit is conceived of as a hypostasis, or even as a personal angelic being.[7] But this is to bring in conceptions which are

---

[1] Str.-B. I, 48–9.
[2] Tg. O. Gen. i. 2; Gen. R. i. 9 on i. 1 etc.
[3] Tanḥ. תזריע, 153a (ed. S. Buber, 1885,'§2, 16b); Midr. Ps. cxxxix. 5 (ed. S. Buber, 1891, 265a).
[4] Str.-B. I, 48–9. Cf. Moore, *Judaism*, I, 389.
[5] Cf. Abelson, 224–37; Str.-B. II, 134–8.
[6] Lev. R. vi. 1 on v. 1; Deut. R. iii. 11 on ix. 1.
[7] E.g. by Ringren, *Word and Wisdom*, 165; against this, Str.-B. II, 134–5; Moore, I, 415–37; Moore, H. Th. R. 15 (1922), 55; Abelson, *op. cit.* 224–37.

strange to the Jewish way of thinking. The Spirit is no angelic heavenly being. In Jewish literature it never appears in the heavenly assembly before the throne of God. It could perhaps be called a hypostasis, if by that one means its independent activity; but this again is a concept taken from an un-Jewish range of ideas, and leads easily to misconceptions. What is intended by using personal categories to describe the activity of the Spirit is not to represent it as a particular heavenly being, but rather as an objective divine reality which encounters a man and lays claim to him. Its presence can equally be described by impersonal expressions: it rests (שׁרה) on a man, it fills him (מלא), it illuminates him (נצנץ), it shines upon a place (הופיע). But this does not mean that any concept of the Spirit is presupposed other than that which lies behind the personal expressions. What is of critical importance is that here a man is confronted by a reality which comes to him from God; a reality which to some extent represents the presence of God, and yet is not identical with him.

B. THE DEAD SEA SCROLLS

Already in the later parts of the Old Testament more and more importance is being attached to the concept that the Spirit of Yahweh is not only a supernatural power but is also an ethical power.[1] The further we penetrate into late Judaism, the more important becomes the ethical decision of the individual, his choice between Good and Evil. During the 200 years that Israel lived under Persian domination, the Persian conception of two opposed spirits[2] which impinge on a man and between which he has to choose must have seemed an ideal expression of this idea.[3] The Spirit is represented as something continually present,

---

[1] Isa. xxxii. 5; xxviii. 6; Hag. ii. 5; Zech. iv. 6; vi. 8, etc. See above, p. 5.
[2] A. Dupont-Sommer in R.H.R. 142 (1942), 16–17.
[3] For the beginnings of this in Jewish thought cf. Asc. Isa. iii. 26, 28.

determining a man's whole existence.   It is the "Good",
for which he has already declared himself in his pre-
earthly existence, and for which he is continually declaring
himself afresh.   Yet he does not think of it just as an
idea, but as a challenging and sustaining power of God.[1]

This is different from Hellenism, for the dualism is felt
as something which permeates both the bodily and the
spiritual world.   Thus the *Manual of Discipline* is dominated by the conception of two spirits contending for a man,
one of "truth" and one of "wickedness" (iii. 18–19; iv.
23 ff.).[2]   Other names for them are "spirit of light",
"angel of truth", "prince of lights" (this occurs also in
Damascus Document, v. 18; iv. 4), "spirit of knowledge", or
"spirit (or angel) of darkness" (iii. 20–25; iv. 4).[3]   The
main significance of this conception is simply to bring out
the element of decision involved in human life; an element
which is similarly brought out in the Old Testament
(where the choice is between Yahweh and Baal) or in the
Rabbis (where it is between Good and Evil).   Thus when
the *Manual of Discipline* (iii. 20–21) talks of "walking in
them" (i.e. the two spirits), this means simply "walking
in the ways of light" or "of darkness".   The "counsels"
of the good spirit lay upon one a whole series of virtues,
while a list of vices enumerates what belongs to the "spirit
of wickedness".   Yet there is an emphasis here, which is
stronger than in the Rabbinic analysis and is closer to the
Old Testament, on man living (or else succumbing to
evil) not by his own strength but by that of God.[4]   In
contrast to the Persian system, it is firmly believed that

---

[1] "The 'holy spirit' is at one moment an aspect of the being of Ahura
Mazda, indeed the most characteristic aspect, if not his actual being
itself; at another moment it is an independent being alongside of him."
E. Abegg in Neue Zürcher Zeitung 11th Jan. 1955.

[2] For war between angels and Azazel see Apoc. Abr. 13–14; Philo,
Abr. 13–14; *Plant.* 23–4; between God's angels and devils, Just. *Dial.* cxvi. 1.

[3] In the *War*, xiii. 10–11, the "prince of light" is opposed to the "angel
of hostility".

[4] *Hymns*, iv. 31: "The way of man cannot be established save by the
spirit which God has fashioned for him."

both of the spirits, or angels,[1] were created by God (*M.D.* iii. 25); and the experience of the overwhelming force of evil is consequently expressed by the conception of a large number of evil spirits (*Hymns*, iii. 18; *M.D.* iii. 14; iv. 20).[2] Indeed, there is such a strong realization that man is controlled from outside himself, that many statements come close to a doctrine of predestination.[3]

Alongside of this, the word "spirit" is used in a different way,[4] to mean the "spirit of man"[5] (*M.D.* iv. 3 (?); viii. 3; xi. 1; *Hymns*, i. 8–9; xv. 32; ii. 15). It can then be identical with the pronoun "I" (*Hymns*, iv. 36; vii. 29). On the one hand this means the "understanding" (*M.D.* v. 23–24; vi. 14, 17), on the other hand it includes both understanding and action (v. 21, cf. ii. 20, iv. 26; ix. 14; *Damascus Document* xx. 24). In fact, the word is on the way to meaning: the existence of a man specifically as he lives before God, i.e. the self which is set over his soul and body.[6]

These ideas were further developed in both Jewish (Testament of the 12 Patriarchs[7]) and Christian literature (Hermas).[8] They never became altogether clear concepts, and the confusion is due to another factor of quite

[1] Spirits and angels are synonymous in *War*, xiii. 10–11.

[2] There is a plurality of *good* angels in *War*, xii. 9; xiii. 10; xix. 1; of evil ones, xiii. 2, 11–12; xiv. 10; xv. 13.

[3] *M.D.* iv. 24–5; *Hymns*, iii. 22–3. Cf. *M.D.* iii. 13–14, 24, and iii. 26–iv. 1, which certainly refer to the two spirits.

[4] Apart from "winds" (*Hymns*, i. 10), "messengers of God", etc. (*M.D.*, ix. 3; *Hymns*, xii. 12; xvi. 12).

[5] Though not imprisoned in the body, as Dupont-Sommer, *op. cit.* 32, infers from *M.D.* iv. 20–1. Cf. *War*, vii. 5: "perfect in spirit and flesh (רוח ובשר)"; *Hymns*, ix. 16, where man appears as "flesh" or as "spirit". Cf. I. P. Hyatt, *The View of Man in the Qumran 'Hodayot*, N.T.St. 2 (1955/56), 276–84.

[6] [This point is discussed by W. D. Davies in *The Scrolls and the N.T.* (ed. K. Stendahl) 77.]

[7] Cf. P. A. Munch, *The Spirits in Test. XII*, Acta Orientalia, 13 (1935), 257–63. I disagree with him in regarding the demonic concepts as primary, the psychological concepts (Test. D. ii–iv: "spirit of wrath" = "wrath") as secondary. Against those who regard Test. XII as Jewish–Christian in origin see W. F. Albright in *Background of the N.T. and its Eschatology*, 166. Cf. M. Burrows, *The Dead Sea Scrolls*, 221.

[8] Cf. J. P. Audet, *Affinités littéraires et doctrinales du M.D.*, Rev. Bibl. 59 (1952), 219–38.

independent origin. Late Judaism already used the God-given "soul" as a name for one's responsible existence before God, and as such had no hesitation in calling this "spirit"; and this brought up the whole question of human responsibility. The immediate solution was to make another distinction, this time between the "spirit" and the "I" of a man which is able either to preserve or to destroy the "spirit" (*Damascus Document*, v. 11 [vii. 12]; vii. 3–4 [viii. 20]); and usually this "spirit" can be clearly distinguished from the biological life-force (Test. N. x. 9, Hebrew). On this view the "spirit" was still God-given, and in the last analysis still belonged to God; but it was now conceived of, not as the active agent of ethical decision, but as passively determined by that decision.[1]

At all events, the problem was now being tackled. It was given a particular twist in Gnosticism; it lies close to the surface throughout the New Testament; and it is given a radical solution in Paul.

c. Gnosticism

In Hellenistic thought, power is conceived of as a substance.[2] When Judaism became involved with the old Greek question about the ἀρχή, which was not merely an inquiry into the First Cause of the universe but also into its Essence (which for a Greek meant also the essence of God), only one answer was possible: Yahweh. To put it in more modern scientific terms, it was necessary to be more specific and say: his Spirit. This word "spirit" was eminently suitable: it conformed to Old Testament doctrine; for the Greeks, it included the concept of the "stuff of life"; and in Egypt, the centre of Hellenistic Judaism, it also suggested the age-old image of God's breath entering

---

[1] In Hermas this becomes God's παρακαταθήκη, which can be returned to him either "deceitful", "useless", or else "unspotted", indeed "renewed" (m. III, ii; s. IX, xiv. 3; xxxii. 2–4).

[2] Nemesius, *De natura hominis*, 30 and 40 (M.P.G. xl. 540b, 561a): "Power (δύναμις) is matter (ὕλη τις)", etc. Cf. Diog. L. VII, 56. See below, p. 56, n. 1.

into matter and giving it life.[1]   And from now on, a new importance was attached to the creative role of the Spirit in Gen. i. 2.[2]

What is new here is that the Spirit is coming to be understood more and more as substance—although no individual would probably be aware how far he was inter-preting this concept according either to Old Testament or to Hellenistic thought.   When the Jew talked of the holy "Spirit" in the sense of human psychology, he meant something that was very important to him: the god-given spiritual existence of man.   But to the Hellenist, this could only evoke the image of the soul which is imprisoned in the body,[3] having descended from the realm of God and ready to ascend thither again after death.   Indeed in the Hellenistic period the unity between God and the world tended to fall further and further apart.   The con-trast between the heavenly realm of light and the material world was sensed more and more acutely.   The soul was felt increasingly to be alien, though of the same substance as God.

It was this kind of attitude towards the world which produced a longing for the Golden Age, which once existed and will one day come again.   In Judaism the Paradise story began to take on new significance.   Adam, as the divine First Man, played an ever more important part.   Two notions consequently gained currency in Judaism—one of a heavenly Being who had "fallen" in the First Age, the other of a "Man" who would come in the Last Age.   This myth of a fallen divine First Man was then combined with the Greek soul-myth, a combination

[1] Diod. S. I, xii. 1–2; Plut. *Is. et Os.* 36.   Cf. Eichrodt, *Theologie des A.T.*[3] II, 19; G. Verbeke, *L'évolution de la doctrine du pneuma*, 335–7.

[2] Herm. s. V, vi. 5; C.H. i. 5; iii. 1 (C. H. Dodd, *The Bible and the Greeks*, 101–34, 217–31; Verbeke, *op. cit.* 318–19); Ascl. 14.   Gnostics: Iren. *Haer.* I, xxx. 1; Hipp. *Ref.* V. xix. 13–19, cf. x. 2; Epiph. *Haer.* 25. v. 1; Ps-Clem. *Hom.* XI, 22–4.

[3] Seneca, *Dialogi* XII, vi. 7; *Epistulae Morales*, lxvi. 12; Porphyrius, *Sententiae*, 29 (ed. B. Mommert, 1907), C.H. xxvi. 13 (Nock-Fest. IV, lxxxv. 3 ff.).

which may have been facilitated by the fact that the old Greek gods had now been given new characters as symbols for the Logos, i.e. the divine part of man. Myths about the gods began to be interpreted as representations of the destiny of the soul, which in turn acquired mythical forms. When the Church preached Jesus as the "Man" of the Last Age who had now come, Hellenists could only see in this the return of the fallen First Man, i.e. the "Second Adam". In Jesus' descent and ascension they saw the destiny of the individual soul, perhaps even encouraged to do so by the Church's conception, taken over from the mystery-religions, that the faithful themselves relive the destiny of God.

However, it appeared to follow from Isa. xxxi. 3 that the divine world is characterized by spirit, and the human world by flesh ($\sigma \acute{\alpha} \rho \xi$).[1] In a Hellenistic context, this could only be understood as a proposition about substances. The "Man" (or Son of Man) is he in whom the original heavenly substance has once more made its entry into the material world in order to free its kindred soul-substance in man, that it may rise into its own original heavenly home. But in that case, how can God and his Spirit be the creator of matter, which in itself is evil?[2] How can there be a divine Spirit in material man?

Gnosticism attempts to answer this question in a great variety of ways.[3] The nature of God is spiritual.[4] At

[1] Cf. Num. xvi. 22; xxvii. 16, where the LXX separates the realm of the spirits from the realm of flesh by altering "God of the spirits of all flesh" to "God of the spirits *and* all flesh". (Similarly 1 Clem. lix. 3; lxiv; Ditt. Syll.³ III, 1181, 2–3.)

[2] This possibility is radically denied by Cerinthus (Iren. *Haer.* I, xxxvi. 1) and the Manichaeans (Acta Archelai, 7): Irenaeus (*Haer.* II, iii. 2) wrestles with the blasphemy that "the world could be a product of the Fall and of ignorance".

[3] Here we attempt only to give the broadest outlines. Necessary distinctions of detail have to be omitted. For Valentine's school, see the excellent detailed treatment by F. Sagnard, *La gnose valentinienne et le témoignage de St. Irenée* (1946).

[4] Heracleon fr. 24 (Orig. *Comm. in Joh.* xiii. 25); cf. C.H. xviii. 3. For parallels in Egyptian religion: Plut. *Is. et Os.* xxxvi (II, 365d); *Quaest. Conv.* VIII. 1 (II, 718ab); Diod. S. I, xii. 2; cf. Verbeke, *op. cit* 292.

the creation, a spiritual substance [1] is in some way [2] united with matter and yearns for release. [3]   Occasionally it may be referred to as "soul", ψυχή, [4] or λογικὴ ψυχή, [5] but mostly the spirit as the divine self is explicitly distinguished from the earthly soul, [6] since it is of the same nature as God or as Christ. [7]   This is particularly evident in Valentine. Here, the "seed" or "embryo" (σπέρμα τῆς ἄνωθεν οὐσίας, κύημα or σπέρμα πνευματικόν), which has the same kind of existence as the angels, is mixed with the soul by the Redeemer, unknown to the Demiurge. [8]   But this seed is "put to death by existence in the world": all that remains alive is its alter-ego, the "angel", [9] which however only exists since the time of Christ, for he is none other than the Christ who enters each individual. [10]   This whole mythology simply represents a concern to separate the spirit, as the substance which is a gift of grace and cannot be lost, from the other two constituents of man, soul and body. [11]   It follows that in Gnostic thought Redemption is nothing other than the reassembly of all the sparks of the Spirit.   It is effected by the Redeemer, whose nature is spiritual, descending into matter, collecting the spiritual fragments, and reascending with them. [12]   His ascension is the beginning of the separating-out process

[1] πνευματικὴ οὐσία (Iren. Haer. I, ii. 4). Cf. Sagnard, op. cit. 398–415.

[2] Basileides even tries to bring creatio ex nihilo into a gnostic system. (G. Quispel in Eranos Jbch., 16 (1948), 120–1).

[3] Cl. Al. Strom. IV, xxvi. 3–4; Heracleon, fr. 23 (Orig. Comm. in Joh. xiii. 20); Hipp. Haer. V, x. 2; xix. 16; xxvi. 17; Acta Archelai, 8.

[4] E.g. Hipp. Haer. V, x. 2; Pistis Sophia 111, 132.   Acta Archelai, 8.

[5] Cl. Al. Strom. II, xx. 112.

[6] Iren. Haer. I, xxi. 4; cf. Hipp. Haer. V, xxvi. 8, 25; VI, xxxiv. 1; VII xxvii. 6.

[7] Heracleon, fr. 24 (Orig. Comm. in Joh. xiii. 25); Odes of Solomon (ed. Rendel Harris), xxvi. 6–7; Iren. Haer. I, v. 6: ὁμοούσιον τῇ μητρί (id est Σοφία).

[8] Iren. Haer. I, iv. 5; v. 6; II, xix. 1, 3; Cl. Al. Strom. II, xxxvi. 2–3; IV, xc. 3–4; Exc. Theod. ii; liii. 2–5.

[9] Cl. Al. Exc. Theod. xxii. 2; Heracleon, fr. 35 (Orig. Comm. in Joh. xiii. 49).

[10] Cl. Al. Exc. Theod. xxxvi. 1–2.

[11] "The spiritual element is not nature, but grace", Tertull. Val. 29; Quispel, op. cit. 262–7, 274–5.

[12] Cl. Al. Exc. Theod. xlii. 2; Eus. Hist. Eccl. I, xiii. 20; Acta Archelai, 8.

by which he gives his body and soul to chaos and his Spirit back to God.[1] Like him, the redeemed also turn into pure spirits by being freed from all ties of body and soul.[2] As soon as they are all once more gathered into the great Spiritual Body,[3] redemption is complete. Despite the mythical imagery, the descent and ascension of the Redeemer is in the end only a paradigm of the destiny of the Spirit that is tied to man. Whether it is thought of as a historical event is immaterial.[4] One way or another, it serves only to remind[5] the spiritual man of the imperishable substance which lives within him, whose nature it is to be saved (φύσει σῳζόμενος).[6] In the last analysis, the Redeemer is none other than the Spiritual Man himself.[7]

Thus Spirit is separated from soul, and the three-fold division of man into body, soul and an added, God-given spirit is clear and complete.[8] In Greek literature there existed already the Platonic three-fold division[9] and the later triad of mind-soul-body.[10] But this was not a real trichotomy: the mind was not separated from the body.[11]

[1] Hipp. *Haer.* V, xxvi. 31–2; VII, xxxvii. 10–12; Cl. Al. *Exc. Theod.* i. 1–2.

[2] Iren. *Haer.* I, vii. 1 (cf. xxi. 5); Cl. Al. *Exc. Theod.* lxiv.

[3] Acta Joh. 100. Evidence in Büchsel, *Kommentar zu den Johannesbriefen* (1933), 285, n. 1.

[4] Cf. Quispel, *op. cit.* 249–50. It therefore remains open to question whether or not the Gnostic Redeemer-figure is pre-Christian.

[5] Act. Thom. 110; Cl. Al. *Paed.* I, xxxii. 1; cf. Iren. *Haer.* I, iv. 1; viii. 2.

[6] Iren. *Haer.* I, vi. 2; Cl. Al. *Strom.* II, x. 2; IV, lxxxix. 4; V, iii. 3; *Exc. Theod.* lvi. 3.

[7] "Le point de départ est toujours l'homme" (Sagnard, *op. cit.* 568). On all this, see R. Bultmann's article in Kittel s.v. γινώσκω, E. T. *Gnosis*, 7–14; R. P. Casey, 'Gnosis, Gnosticism and the *N.T.*', in *The Background of the N.T. and its Eschatology* (1956), 52–80; W. F. Albright, *Discoveries in Palestine and the Gospel of St. John, ibid.* 162–3.

[8] Iren. *Haer.* I, v. 6; vi. 1. Correspondingly there are three classes of men, vii. 5. Further instances in Sagnard, *op. cit.* 172–98.

[9] *Phaedrus*, 247c; *Rep.* VI, 508d; taken over by e.g. Philo, *Leg. All.* I, xxii–xxiii.

[10] For Aristotle and Plutarch, see E. B. Allo, R.B. 43 (1934), 335. Also M. Ant. XII, iii. 1 (cf. xiv. 5); V, xxxiii. 6; VIII, lvi. 1–2; II, ii. 1.

[11] In his general appraisal, Burton (*Spirit, Soul and Flesh*, 205–7) does not allow for the fact that there are no Greek parallels to the superiority of πνεῦμα over ψυχή which may not have been influenced by Judaism or Christianity. The same goes for magic texts (cf. Verbeke, *op. cit.* 322–37).

By contrast, the concept of the Spirit of God standing over against the body and soul of man is central in Judaism, and is applied also to the Spirit which dwells in man. The transition is particularly clear in Irenaeus, where the Spirit of God is grasped as the power which resurrects body and soul.[1] while at the same time it is maintained that man is only perfect when the Spirit is added to body and soul.[2] The Jew is aware that in the Old Testament the soul belongs to the flesh,[3] but he also wishes to portray the natural man as one who thinks, and wills, and lives a conscious life. Therefore when he wants to talk about the opposite of "spiritual" he may just as well say "of the soul" ($\psi\upsilon\chi\iota\kappa\acute{o}s$) as "of the body" ($\sigma\omega\mu\alpha\tau\iota\kappa\acute{o}s$).[4] Since this opposition of spirit and soul has so far only been found in literature which is either Jewish or Christian or else influenced by them, it appears that the decisive conception must have been the Jewish one of the Spirit which both transcends a man and dwells within him.[5]

[1] *Epid.* xlii. Also Mart. Polycarpi xiv. 2 (Eus. *Hist. Eccl.* IV, xv. 34).
[2] Iren. *Haer.* V, vi. 1. Also Cl. Al. *Strom.* V, lxxxvii. 4–lxxxviii. 4; Tat. *Or. Graec.* xv. 2.
[3] Eth. Enoch, xvi. 1: "flesh-soul"; J. A. T. Robinson, *The Body* (1952), 23, n. 2. Yet this use of words cannot be derived from Gen. ii. 7 (R. Bultmann, *Gnosis*, J.T.S. (N.S.), 3 (1952), 14–16).
[4] E.g. Epiph. *Haer.* 33, v. 13, or $\sigma\alpha\rho\kappa\iota\kappa\acute{o}s$ Ign. *Eph.* vii. 2; x. 3; *Sm.* xii. 2; xiii. 2; *Mag.* xiii. 2; *Pol.* i. 2; ii. 2. See below, p. 87.
[5] See above, p. 17. Cf. Allo, *op. cit.* 336–41; Verbeke, *op. cit.* 538–43.

THE NEW TESTAMENT

LONG before the Spirit was an article of doctrine it was a fact in the experience of the primitive Church. This explains why the New Testament statements about it exhibit both such diversity and such unity.

A. MARK AND MATTHEW

1. *Demonic and psychological "spirit"*

Out of 23 occurrences of the word spirit (πνεῦμα) in Mark, 14 are in a phrase like "unclean spirit" (πνεῦμα ἀκάθαρτον), meaning "demon" (δαίμων or δαιμόνιον) [1]— a concept which is familiar from contemporary Judaism. Matthew usually avoids this term, and in viii. 16 goes to the other extreme when he renders "demons" (δαιμόνια in Mark i. 34) by "spirits" (τὰ πνεύματα) without any qualifying word.

In Mark ii. 8 "spirit" seems to be purely psychological ("Jesus knowing in his spirit . . .", cf. v. 30 "knowing in himself"); in Mark viii. 12 it is the seat of perception and emotion, and in Matt. xxvii. 50 it is the life-force.

There is a special shade of meaning in Mark xiv. 38, where the "willing spirit" (πνεῦμα πρόθυμον) is contrasted with the "weak flesh" (σὰρξ ἀσθενής). This reflects the experience of a conflict within man, which can already be seen in the *Manual of Discipline* and elsewhere in Hellenistic psychology. It implies that the opposite of (sinful) flesh is not some better part of man's

---

[1] The synoptic parallels to πνεύματα ἀκάθαρτα in Mark v. 13 are δαίμονες and δαιμόνια. Cf. E. Langton, *Essentials of Demonology* (1949), 147–71; S. Eitrem, *Some Notes on the Demonology in the N.T.*, Symb. Osl. xxvii. (1950); V. McCasland, *By the finger of God* (1951).

nature, but is the effect of God's will. Once it is realized that the expression "willing spirit" derives from the Hebrew text of Ps. li. 12,[1] where it is identical with the "Holy Spirit" of God, and that here the prayer is for strength in temptation, it becomes clear that what is meant by "spirit" is the Spirit of God which is temporarily imparted to a man and fights against human weakness.

2. *The Spirit as the Power of God*

However, the meaning of "spirit" ($\pi\nu\epsilon\hat{\upsilon}\mu\alpha$) in Matthew and Mark is to all intents and purposes determined by the Old Testament concept of God's power to do certain things.[2] The "blasphemy against the Holy Spirit" is committed, according to Mark iii. 28–30, by those who, when Jesus casts out devils, mistake the power of God for the apparently similar[3] power of the devil.

The formation of this *Logion* is hard to determine. In its Marcan form, the blasphemy against the Spirit is contrasted with all other sins and blasphemies, in its Q form only with blasphemy against the Son of Man. Matthew places both versions side by side, Luke adopts only Q. It may be conjectured that a pre-Marcan version had $\tau\hat{\omega}$ $\upsilon\dot{\iota}\hat{\omega}$ $\tau o\hat{\upsilon}$ $\dot{\alpha}\nu\theta\rho\dot{\omega}\pi o\upsilon$,[4] which in one tradition turned into the completely unambiguous $\tau o\hat{\iota}s$ $\upsilon\dot{\iota}o\hat{\iota}s$ $\tau\hat{\omega}\nu$ $\dot{\alpha}\nu\theta\rho\dot{\omega}\pi\omega\nu$ of Mark, and in another, at a time when "Son of Man" was only understood as referring to Jesus,[5] into the Q version. But it is more likely that the saying was originally a missionary slogan, intended to show the Jews the gravity of their decision.[6] There is

[1] Lohmeyer, *Komm. zu Mk. ad loc.*
[2] E.g. Ezek. i. 12, 20; Judges xiii. 25; xiv. 6, 19; xv. 14.
[3] That is why both can still be described as $\pi\nu\epsilon\hat{\upsilon}\mu\alpha$, though this usage is avoided more and more. Yet the $\delta\alpha\iota\mu o\nu\iota\zeta\dot{o}\mu\epsilon\nu os$ of the synoptics is never contrasted with the $\pi\nu\epsilon\upsilon\mu\alpha\tau\iota\kappa\dot{o}s$ of the Epistles as his good counter-part (Jackson-Lake, I, v. 102–3).
[4] Apart from this, the title Son of God hardly occurs in Mark before Peter's confession (T. W. Manson, *The Teaching of Jesus*, 214). See further, Jackson-Lake, I, i. 380–1.
[5] Wellhausen, *Mt.*, *ad loc.*; A. Loisy, *Les évangiles synoptiques, ad loc.* For the fact, cf. Did. xi. 7; II Cor. vii. 2, 17.
[6] The saying can hardly go back to Jesus, despite R.N. Flew, *Jesus and His Church*, 49.

something similar in Acts iii. 17. In its certain knowledge of possessing the Spirit (I Thess. i. 6, etc.) the Church sees the end of the age of uncertainty. The title "Son of Man" in this case denotes the earthly man who is not yet installed as the Son of God κατὰ πνεῦμα (see below, pp. 57–8).

In any case, the *Logion* is evidence for the Church's boundless conviction that it possessed the Spirit. In this connection it is noticeable how in Mark iii. 28 and Matt. xii. 32α[1] it is the incredible magnitude of what is forgiven that is especially emphasized. It is as a corollary to this that one must understand the severity with which resistance to the manifestation of the Spirit is castigated. Granted the Church's conviction of the reality of the Spirit working within it, such resistance could only be regarded as wilfulness against the overpowering force of the Spirit.[2] No forgiveness is available, because none is asked for.[3]

Matt. xii. 28 ("If I, by the Spirit of God, cast out demons . . .") belongs to the same context. "Spirit" (πνεύματι) is presumably a correction by the primitive Church (which had experienced the working of the Spirit in its midst) for the original "finger" (δακτύλῳ Luke xi. 20). Now the Spirit of God does not appear among the various means of casting out devils known to the Rabbis.[4] Therefore this attitude is completely new; and what is remarkable in this passage is that the presence of the Spirit (casting out devils) is interpreted as the presence of the kingdom (βασιλεία).[5] In the same way, the promise that God will put his Spirit upon his Servant is seen to be fulfilled, according to Matt. xii. 18, in Jesus' work of

[1] Matt. xii. 32α is better adapted to a situation after Pentecost, while Mark refers it to an event before Pentecost (iii. 30).

[2] Kittel, art. *Sin*, E.T. 68.

[3] Consequently the saying cannot be addressed to those who are anxious about being guilty of it.

[4] Str.-B. IV, 532–5 (cf. the dramatic casting out of devils in front of Vespasian).

[5] Kittel, art. *Basileia*, E.T. 42. The saying, at least in essentials, may well go back to Jesus.

healing; and this is of a piece with the Church's conviction that with the coming of this miraculous Spirit the Last Age is breaking in.

There is nothing further to be learnt from Mark i. 12 ("immediately the Spirit drove him out (ἐκβάλλει) into the wilderness"), where the Old Testament colouring[1] comes out so crudely that is already modified in Matthew. Here, the Spirit is not understood as anything like help in temptation, but as the irresistible power of God which goes off with its victim.[2]

3. General endowment with the Spirit

It is significant that the Rabbinic identification of the Holy Spirit with Scripture (see above pp. 28-9) only crops up once, in Matt. xii. 36. The Church is conscious that it has received the prophetic Spirit not only in the past epoch of salvation—the time of the scriptural prophets— but also in the present (Mark xiii. 11 and parallels[3]). The Old Testament view is that the Spirit mediates the word of God (II Sam. xxiii. 2); but this is now understood in a different way, in that the utterance of the Spirit is a sign of God's help in the eschatological time of need.[4]

It is true that a general endowment with the Spirit is only referred to in Mark i. 8 ("He will baptize you with the Holy Spirit"). Mark certainly saw the fulfilment of this saying in the pouring out of the Spirit upon the Church[5]—which is also the interpretation in Acts (i. 5; xi. 16).

The Q version is doubtless the more original. It is easily understandable that the incomprehensible καὶ πυρί

---

[1] Cf. II Kings ii. 16 (hi. שלך); Ezek. viii. 3; xi. 1, 24; xliii. 5 (hi. בוא); Ezek. xxxvii. 1 (hi. יצא).

[2] See below, p. 44 top.

[3] The form in Q is probably original (Lohmeyer, Markus, 273).

[4] The saying which limits endowment with the Spirit to particular times of need may well be dominical (Loh. Markus, ad loc., W. F. Howard, Christianity according to St. John, 78); the replacement of the Spirit by the ascended Christ and the broadening of the promise (Luke xxi. 15) are secondary.

[5] Did Mark xvi. 9 ff. once recount this? (Barrett, Gospel Tradition, 125.)

should have been left out, but not that it should have been added; for no fire-baptism in fact took place. Even Luke did not see it happening in Acts ii. 3, since in i. 5 he only quotes the saying in its Marcan form. In this case it must go back to the Baptist (or to Jesus) and belongs to the circles of intense eschatological expectation. Fire is a widely-known symbol of judgment,[1] and this more than anything is its meaning in the verses which immediately surround this *logion*, viz.: Matt. iii. 10, 12 = Luke iii. 9, 17 = Q. Thus baptism by fire,[2] in the oldest form of the saying which we can trace, was understood as eschatological judgment. But in this case "He who cometh" is surely not only Elijah, but the Messianic judge.[3] It is questionable whether this also explains satisfactorily the promise of a baptism by the Spirit, or whether this promise was originally a Christian addition.[4]

Eschatological expectations are met by endowment with the Spirit—often in the imagery of cleansing water [5] —and also by the Fire of Judgment. Both appear also in the Dead Sea Scrolls (*M.D.* iv. 13, 21). In this case the Messiah would have the double task of both destroying the ungodly and of saving the devout. In fact, however, the two concepts are not so strictly connected, and the Messiah is seldom regarded as a dispenser of the Spirit (see above, p. 11). Moreover, unless this distinction were made clear, it would not be easy, within the single image of judgment, suddenly to conceive both of Spirit as a gift of grace and of fire as the instrument of judgment. It is more likely that "spirit" originally meant

---

[1] Isa. lxvi. 15–16 (cf. i. 31; xxx. 30, 33; xxxi. 9; xxxiv. 9–10); Amos. i. 4; vii. 4; Mal. iii. 2; Ps. Sol. xv. 4; IV Ezra xiii. 4, 10; Syr. Baruch xlviii. 39; Test. Abr. 14 (ed. M. R. James, xciv. 18); Mark ix. 43–9; I Cor. iii. 13; II Thess. i. 8; II Peter. iii. 7; Rev. xx. 9; Qumran, *Hymns*, iii. 28–31; vi. 18; *M.D.* ii. 8, 15; iv. 13.

[2] The phrase was formed by analogy to John's water-baptism (C. H. Kraeling, *John the Baptist*, 114–18). In Mark x. 38–9, Luke xii. 50, βαπτισθῆναι is used figuratively.

[3] At most a "Messianic" Elijah: W. H. Brownlee, *John the Baptist in the New Light of Ancient Scrolls*, Interpretation 9 (1955), 86–7.

[4] See most recently, V. Taylor, *Mark, ad loc.*

[5] T. F. Torrance, *Proselyte Baptism*, N.T.St. 1 (1954–5) 152–3. Schlatter, *Joh.* on iii. 5.

"wind".[1] Storm-wind and fire are often mentioned together, e.g. in the description of the "Son of Man" who comes to the judgment on the clouds of heaven.[2] And in particular, both are presupposed in the immediately adjacent sentence in Matthew (iii. 12): the winnowing is done in the storm-wind (Isa. xli. 16; cf. xxvii. 12; Jer. iv. 11; Amos. ix. 9) and the chaff is consumed with fire.[3]

If then the baptism of John was originally understood as the rite by which a throng of penitents hoped to escape imminent judgment,[4] a decisive step forward was made by the Synoptics' understanding of it: having a share in the Spirit in the Church of Jesus is already an anticipation of salvation from the eschatological judgment. Baptism "by Spirit and Fire" has become the fulfilment of the saving function of John's baptism. It is still understood as judgment by separation and purification; but this is no longer merely awaited in the future: it is experienced in the present—experienced, that is, as salvation for all who submit to it.

4. Jesus' endowment with the Spirit at his Baptism

The account of Jesus' baptism is preserved only in the form which it has in Mark i. 9 ff.[5] Even this is an account of something other than the call of a prophet. Of all the possibilities, the most likely is that this is an account of the

---

[1] As frequently in the O.T. Cf. Barrett, *Gospel Tradition*, 126; Kraeling, *op. cit.* 63; Taylor, *Mark, ad loc.* (as a possibility).

[2] IV Ezra xiii. 10, 27 (spiritus, ignis, tempestas). Cf. Isa. xxix. 6; xxx. 27; Ezek. i. 4, etc. In particular, in Gen. R. 83, the judgment of the heathen is compared with winnowing, helped by fire (Mal. iii. 19) and storm-wind (Isa. xli. 16).

[3] M. Goguel, in Rev. H. Ph. R. 5 (1925), 68, sees the influence of this saying in Rev. xiv. 14–20 (18 πυρός).

[4] Kraeling, *op. cit.* 118–22; Barrett, *Gospel Tradition*, 31–4.

[5] Matt. iv. 3α, 6α suggests that Q already knew of a proclamation of the Son of God. Against the view that the story is a cult-legend (A. Loisy, *Luc, ad loc.*), must be set the lack of an institution-narrative (as in Matt. xxviii. 19); against the view that it is a Baptist-legend proving Jesus' inferiority (M. Goguel in Rev. H. Ph. R. 13 (1933), 424, n. 13), the total withdrawal of the Baptist and the voice from heaven. πνεῦμα used absolutely is not necessarily Hellenistic (*M.D.* iv. 6; *War*, vii. 6?), and "son" for "king" is certainly not.

gift of the Spirit to the Messiah. The Messiah has the Spirit of God: that is an Old Testament promise which is repeated in Judaism (see above p. 11);[1] and that this event is quite different from anything in the prophets is made explicit (apart from the visible apparition of the dove and the audible testimony of God), not through any new doctrine of the Spirit,[2] but through the fact that *this* gift of the Spirit takes place at the End of the Age, after a long period when the Spirit was extinct (see above p. 13).[3] In this way the event is pin-pointed as the beginning of the new Divine Age. For this reason also it is in a completely different class from Hellenistic accounts of ecstatic phenomena.[4] The original significance of the gift of the Spirit in Baptism is that it marks the beginning of Messiahship; but, unlike later Adoptianism, this is not a doctrinal proposition which excludes other possibilities.[5] No difficulty is felt at this stage about the place of the story alongside that of the miraculous conception by the Spirit. It is not a question of giving concrete form to the appearance of a Wonder Man; both stories are concerned to announce the already accepted uniqueness of Jesus by recounting God's direct intervention at certain points in his life. This is their way of saying that, in Jesus, God himself is at work.

5. *Passages peculiar to Matthew*

The first of these to be mentioned is Matt. v. 3. οἱ πτωχοὶ τῷ πνεύματι cannot mean those who are poor in the Holy Spirit. But it is also impossible to take πνεύματι as an instrumental dative. It must be a dative of

---

[1] Barrett, *Gospel Tradition*, 42–4.

[2] No acts of the Spirit are presupposed beyond those in the passages mentioned.

[3] In Judaism, when individuals appear in possession of the Spirit, they too are regarded as a sign of the Last Age.

[4] These are self-induced and remain a private experience of the individual, not a sign of a new act of God. εἰς αὐτόν means no more than ἐπ' αὐτόν (Bl.-Debr. §207, Mark iii. 13, unlike Gosp. Hebr. iv).

[5] Unlike Just. *Dial.* 87–8.

respect,[1] parallel to καθαροὶ τῇ καρδίᾳ and the Rabbinic phrase שִׁפְלַ רוּחַ (Prov. xxix. 23; Isa. lvii. 15). πνεῦμα therefore signifies the human spirit. However, what is new in this, as against the parallels from Judaism,[2] is that this disposition is not demanded as a virtue to be acquired by men, but rather those men are esteemed to whom it is given. Nevertheless, just as "spirit" (רוח) in Judaism was continually taking on more overtones of the religious individuality of man (see above, p. 17), so Matt. v. 3 esteems blessed the poor "people of the land" (אם הארל) who put their whole trust in God, as opposed not so much to those who are materially (Luke vi. 20, 24) or intellectually rich, but to those who are rich in religious knowledge and practice.

A special place belongs to the command to baptize in Matt. xxviii. 19.

It is open to question whether the triple formula may not be an ancient interpolation.[3] Eusebius, 21 times out of 25, quotes it without the formula, and quotes the triple formula only after Nicaea. Justin (*Ap.* I, 61) supports baptism in the triple name with Isa. i. 16 ff. and the apostolic tradition, but does *not* cite Matt. xxviii. 19. In the practice of the Church, the formula appears for the first time in Didache vii. 1. On the other hand, Didache ix. 5 shows that at the same time the single formula was still current. It may be that since it was not based on any particular Trinitanian doctrine, it could crop up from time to time without being felt as anything sensationally new—just as triadic formulae occasionally appear in Paul. Therefore it is not impossible for the time of Matthew.[4] But it cannot go back to Jesus; for Luke, John, Paul and even Mark xvi. 15 have no knowledge of it, and the primitive church knows of no triple formula, nor indeed of any commission to the Gentiles.[5]

---

[1] Bl.-Debr. §197—exactly as in Ps. xxxiv. 19 (LXX). Qumran, *War*, xi. 9–13 is very instructive: "those who are bruised in spirit" or "the poor" are those who are fighting on God's side: cf. xiii. 14; xiv. 7. Other references in A. Dupont-Sommer, R.H.R. 148 (1955), 160, n. 4.

[2] Str.-B. *ad loc.*

[3] Barrett, *Gospel Tradition*, 102–3.

[4] So A. H. McNeile, *The Gospel acc. to St. Matthew, ad loc.*

[5] Cf. Flemington, *N.T. Doctrine of Baptism*, 108.

What is astonishing about this is not the reference to the
Spirit at baptism (see below p. 50), so much as the naming
of the Spirit's name (ὄνομα τοῦ πνεύματος) alongside the
other two names. This means that here πνεῦμα is
understood in a completely different sense from that in
any other passage in Matthew. Matthew must have
known the formula already as a baptismal formula (perhaps in a very restricted circle). Once the "Lord",
κύριος, was placed next to God, it would have been very
easy for the Spirit to be added. This did not involve
speculation over their mutual relationship; it was rather
a proof that God cannot be demonstrated as the apex of a
monotheistic system, but can only be encountered when
he meets the Church in person: in the Son, or else (for
the individual) in the Spirit, in which this encounter with
the Son takes place.[1]

6. *The supernatural conception of Jesus by the Spirit*

Finally, Matt. i. 18, 20 must be mentioned: the reference to Jesus' conception.

> This tradition is secondary to that of Luke, since it
> presupposes polemical opposition to it. The episode is
> not narrated, but simply reported by the angel to allay a
> suspicion. An analysis of Luke gives the following
> results: (1) The Baptist stories were originally indepen-
> dent and nowhere allude to Jesus; (2) the Christmas
> story does not presuppose i. 26–38. In an attempt at
> harmonization, Baptist and Jesus stories are woven
> together, so that they run parallel, and yet give prece-
> dence to the Jesus stories (most noticeable in i. 26–38).
> The most likely conclusion seems to me to be: (a) i.
> 26–38, ii. 1–20 were originally independent legends; (b)
> Luke or his predecessor uses them to provide a parallel
> and to emulate the already current Baptist stories; (c) this
> motive affects the tradition behind i. 26–38 right from the
> start, making the parallels clearer here than in ii. 1–20.

---

[1] It is true that it is impossible to distinguish sharply between liturgical
formulae and creeds (but see O. Cullmann, *Early Christian Creeds*, p. 36 n.1.);
but this does not mean that formulations of this kind could not have existed
before there were any literary examples of triple credal forms.

In Matt. i. 18, 20, as in Luke i. 35, πνεῦμα is the divine creative power, creating the life of this unique child—a conception which we certainly cannot find in Rabbinic Judaism,[1] though we can find it in popular writings.[2] Now it may be that the creative intervention of God in the process of conception was currently believed in, in which case it was but a short step to Luke i. 35 and Matt. i. 20. However, the ground had also been prepared from another direction. In Egyptian-Hellenistic Judaism Isa. vii. 14 had once been interpreted in the sense of a miracle of fatherless birth; furthermore, it is precisely in Egypt that the notion of conception through the Spirit of God was developed; finally, a mass of parallels from comparative religion show that some kind of divine conception was regarded, especially in contemporary Hellenism, as an absolutely indispensable characteristic of the Saviour.[3]

The result was a combination of the belief in a unique example of the creative intervention of God, with the concept (already explicit in the Old Testament) of the creative power of God's Spirit[4]—a concept, which, through Graeco-Egyptian parallels, was applied in Hellenistic Judaism to the process of conception.

7. Recapitulation

One conclusion from this survey is that Matthew and Mark contain astoundingly few statements about the Spirit. Only one of these (Matt. xiii. 11 and parallels) or the gist of it, can be attributed with any certainty to Jesus. This shows, in the first place, the astonishing fidelity of the tradition: the early Church's experiences of

---

[1] Indeed, our story is told in order to outbid the story of the direct intervention of God at the birth of John, for which parallels can be found in Str.-B. I, 49–50.

[2] See above, p. 14.

[3] In Philo (*Cher.* 40–52; *Fug.* 108–9; *Ebr.* 30; *Leg. All.* ii. 49–51, on which see Barrett, *Gospel Tradition*, 9–10) the mythical background of Egyptian thought is still visible. For Philo himself the event is purely spiritual. See Barrett, *Gospel Tradition*, 10–15, on other lines of interpretation.

[4] Cf. Barrett, *Gospel Tradition*, 17–24.

the Spirit have hardly been read back at all into the description of Jesus' life.[1] There is also, however, a significant theological point to be considered.

The temptation to portray Jesus as a Man of the Spirit must have been considerable. Even if Jesus did not betray many of the marks of ecstatic piety, nevertheless, even under critical analysis, the tradition about him still has quite a large "spiritual" element compared with anything in Rabbinic literature. Thus even the references to his power (ἐξουσία, δύναμις) are really only a variation on the popular and Old Testament sense of "Spirit". Why then is the Spirit mentioned so little? Reference to Isaiah and Jeremiah[2] does not help, since the relevant passages represent a reaction to the abuses of the *Nebiim*; but Jesus does not compete with such figures, even though they occasionally did make their appearance in Judaism. Another possible explanation[3] is that Jesus was originally portrayed as a Man of the Spirit, but that these traits were subsequently suppressed in the interests of a more advanced Christology. But this is an unlikely hypothesis. After all, Judaism knew that the Messiah would be a bearer of the Spirit; so that an accretion of clearly Messianic characteristics might have been expected, but not the suppression of "spiritual" ones. Again, the suggestion that the Spirit, being an "intermediary", would make God seem more distant, while Jesus was proclaiming the direct nearness of the Father,[4] does not work; for it is precisely in the Spirit that the Church experiences the presence of God. Finally, it makes the facts no clearer to say that the presence of the Spirit was so manifest that there was no need for anything to be said about it; for the gospels are not concerned just with settling

---

[1] R. N. Flew, *Jesus and his Church*, 49; Barrett, in J.T.S. (N.S.) 1 (1950), 1. Flemington, *op. cit.* 95, makes the same point for baptism.

[2] J. E. Fison, *The Blessing of the Holy Spirit*, ch. 5. Barrett, *Gospel Tradition*, 152, is sound on this.

[3] Windisch, *Syn. Ueberlieferung*, 230–4.

[4] E. F. Scott, *The Spirit in the N.T.*, 79.

doubtful points:[1] they report and proclaim. Moreover, Acts and Paul speak constantly about the Spirit.

Therefore it may be taken as a historical fact that Jesus himself said hardly anything about the Spirit.[2] This may have been because he thought of himself at first as Messiah-designate; or else because it was only after the completion of his ministry that his disciples were ready for it;[3] or again because he simply did not expect an out-pouring of the Spirit.[4] But at least in this respect the Johannine view is confirmed (see below p. 96) which bases the full understanding of Jesus, not on his sayings, but on the post-resurrection proclamation of the Church. It was this Church which experienced the gift of the Spirit as a divine sign marking it out as the People of the Last Age. It knew, of course, that this was dependent on the coming of Jesus and on faith in him; but it was a long time before it reached a clear formulation of this belief (see below pp. 54 ff.). On the other hand, the fact that the Church so consistently avoided portraying Jesus simply as the first Man of the Spirit, throws into startlingly high relief its conviction that the role intended for it by Jesus was neither that of being an example of the "spiritual" life, nor the teacher of the People of the Last Age. The only impor-tant point was that God encountered his people in Christ. Therefore all that is said about Jesus and the Spirit only underlines Jesus' uniqueness, his "eschatological" status, the fact that God is really present in him as he is nowhere else.[5] This is the purport of the small number of passages

[1] Barrett, *Gospel Tradition*, 141–2.
[2] For another view, see W. F. Lofthouse in Exp. Times, 52 (1940–1), 334–6.
[3] Flew, *op. cit.*, 51.
[4] So Barrett in Exp. Times, 67 (1955–6), 142–5. Some scholars (e.g. Leisegang, Bultmann (*T.N.T.* I, 41), Goguel) attribute the experience of the Spirit to the Hellenistic church.
[5] The position is the exact opposite of that in Judaism, where only the Good Men of the Last Age occupy a central position, and the Messiah, as their mediator, is of secondary importance (Bousset-Gressmann, 222–3). The statement about possession of the Spirit is much less firmly rooted in the early Kerygma than that about the Messiah, cf. C. H. Dodd, *The Apostolic Preaching* (1936), 133–5 = (1944), 57–8.

which portray Jesus as the bearer of "spiritual" power (Matt. xii. 18, 28; Mark iii. 29–30), and still more distinctly of those other passages which, on account of the activity of the Spirit in Jesus, lift him right above his predecessors (Matt. i. 20; Mark i. 10) or describe him as the eschatological Spirit-baptist (Mark i. 8, cf. xiii. 11).

Matthew and Mark therefore have substantially the same conception of the Spirit of God as the Old Testament. Words and deeds which would otherwise lie outside human capacity are made possible by the power of God. Only once (in the notion of the Spirit's part in the conception of Jesus) do more modern ideas from Hellenistic Judaism make their appearance. But what is completely new is the strict subordination of Spirit episodes to the conviction that in them the messianic Last Age has dawned.[1] All statements about the nature of the Spirit are there purely for their Christological importance.

B. LUKE AND ACTS

That the Spirit received a new importance in these circles can be seen at once from the fact that πνεῦμα, as the term for the divine Spirit, is used at least three times as often in Luke as it is in Mark.[2] As for Acts i–xii, which has 37 πνεῦμα-passages, this is relatively the highest incidence in the New Testament.[3] Moreover, it appears from the material that Luke has a new conception of the Spirit. Usually this is regarded as "influence from Greek Asia Minor".[4] But it will become clear that the development was strongly moulded by Judaism. Our method

[1] Barrett, *Gospel Tradition*, 153.
[2] πνεῦμα ἀκάθαρτον, etc.: 12 times. For psychological πνεῦμα see below, p. 54.
[3] Acts xiii–xxviii has only 18 instances, although it is about a third longer than i–xii.
[4] E.g. by P. Volz. *Der Geist Gottes*, 198 ; but it would be hard to imagine the Palestinian Church as "unspiritual". Cf. E. F. Scott, *The Varieties of N.T. Religion*, 32–3; C. C. Torrey, *The Aramaic Period of the Nascent Christian Church*, Z.N.W. 44 (1952–3), 207–8.

will be to start in each case from Luke (since Luke shows most clearly the progress of the concept compared to Mark) and then to complete the picture from Acts.

1. The relationship between the Spirit and Jesus

Mark i. 12 runs: "The Spirit cast him out into the wilderness", τὸ πνεῦμα αὐτὸν ἐκβάλλει εἰς τὸν ἐρημόν. Contrast the version in Luke iv. 1 : "Jesus being full of the Holy Spirit returned . . . and was led in the Spirit into the wilderness", ἤγετο ἐν τῷ πνεύματι ἐν τῷ ἐρήμῳ. In other words, Luke avoids giving the impression that the Spirit is an agent set over Jesus. He is not satisfied with the Old Testament idea of the power of God falling upon a man (see above p. 4). Instead, Jesus becomes the agent—"in the Holy Spirit".[1] He is no longer a Man of the Spirit, but is now Lord of the Spirit. In iv. 14, Luke introduces the Spirit again, and from then on the dominant description of Jesus is that of one who possesses the power of the Spirit.[2] iv. 18 also (peculiar to Luke) emphasizes the resting of the Spirit upon Jesus. There is a notable reinterpretation in xii. 10, where Luke takes the saying about the sin against the Holy Spirit out of the context which it has in Mark,[3] for the reason that it is impossible for him to see the decisive manifestation of the Spirit in the casting out of demons by the Man of the Spirit, Jesus. ii. 40 is completely parallel to i. 80 ; but a growing "in the Spirit" is not attributed to

---

[1] Jesus is led "in" (not "by") the Spirit. πλήρης, as opposed to πλησθείς, indicates being continually full. This is the first instance of the Spirit being a power in the struggle against Satan (G. W. H. Lampe, The Holy Spirit in the writings of St. Luke, in Studies in the Gospels, ed. Nineham, 170).

[2] Lampe, op. cit. 170–1. Luke iv. 14β, 15, describe this possession. Thus it would be wrong to interpret these passages, "on an impulse of the Spirit".

[3] See above, p. 25. It is unlikely that this was already so in Q; for Matt. is not aware of this connection, and Luke xii. 10α, when compared with xii. 9, can hardly be original (although the phraseology, with its asymmetrical πᾶς ὅς . . . , ὁ δέ . . . or τῷ δέ . . . is exactly similar). In any case Luke avoids the interpretation (which he must have known) given in Mark iii. 30. See below p. 41.

Jesus as it is to the Baptist.[1]   On the other hand, Luke is able to accept the story of the conception of Jesus by the Spirit, i. 35 (see above, p. 32).   Here, still more than in Matthew, the Spirit appears as the life-begetting creative power of God;[2] but only the event is important, not the manner of its happening: as one born of the Spirit, Jesus, right from the start, is in possession of the Spirit, and not only (like a Man of the Spirit) an object of its activity.   It is no objection to this, that Luke accepts the tradition of the gift of the Spirit at Jesus' baptism (iii. 22),[3] that he records Jesus being filled with the Spirit before an inspired utterance (x. 21),[4] or that he places the final reception of the Spirit after the Ascension (Acts ii. 33).   No phased programme of growth in the Spirit is implied in this; for there stands behind it the Biblical recollection[5] that even when the Spirit is given to a man it is still God's Spirit, so that every time it is active there is ultimately a new act of God (see below, p. 40 n. 2).   That the baptism in the Jordan and the Pentecost story are in no way assimilated to each other is an indication that for Luke the gift of the Spirit to Jesus is on an altogether different level from the gift to the Church.

On the one hand, Jesus is in full possession of the Spirit from the beginning.   On the other hand, after the Resurrection, he is also, for the Church, the donor of the Spirit (Luke xxiv. 49; Acts ii. 33).[6]   This must explain the

---

[1] Lampe, op. cit. 168.   The insertion of τὸ πνεῦμά μου into the O.T. sequence (i. 47) shows that although πνεῦμα is here interchangeable with ψυχή, nevertheless Luke wishes to emphasize that it is not simply a human faculty which is the agent here, but the self which ultimately cannot be separated from God's Spirit and is bestowed on man.   The same goes for i. 80 and ii. 40.

[2] The pattern Creation/New Creation can hardly be alluded to (despite C. F. Burney, The Aramaic Origin of the Fourth Gospel, 44, 47, who sees Christ as the new Adam in i. 78–9; ii. 32; iii. 38).

[3] Indeed, he emphasizes it even more strongly than Mark and Matt.

[4] In Luke x. 21 it is πνεῦμα ἅγιον, whereas πνεῦμα αὐτοῦ of Mark ii. 8 (viii. 12) is not adopted.

[5] See above, p. 2.

[6] The underlying tradition holds (unlike Luke) that the Spirit was first received by the Ascended One (cf. John xx. 22; Eph. iv. 7–12; and the fixing of Ascensiontide in the ancient Eastern Church on the fiftieth day).

growth of the idea that the risen Lord himself is encountered in this his gift, so that either the Spirit or the risen
Lord can be referred to interchangeably (compare Luke
xii. 12 with xxi. 15, Acts x. 14 with 19 and xvi. 7).

Luke therefore has made a clear theological decision.
Mark and Matthew could still naïvely describe Jesus as a
"Man of the Spirit", even though at the same time they
were evidently already trying to present him as the unique
eschatological saviour. Luke has brought this insight
into the open: Jesus is not a "Man of the Spirit" in the
sense in which men of the Spirit exist in the Church, nor
is he an agent of that Spirit which is at work also in the
Church. In Jesus, God's Spirit is made manifest for the
very first time; it is through Jesus that the Spirit is given
to the Church.

2. The "abiding" of the Spirit in the Church

An analogy to all this can be established with reference
to the Church. Here again, Luke is trying to rise superior
to the concept of the Spirit as a power which at one leap
overtakes a man and subsequently abandons him.[1]
Typical of this is the fact that alongside the originally
animistic concept of the Spirit as an independent being
which seizes upon a man and yet is alien from him, there
now appears the originally dynamic conception of it as a
fluid which fills a man.[2] This conception is better adapted
for describing a spirit which leaves its mark on a man's
whole existence. At the same time the Gnostic danger is
avoided: the Spirit is not automatically a possession of the
believer. Thus Luke not only preserves the terminology
of the "animistic" conception (since this underlines the
divinity of the Spirit, its complete separateness from man);
but even when he uses a "dynamic" expression, we find,

[1] Cf. Gen. xli. 38; Num. xi. 17; xxvii. 18; Isa. xlii. 1; lxi. 1; Zeph. iii. 4,
LXX; Hos. ix. 7.
[2] The first is mainly in the O.T., the second in Hellenism. Evidence for
both in Bultmann, *T.N.T.* I, 155–6. Cf. J. E. L. Oulton, *Holy Communion
and Holy Spirit*, 42–8.

besides the phrase "full of the Spirit", πλήρης πνεύματος (which emphasises the abiding association with the Spirit),[1] the phrase "filled with the Spirit", πλησθῆναι πνεύματος (which preserves the conviction that every manifestation of the Spirit is always an act of God and proceeds from God).[2] The believer "has" the Spirit in exactly the same way as, through Jesus Christ, he "has" a faithful God, in whose continually renewed action he can put his trust.

3. The physical manifestations of the Spirit

In the story of Jesus' baptism, Luke adds that the Spirit descended "in bodily form" (σωματικῷ εἴδει): and he no longer means this to be regarded as merely something which Jesus saw in a vision.[3] He attaches importance to the objective character of the descent of the Spirit. It is the same when he is so ready to report the visible apparitions at Pentecost,[4] or when he takes an earthquake as evidence for the reality of the event (Acts ii. 3–6; iv. 31). It is in this connection, too, that prophesying (προφητεύειν) in times of crisis takes the form of speaking with tongues (Acts ii. 4; x. 46; xix. 6), a phenomenon astounding enough to convince even those who are not yet involved.

Luke is a Hellenist. This means, among other things, that he can only conceive of power in the form of a substance (see above p. 18, n. 2). Nevertheless his real interest is elsewhere. Unlike a Hellenist he never describes *how* the Spirit impinges upon men. Thus al-

---

[1] Acts vi. 3; xi. 24; cf. vii. 55; Luke iv. 1. It is also presupposed in Acts ii. 38; xix. 2; Luke ii. 25. Cf. also the imperf. ἐπληροῦντο Acts xiii. 52.

[2] For the individual, Acts iv. 8; xiii. 9; for the Church, iv. 31. This passage is too thin to be an old variation on the Pentecost story, and iv. 8 would then be impossible. See further Luke i. 41, 67 and i. 15; Acts ii. 4; ix. 17, where it is thought of as a permanent possession.

[3] Matthew had already avoided this by saying that the "heavens opened".

[4] It is not quite certain whether the flames were thought of as perceptible to everyone, though the noise certainly was. Nevertheless the Spirit is not *identified* with the dove or with the fire and wind (ὡς, ὥσπερ, ὡσεί).

though he takes for granted the concept of Spirit as a substance, this is not his real concern. What concerns him is that the manifestations of the Spirit are visible and ascertainable. Accordingly it is precisely these manifestations which are important to him, indeed more important than to the other New Testament witnesses.[1] The Spirit sends those unambiguous pointers from God which admit of no contradiction.[2]

Many of these statements doubtless need to be corrected in the light of other New Testament passages; but the important thing is the conception of the Spirit making man's corporal nature subject to God. Such is the extent of its activity.

4. *The working of the Spirit*

The sin against the Spirit is unpardonable; but according to Luke xii. 10 (see above p. 37) the Spirit as the power of God no longer manifests itself in casting out demons,[3] but (as xii. 12 makes clear) in the inspired speech of those who witness to Jesus.[4] Thus Luke is taking over the typically Jewish conception of the Spirit as the Spirit of prophecy (see above p. 7). Another indication of this is Luke iv. 23–27, where it is in fact denied that the miracles named in iv. 18 are manifestations of the Spirit, and the fulfilment of the prophecy is seen only in the authority of

---

[1] Acts x. 47; xi. 17; xv. 8. Yet for all that he does not forget that for those who have not faith none of these manifestations is unambiguous, Acts ii. 13.

[2] It is true that, strictly speaking, xxi. 4 asserts that the Spirit can also give a false direction. Thus here too man's responsible decision is not dispensed with. Yet in fact Luke is only emphasizing the correctness of the Spirit's prophecy: it was the advice with which it was combined which was false (though humanly understandable).

[3] This tends to fade out in Acts (Jackson-Lake, I, v. 108).

[4] So Lampe, *op. cit.* 190–1. The only question is whether the disciples are being encouraged (in which case it is their persecutors who commit the sin) or warned (in which case it is themselves, when they do not heed the voice of the Spirit, and fail to confess). Two reasons make the second alternative preferable: (i) the similarly phrased saying in xii. 8–9 is certainly addressed to the disciples; (ii) in Acts xxvi. 11, where the context is the same, βλασφημεῖν refers to the disciples. Luke xii. 10 raises the previous two verses to a higher key.

the new preaching.[1] Although the miracles are of the greatest importance for Luke, they are never once ascribed to the Spirit. What brings salvation is the name of Jesus, faith in Jesus, Jesus himself, prayer, physical contact with the disciples, a shadow or a handkerchief[2]—in other words, the power ($\delta\acute{v}\nu\alpha\mu\iota\varsigma$) of Jesus.[3] And although Luke is able to use power ($\delta\acute{v}\nu\alpha\mu\iota\varsigma$) and Spirit ($\pi\nu\epsilon\hat{v}\mu\alpha$) almost synonymously,[4] in this case the distinction is clear. Not that Luke does not regard the evidence afforded by the Spirit as miraculous. He certainly does so where it is a case of speaking with tongues,[5] and also in a case where a momentary inspiration produces a vision of the future.[6] The same goes for the prophetic insight by which the apostle, under the influence of the Spirit, sees into the normally hidden thoughts of another and declares to him his own heart.[7] The activity of the Spirit which is emphasized most strongly is the apprehension of God's otherwise mysterious will, and this in such a way that it provides direct instructions for concrete action.[8]

However, the chief thing for which the Spirit is res-

[1] Unlike Matt. xi. 5=Luke vii. 22, though there $\pi\nu\epsilon\hat{v}\mu\alpha$ is not mentioned.
[2] References: Acts iii. 6, 16; iv. 30; v. 15; ix. 34, 40; xvi. 18; xix. 13; xx. 10; xxviii. 8. The distinction is particularly clear in iv. 31β, despite W. Knox, *Acts*, 88).
[3] Luke v. 17; vi. 19 (an addition to the tradition).
[4] Luke xxiv. 49; Acts. i. 5, 8; Luke i. 17; iv. 14—already connected in Micah iii. 8 (H. A. Guy, *N.T. Prophecy*, 90, A.b.).
[5] Acts ii. 4 (see below, p. 47). x. 46; xix. 6; and also viii. 18.
[6] Luke i. 41, 67; Acts xi. 28; xx. 23; xxi. 4, 11; cf. i. 16; iv. 25; xxviii. 25. In two borrowed passages, Luke i. 41, 67, it is in a more general way the disposition of the speaker which is described as controlled by the Spirit, whereas in Acts it is the utterance itself. People prophesy $\delta\iota\grave{\alpha}$ $\tau o\hat{v}$ $\pi\nu\epsilon\acute{v}\mu\alpha\tau o\varsigma$, or else $\pi\nu\epsilon\hat{v}\mu\alpha$ itself is the subject. Luke x. 21 is original to Luke (see above p. 38, n. 4); as the other passages show, it is not $\dot{\alpha}\gamma\alpha\lambda\lambda\acute{\iota}\alpha\sigma\iota\varsigma$ as such, but, only as expressed in prophetic testimony, which is an activity of the Spirit.
[7] Acts xiii. 9.
[8] Acts viii. 29; x. 19; xi. 12; xiii. 2, 4; xvi. 6–7. xx. 22 is also to be understood in this way ($\check{\alpha}\gamma\iota o\nu$ is often omitted in references to the divine $\pi\nu\epsilon\hat{v}\mu\alpha$), in which case the instruction of the Spirit is made directly to Paul, whereas xx. 23 refers to instructions given to other brethren. Presumably the same goes for vii. 51, though vii. 55 is somewhat different, since here the Spirit makes possible a vision of heaven in the hour of death —although this too leads to $\mu\alpha\rho\tau\upsilon\rho\epsilon\hat{\iota}\nu$ in word and deed.

ponsible is the preaching of the disciples. This is a wondrous work of God; it takes place in the face of a hostile and persecuting world.[1] That Luke regards prophesying, προφητεύειν, as the central and decisive activity of the Spirit, is shown by his insertion of this word into the long and otherwise almost unaltered quotation from Joel about the eschatological outpouring of the Spirit.[2] For Luke, the Church of the Last Age is a church of prophets. It is only as an afterthought that certain phrases appear in which the Spirit is understood in a general way as abiding in the individual or in the Church.[3]

It is not easy to come to a decision about Acts v. 3, 9. It is very unlikely, at least as far as Luke is concerned, that this is a description of the sin against the Spirit on the lines of Mark iii. 28–9. Moreover the idea can hardly be that the apostles as such are in possession of the Spirit: it is more likely to be the same as in xiii. 9. It is perhaps a prior question, whether xv. 28 (and perhaps xx. 28) does not betray the attitude of a later age, according to which the decision of the Church authority is *eo ipso* the decision of the Holy Spirit. Nevertheless the fact that πνεῦμα and ἡμεῖς crop up side by side, and that there is no mention of anything like πνεῦμα ἐν ἡμῖν makes it probable that Luke, here as elsewhere, means the prophetic Spirit, with which the ἡμεῖς are associated.[4] In this case xx. 28 is also to be explained on the lines of xiii. 1–3; and the important thing to notice is that Luke presupposes the working of the Spirit on all occasions and not just on exceptional ones. Herein lies the possibility of a subsequent misconception, which

[1] Luke xii. 12 is taken from tradition, but given greater emphasis by juxtaposition to xii. 10 (see above, p. 41). Also Acts i. 8; iv. 8, 31; vi. 10; v. 32 is also to be taken in this way: the testimony of the Spirit does not consist in the visible event of Pentecost, but in the preaching of the Apostles and all "those who obey". In Acts xviii. 25 (see below, p. 51), as also in v. 32; vi. 10, a permanent qualification for giving testimony is mentioned; and the power of God referred to in Luke i. 17 and iv. 14 seems to be mainly expressed in the form of proclamation.

[2] Acts ii. 18. D it. read the O.T. text. Cf. Luke ii. 26.

[3] It corresponds to σοφία (Acts vi. 3), πίστις (vi. 5; xi. 24), φόβος τοῦ κυρίου (ix. 31), χαρά (xiii. 52).

[4] Cf. v. 32 and n. 1 above.

automatically associates the Spirit with a correctly performed commission of the Church (see below, p. 108).

One passage is peculiar: Acts viii. 39, where the
catching away of Philip is attributed to the Spirit. One
cannot get round the miraculous element simply by
taking the (dubious) reading ἀπ' αὐτοῦ into the text.[1]
In any case there are numerous parallels to a miraculous
snatching away (I Kings xviii. 12; II Kings ii. 16; Ezek.
iii. 14; viii. 3; Ev. Hebr. (Orig. *Comm. in Joh.* II, 12);
Bel and the Dragon 36; Herm. v. I, i. 3; II. i. 1; Philostr. *Vit.
Ap.* VIII, 10—in Rome in the morning, at Puteoli in the
afternoon). On the other hand, it is possible that the A
reading is original, which attributes the snatching to the
angel. The peculiarity of the Spirit-concept in the usual
text and the regularity with which otherwise, right up to
chapter x, the outpouring of the Spirit is reported or at
least promised, is an argument for this. The omission
could have arisen either from a mechanical slip from
πνεῦμα to κυρίου or from dogmatic considerations (there
is no apostle here to pass on the Spirit). Otherwise it
must be a passage left over from pre-Lucan tradition.

'In short, Luke shares with Judaism the concept of
spirit as essentially prophetic Spirit.[2] This prevents him
from regarding the Spirit as the direct source of gifts
of healing, χαρίσματα ἰαμάτων,[3] on the one hand, and
on the other hand of more distinctly ethical phenomena
such as the community life of the early Church.[4] Luke
is still fairly close to the way of thinking which measures
the work of the Spirit by its extraordinariness. Nevertheless it is not the extraordinariness of it as such which
concerns him so much as the fact that God gives to his
Church clear directions and visible signs of his activity.
Preaching, a gift of the Spirit, is certainly always conceived of as a miracle, but not usually as something extra-

---

[1] Th. Zahn, *Apostelgeschichte, ad loc.*

[2] Guy, *op. cit.* 93, A.a. Lampe, *op. cit.*, 193.

[3] I Cor. xii. 28. Similarly in the O.T. miracles are not ascribed directly
to the יהוה, but only to the possessor of the Spirit.

[4] L. S. Thornton, *The Common Life in the Body of Christ*, 6, 74–5, and
C. H. Dodd, *The Apostolic Preaching*, 137, overlook the fact that this is not
actually stated to be due to the Spirit. For Luke, it is not moral renewal
but missionary enterprise which is the gift of the Spirit.

ordinary[1]; for it is particularly in preaching that the activity of the Spirit is bestowed on the Church. However strongly Luke the Hellenist is interested in the *visible* activity of the Spirit, the limitation of this to prophetic preaching remains thoroughly Jewish.[2]

5. *The Spirit as a characteristic of the Age of the Church*

In Luke xi. 13, those who pray to God are promised the πνεῦμα ἅγιον, the Holy Spirit. Originally the promise was simply of "good things" ἀγαθά (Matt. vii. 11)[3]. This correction on Luke's part is understandable in so far as he regards ἀγαθά as worldly goods and therefore suspect; but it also indicates that for him the Spirit is quite simply the gift which is given to the faithful in Jesus' Church.[4] Mark and Matthew saw the Spirit as an eschatological event. But loyalty to the Old Testament view that the Spirit's appearance was something out of the ordinary was still so strong that apart from the Baptism formula only *one* Church *Logion* invoked the momentary aid of the Spirit in particular cases of need. But Luke knows that the Old Testament prophecies promising the Spirit to the people of the Last Age (Num. xi. 29, see above p. 12) are fulfilled. And this means that the Spirit

[1] In the second half of Acts, where fewer sources are drawn on, there is in general less of the miraculous element, in the sense of the extraordinary, and direct injunctions of the Spirit take the place of those given through angels in the first part (Knox, *op. cit.* 91–2; Acts xxvii. 23 is a dream). Even in iv. 31 the Church prays for παρρησία, not γλωσσολαλία. In Acts ix. 27–8 παρρησία is *proof* of the genuineness of Paul's conversion, a reference to which forms the conclusion to Acts (xxviii. 31).

[2] Luke's lack of interest in the process by which the spiritual substance penetrates a man (cf. Verbeke, *op. cit.* 396–7) sets him apart from the Hellenistic conception of πνεῦμα μαντικόν. This is the only mode in which it is true that Acts "represents the power of the Spirit of Jesus assuming historical form in the apostles" (Harnack).

[3] πνεῦμα ἅγιον is a Lucan expression, which he is apt to introduce in other places.

[4] This would receive still greater emphasis if the prayer, "may thy holy Spirit come upon us and cleanse us" (Luke xi. 2), is the oldest reading (Klostermann, *Lukas, ad loc.*; Lampe, *op. cit.* 184; R. Leaney, *The Lucan text of the Lord's Prayer*, Nov. Test. 1 (1956), 103–11).

is given to all members of the Church, and given to them for ever.

Thus it is presupposed in Acts xix. 2 that everyone who is baptized possesses the Spirit, and moreover possesses it visibly and tangibly. The same goes for ii. 38–9, where the promise of the Spirit is explicitly extended to everyone; also for xv. 8–9, where in particular the Gentiles are included; and for those passages (viii. 16–18, 39 (see above); ix. 17; x. 44; xi. 16–17; xix. 6) which see the gift of the Spirit as the natural consequence of accepting the faith.[1]

In Luke's account of the outpouring of the Spirit one is at first inclined to see the decisive eschatological event. At any rate, the quotation from Joel describes it as such (Acts ii. 17–21),[2] and indeed there is an eschatological colouring to the description of the happenings at Pentecost. The one common language is a phenomenon of the Last Age.[3] Nevertheless, despite ἤκουον in ii. 6 and ἀκούομεν in ii. 8, the author is not dealing simply with something miraculously heard.

> The analysis of the section is very difficult. It is historically probable that there was some decisive experience in the original Church of an outpouring of the Spirit, and this may possibly have been the first appearance of speaking with tongues.[4] But the question is, how this came to be understood as a linguistic miracle. It is impossible to explain the story by reference to the Greek custom of calling on the Godhead πάσῃ φωνῇ καὶ πάσῃ

---

[1] From xi. 19 onwards there are no references to a pouring out of the Spirit except in xix. 6. But this only means that Luke takes from the tradition reports of objectively authenticated gifts of the Spirit, and sees in them a particular instance of God's guidance at moments of crisis.

[2] The addition of ἐν ταῖς ἐσχάταις ἡμέραις (ii. 17) stamps the pouring out of the Spirit as an eschatological event, though this may be a later correction.

[3] Test. Jud. xxv. 3; Plut. *Is. et Os.* 47 (II, 370b); cf. Isa. lxvi. 18–19. Paul also takes Isa. xxviii. 11 as referring to γλωσσολαλία, and so earmarks it as a phenomenon of the Last Age (I Cor. xiv. 21).

[4] Only as regards ii. 13. The misunderstanding, which is then answered by an apostle, is an invention by Luke in his usual style (Acts iii. 11–12; xiv. 11–15; cf. iv. 9–10; vi. 13–14; xvii. 22–3). Elsewhere in Acts, speaking with tongues accompanies moments of decisive progress.

διαλέκτῳ. Again the suggestion that Luke simply mis-understood γλῶσσα since he no longer had any knowledge of speaking with tongues, is incompatible with x. 46 and xix. 6. Nevertheless, it could be Luke who was res-ponsible for the details of the story. He understood the first gift of the Spirit as something *sui generis* and so he could place an event of this kind at the beginning of Acts just as he placed Luke iv. 16–30 at the beginning of his gospel.[1]

However, it is far more likely that well before Luke's time the concept of the New Covenant, of the renewal of the Law for Judaism all over the world,[2] powerfully moulded the story of the Spirit's first appearance. There is no doubt that Jub. vi. 17, 19 is anyhow pre-Christian, as is Philo's description of the divine voice on Sinai, which produces a particular echo in each individual soul, turns itself into a flame, and passes like a πνεῦμα through a trumpet, so that it is heard by the nearest and the farthest and reaches to the end of the earth (*Decal.* 33, 35; *Spec. Leg.* II, 189).[3] If by A.D. 70 Pentecost was already observed as the conclusion of the Passover which celebrates the release from Egypt, and if the day of the gift of the Law (Deut. iv. 10; ix. 10; xviii. 16 LXX) was already referred to as ἡ ἡμέρα τῆς ἐκκλησίας, this kind of interpretation would have been a natural one. It is likely that in the (unorthodox) circles of Jubilees and perhaps also among the sects, Pentecost was celebrated as the "Oath Festival", on which the covenant was renewed and the spiritual year began. The Baptist's saying about one who would baptize with storm and fire[4] could have been turned into history, and so could have determined the formulation of Acts ii, 2–3. Luke takes over the story, not attaching much importance to it (unlike Matthew) as a statement of the new Law,[5] but regarding it as the beginning of the period of the Church and at the same time as a precursor of the progress of the Gospel among the nations. This presumably leads him to think

[1] Lampe, *op. cit.* 159.
[2] Knox, *op. cit.* 80–2. On the list of the peoples, *ibid.* 84, n. 1. The eschatological reunion of all the dispersed was a living hope.
[3] Law and Fire are also combined in Rabbinic literature (Str.-B. II, 603–4).
[4] See above, pp. 28–9.
[5] Luke no longer makes the Sermon on the Mount correspond to the Sinai proclamation, as Matthew does (so Knox, *op. cit.* 81–2, rightly). But this is not because Pentecost takes its place.

of the language of the Spirit as a new miracle language understood by all; and maybe the idea of an antitype to the Babel story in Gen. xi. played its part also.[1]

Yet this episode, for Luke, is not the decisive eschatological one. It introduces a new age, but not *the* new age. Between the O.T. salvation-narrative and the history of the mission, he makes the Christ-event "the mid-point of time".[2] Consequently it is possible for the outpouring of the Spirit to be repeated whenever men are drawn to the faith. It takes on special forms, when a new step is taken into the world of the Gentiles (Acts viii. 17–18; x. 44 ff.). That the beginning of Luke's gospel allows for men being filled with the Spirit shows only that this was drawn from tradition,[3] and was regarded by Luke as a presage of what was to come. On the other hand, Luke occasionally avoids the expression that an O.T. writer speaks "in the spirit". (Contrast Mark xii. 36 with Luke xx. 42; but cf. Acts i. 16; xxviii. 25.) The same goes for the corresponding concept of δύναμις at the Parousia (Mark ix. 1).

Luke has gone ahead of Mark and Matthew by an important step. He is not content with occasional spiritual traits or even with the nativity and baptism narratives for portraying Jesus as the bearer of the Spirit. His real concern is with the age of the Church. This is where the prophecies about the People of God are fulfilled; for it is to this people in its totality that the Spirit is given. Prophets no longer come by ones and twos. All the members of the ultimate Church are prophets.

[1] J. G. Davies, *Pentecost and Glossolalia*, J.T.S. N.S.3 (1952), 228–9.

[2] Cf. G. Vos, *The Eschatological Aspect of the Pauline conception of the Spirit*, Biblical and Theological Studies, Princeton (1912), 223–4. Yet the differences from Paul, in view of Rom. ix–xi, must not be exaggerated. For Luke, too, nothing more can happen in history greater than the salvation wrought by Christ. History, in fact, is now the history of faith in that salvation, i.e. the history of the mission.

[3] Goguel, *Notion*, 45, n. 1. Lampe, *op. cit.* 167, thinks differently. This is indicated by the strong connection with temple worship of all those who are endowed with the Spirit (except Mary). It is consequently very unlikely that Luke consciously composed this prelude under the influence of Joel iii. 1–2 (Guy, *op. cit.* 28–9).

The limitations of his vision and his indebtedness to Jewish tradition become apparent here. Basically, he cannot get away from understanding the Spirit only as an exceptional power which makes possible unusual feats of strength. It is true that this conception was counteracted by two things; first by the Jewish tradition, which almost confined the Spirit to the activity of inspiring prophetic utterance; secondly, by what was now an article of faith, that all members of the new Church possess the Spirit. This implied that the Spirit could not be present *only* in paranormal manifestations. Nevertheless Luke remained true to the old conception. Granted that the Spirit must have ways of showing itself which are not outwardly abnormal, for instance, in παρρησία (see above, p. 45 n. 1), nevertheless it does not automatically launch the believer on a completely new "eschatological" way of life; it simply imparts to him a special gift to equip him for quite definite additional expressions of his faith, things which are essential for the still incomplete, still expanding history of the mission—things indeed which alone make the mission possible.

There is also a negative side to this: faith is never derived from the Spirit, even in places where Luke goes out of his way to underline the fact that "believing", πιστεῦσαι, is not a natural phenomenon, but something which is miraculously given by God.[1] Even the ideal condition of the Church can be described without any mention of the Spirit,[2] nor is salvation ever based upon it.[3] According to Acts ii. 38, those who repent and are baptized receive the Spirit; but v. 32 adds, that obedience is a condition of receiving it. Days, or in exceptional cases even weeks or years, can elapse before the gift of the Spirit follows faith, though this does not mean that the believer returns to the

---

[1] Acts xvi. 14: ὁ κύριος διήνοιξεν τὴν καρδίαν; iii. 16: ἡ πιστις ἡ δι' αὐτοῦ (=Jesus).
[2] E.g. Acts ii. 42–7.
[3] This is an entirely Jewish attitude. In Hellenism salvation comes by apotheosis and rebirth, Jackson-Lake, I, i. 326.

status of a non-believer (ix. 17: viii. 16; xix. 2). In the same way prayer is never understood as an act of the Spirit, but as a preparation for receiving it (see below p. 52 n. 3).

Thus it would certainly not be correct to connect only "extraordinary" religious activity with the Spirit;[1] nevertheless in Luke the Spirit only gives the power necessary to fulfil a particular task, or to express faith in some concrete action. Therefore the difference between this concept of the Spirit and the Old Testament attitude consists only in that in the new Age of Salvation not only the individual but the whole Church is a bearer of the Spirit, and that, as a result of the recent development of the Spirit-concept in Judaism, the operation of the Spirit is almost entirely understood in connection with prophecy.

In other words, the peculiarity of Luke's testimony lies in its demonstration that a church which has no special power to fulfil its missionary task in a concrete way is a church without the Spirit. By not yet ascribing to the Spirit the very existence of the Church, Luke reminds the Church how necessary is that activity which is the gift of the Spirit.

6. *How the Spirit is received*

Normally the Spirit is given by baptism in the Name of Jesus. The reason why the disciples in Acts xix. 2 have not received the Spirit is presumably that they have not been baptized. In ix. 17 Paul is promised the gift of the Spirit, and this seems to be automatically fulfilled by the baptism in the next verse. In ii. 38, baptism at any rate precedes endowment with the Spirit. But in x. 44–48 it is the other way round. The pouring out of the Spirit precedes baptism, although it still does not make baptism unnecessary.

---

[1] Thus (a) παρρησία is derived from the Spirit, even when it has no abnormal form; (b) miracles of healing are not.

It is questionable how far these passages are based on correct historical recollection. In xi. 15–17 baptism is not mentioned at all. Instead of κωλῦσαι τὸ ὕδωρ (x. 47) appears κωλῦσαι τὸν θεόν. The quotation in xi. 16β only makes sense so long as no baptism by water follows, or at least so long as it remains unimportant. According to xi. 3, Peter is only accused of sharing table-fellowship, not baptism; yet it cannot be inferred from this that the baptism in x. 44–8 is a later addition. If Luke had added this here, why not also in xi. 3 and 17? On the contrary it must be inferred that in x. 47–8 he took over from tradition the reference to baptism without attaching any great importance to it. For xi. 6, as i. 5 shows, is certainly a Lucan addition, and proves that Luke thought of baptism as at most incidental to the all-important outpouring of the Spirit.

Further, the precise meaning of ii. 38 is that for Luke baptism is simply a natural episode in what he regards as much more important, namely conversion.[1] Consequently he does not pause to consider that, a moment before, the Spirit had been poured out on the 120 (I. 15) without baptism—which proves that he did not regard baptism as essential for acquiring the Spirit. The same goes for xix. 1–7, especially if one considers it along with xviii. 25. xix. 1–7, according to Luke, is about Christians who have had no experience of the Holy Spirit. It is historically possible that twelve disciples of John were converted by Paul, so that in the earliest narrative the baptism of John, which involves no gift of the Spirit, was distinguished from the baptism of Jesus, which does.[2] Similarly, Luke regards Apollos as being already a Christian, whereas historically he was probably a Jewish missionary who again was first converted in Ephesus. In the one case a baptism was in the tradition, in another case not. In Luke's account there is no room either for a Jewish missionary working "in the spirit" or for a group that has remained loyal to the Baptist. Both stories serve him as illustrations of the progress of salvation

[1] In Qumran, *Manual of Discipline*, iii. 4–12; v. 13, baptism is an outward sign of the conversion which has already happened, and which alone purifies.
[2] The passage certainly does not prove that the Baptist said nothing about the Spirit, but only that those disciples had not experienced the actual outpouring of it. Cf. B. W. Bacon in *The Expositor*, VI, 10 (1904), 14.

from the O.T., through the Baptist, to the Church. But we cannot infer from this that there was a time when spirit-baptism made water-baptism seem unnecessary.[1] It is unlikely that even at the beginning baptism could have had merely a negative significance as a cleansing rite and been disconnected from the pouring out of the Spirit.[2]   At the very least baptism was always a necessary condition for receiving the Spirit.

It looks then, as if Luke either takes over from tradition the connection between baptism and reception of the Spirit, or else uses the word baptism as a natural expression for conversion, without laying any special emphasis upon it.   As a preparation for receiving the Spirit, Luke regards prayers as far more important than baptism,[3] and as a condition for it, he always mentions faith ($\pi\iota\sigma\tau\epsilon\hat{\upsilon}\sigma\alpha\iota$ ii. 38, viii. 12; ix. 1–19, etc.)   According to xv. 8–9 it is faith, not baptism, which cleanses one for receiving the Spirit.   Nevertheless, Luke does not regard water-baptism as an unnecessary external rite.   He is no "spiritualist" who knows only of spirit-baptism.[4]   What is more imporant is that in Acts it is the freedom of the Spirit which is most strongly emphasized.   The Spirit does not limit itself to baptism.   At one time it falls upon men before their baptism (x. 44), at another time without any baptism at all (ii. 1–4) and once (xviii. 25) upon a disciple who only knows of the baptism of John which, according to xix. 3–4, is unable to confer the Spirit on others.[5]

But is there not evidence in viii. 14–17 that the gift of the Spirit is dependent upon a laying on of hands by the

---

[1] Flemington, *op. cit.* 44, n. 1; 45.   Contrast Jackson-Lake, I, i. 337–43. On the historical question of the appearance of Baptism see Kraeling, *op. cit.* 171–5.

[2] On the other side see Bultmann, *T.N.T.* I, 139.

[3] Luke iii. 21; Acts ix. 9, 11 for the first, and Acts iv. 31; xiii. 1–3 for a repeated reception of the Spirit.   In viii. 15 the Apostles pray for it, and in viii. 18–20 a misunderstanding in terms of magic is sharply repudiated.

[4] Otherwise he could neither write ii. 38 nor incorporate x. 47–8; xix. 5.

[5] On the freedom of the Spirit cf. also x. 20 (where $\dot{\epsilon}\gamma\dot{\omega}$ is emphasized); xiii. 1–4; xvi. 6–7; xx. 22–3; xxi. 4, 11.

apostles? Is not this passage at least an early instance of
"Catholicism", where the Spirit appears to be dependent
on order and ritual, and no longer the other way round?
Hardly, for this passage is peculiar. In ii. 38 and x. 48,
no laying on of hands is mentioned.[1] In ix. 12 the action
is taken by an ordinary member of the Church, and although laying on of hands is mentioned, it is only in order
to heal![2] No, Luke's main interest is in the free working
of the Spirit, even in passages where in fact the decisive
issues are ones of "ecclesiastical politics". He knows, for
instance, about the collection for Jerusalem (Acts xxiv.
17), which Paul himself regarded as a kind of token of
loyalty towards Jerusalem, rather like the Jewish Temple
tax. (Gal. ii. 10; Rom. xv. 27). But Luke does not describe this in any way as an expression of an integrated
ecclesiastical organization, but prefers to give an account
of it which derives such a collection from free prophetic
inspiration (xi. 28). Again, in viii. 14–17, it does not
seem to be the ritual laying on of hands or the authority
of the apostles which is important, but only the connection
with Jerusalem. Just as the beginning of Luke's gospel
is linked to Jewish piety, so Acts viii. 14–17 is evidence that
the Spirit does not lead the Church at one leap into completely new territory, but that its activity is closely related
to the history which preceded it. That is why not only
apostles have to "come down from Jerusalem" (viii. 14–
15), but also prophets who speak from the occasional
inspiration of the Spirit (xi. 27). That is why, again,
Paul's journey to Jerusalem is so strongly emphasized, just
as Jesus' is in the gospel. The movement of God's
history is from Jerusalem outwards and then always back

[1] Even if this were because it was taken for granted and therefore not
mentioned (Flemington, *op. cit.* 44, n. 1—is that why it is never mentioned
in Paul at all?), it would still not be essential for Luke. The same goes
for Luke xix. 6, where the whole *pericope* shows that it is not the laying on of
the apostles' hands which matters, but Jesus' baptism.
[2] And this is not because only an apostle could pass on the Spirit: for in
ix. 17 it is expected that it will be passed on *by* Ananias. In xiii. 3, too, it
is not the apostles who lay on hands. Cf. also viii. 39 (A text).

again.   Later on, the idea develops into something like
a caliphate at Jerusalem; but for Luke it only goes to confirm the progress of God's work of redemption.

Appendix: miscellaneous usages of πνεῦμα

In Luke i. 47, 80, πνεῦμα appears in a psychological
sense; nevertheless in both passages it seems that there is
still a strong echo of the concept of God's power standing
apart from a man and being only temporarily imparted
to him (see above, p. 38 n.1).   Acts xvii. 16 is to be understood as equivalent to Luke i. 47, whereas in Acts xix. 21,
as in Luke ii. 27, the reference is to the Spirit of God; so
also in Acts xviii. 25; xx. 22 (see above, p. 51). πνεῦμα
appears (a) as that part of a man which survives death[1] in
Luke viii. 55 (which is new compared with Mark), (b)
in a quotation in Luke xxiii. 46, and (c) in a passage
dependent on this, Acts vii. 59. It is questionable
whether one can conclude from Luke xxiii. 43, Acts ii. 24,
31–2, that Luke thought of Jesus existing during the
triduum mortis in the form of πνεῦμα as distinct from the
(incorruptible) σάρξ.[2]   Luke xxiv. 37, 39; Acts xxiii. 8–9
are anyhow completely unhellenistic in that πνεῦμα
means a ghostly, bodily existence which is precisely the
opposite of ἐγὼ αὐτός (Luke xxiv. 39).

C. PAUL

1. Old Testament and Hellenistic antecedents[3]

All that has been discussed so far has taken its basic
character from the Old Testament.   As in the Old Testament and as throughout Judaism, the Spirit has appeared,
not as a necessary condition of salvation, but as the power
required for special feats.   Granted this conception, it was

---

[1] Jub. xxiii. 26–31; Eth. Enoch xxii; xxxix. 4 ff. etc.
[2] Cf. the disembodied souls of the blessed in Lucian Verae Historiae, II,
12.
[3] On the one hand, in Judaism (and still more in the development of
Christendom) Hellenistic and Palestinian communities exercised a powerful
influence on each other; and on the other hand, Gnosticism seems inseparable from a heterodox Judaism which was under the influence of Iranian
and Hellenistic dualism.   In Paul, too, it is hard to distinguish between
the two.

hardly possible that the Spirit could appear as anything but a sign of some still imminent reality. In the quotation from Joel (Acts ii. 19–21) the pouring out of the Spirit is still clearly represented as the beginning of the cataclysm of the Last Age, and in Hebrews vi. 4–5 the Spirit which works miracles is a foretaste of the good things of the world to come. But this is to make the Spirit no more than a somewhat irregular prelude to the Parousia, a welcome but basically inessential presage of the impending reality. After all, the existence of all kinds of new miraculous powers does not amount to an assurance of one's own salvation.

Luke could attempt to get over this, since he lived at a time when there was no longer a lively expectation of the Parousia. But this is precisely where the dilemma arose. The Parousia was displaced by the mission period. Therefore the Spirit could no longer be a warrant of eschatological salvation; it must be a power working through the history of the intervening period. Yet, despite all the different interpretations, the main question remained. How was the proclamation of the Spirit connected with that of the crucified, risen and coming Lord?[1]

When the witness of Christianity spread to men who were influenced by Greek thought, it was transplanted into a community unfamiliar with the concept of a progressive and purposeful history.[2] Such people were not accustomed to the old idea of one age succeeding another: if they were dualists at all, they thought in terms of opposing spheres.[3] Therefore they certainly could not conceive of the Spirit as a mere *sign* of that which is to come. If it were part of the heavenly world, it must be the reality itself. Now the Hellenist always thought of power as a material substance;[1] therefore for him the coming of the

[1] This is the decisive question for primitive Christianity.
[2] O. Cullmann, *Christ and Time*, E.T. 51–58. Gnosticism is a "révolte contre le temps", G. Quispel in Eranos Jbch. 16 (1948), 122, n. 23.
[3] For the Gnostic view, see above, p. 19.

Spirit could only mean the irruption of celestial matter.
If Jesus were the bringer of the Spirit, he must have been
a bearer of celestial matter, with which he endowed believers and so united them with the celestial world.   Thus,
for the first time, a radical solution became possible.   The
meaning of Jesus' mission lay in his bringing the celestial
power-substance, πνεῦμα, into the world.   Union with
him meant union with this substance, that is to say with
heaven, that is to say, salvation itself.

We can still see in second-century Gnosticism (where
this possibility was taken to its logical conclusion) how
this interpretation must have looked in its early stages.
The meaning of Jesus' whole mission lay entirely in his
bestowal of the Spirit; and the Spirit meant salvation—
though at the same time it meant the nature, φύσις, which
saves the "spiritual" man.[2]

It followed inevitably from this last point that the
"spiritual" nature of man should be thought of as having
existed all along.   In that case the act of redemption
could not create any change in him, but could only help
him to understand it.[3]   Did it not follow that all that was
necessary to give him this understanding was a myth?
Was it not completely unimportant whether anything had
actually happened or not?   It is no accident that the
Cross had no place in this system, nor that the entire
Incarnation could be understood as a piece of deception
played on the hostile powers.[4]

In Paul, eschatology is critical.   More clearly than all
his predecessors, he understood the cross and resurrection,

---

[1] See above, p. 18 n. 2.   This Hellenistic substance-concept was of
course indebted to primitive concepts which occur just as much in the O.T.
as anywhere else (cf. W. D. Davies, *Paul and Rabbinic Judaism*, 184, for
Rabbinic examples); but only in Hellenism did it become normative for
theory about the spirit.

[2] See above, p. 21, and (for φύσει σῳζόμενος), p. 22 n. 6.

[3] It is agreed that the Gnostic's knowledge is an understanding of himself.
But does not this show precisely that this is *all* it is, and that man *only* meets
himself in it?

[4] Lietzmann, *Komm.* ad I Cor. ii. 6 (Exk.).

not as an overture to the Parousia, but as the great turning point in time; life in the Spirit meant life in the new κτίσις, the new created order.[1] In this way he was able to take the Hellenistic interpretation of the Christ-event a stage further. The presence of the Spirit was already clearly connected with the descent and ascent of the Redeemer; it was now no longer just an additional phenomenon, but was manifest in the new existence of the Church itself.

It is clear from Rom. i. 3-4 that "Spirit" (πνεῦμα) was already used to describe the celestial sphere or the celestial substance, and that Paul, for his part, took over this conception.

> The related formula in I Tim. iii. 16 is constructed in rigidly chiastic pairs: a–b/b–a/a–b. σάρξ, ἔθνη, κόσμος correspond to πνεῦμα, ἄγγελοι, δόξα.[2] It follows that ἐν πνεύματι, which is contrasted with ἐν σαρκί, must be rendered " in the sphere of the Spirit ". Salvation consists in the new-found unity of the two spheres.[3] πνεῦμα then not merely describes a spatial realm, but qualifies this as the realm of celestial substance. It is taken for granted in all this that the nature of the Redeemer is "spiritual"—that is why the μυστήριον begins with the φανερωθῆναι ἐν σαρκί. The same goes for the phraseology in I Pet. iii. 18β. It would be easy to understand πνεύματι as an instrumental dative,[4] but this is out of the question for σαρκί. Therefore the interpretation here, as in I Tim. iii. 16, must be: in the corporal sphere, in the spiritual sphere.[5]

It is stated in the same passage (Rom. i. 3-4) that Jesus Christ in his corporal existence is the Son of David, in his spiritual existence the Son of God in power. Originally

---

[1] It is to the lasting credit of A. Schweitzer (*Mysticism of Paul the Apostle*, E.T., 160–76), that he pointed this out.

[2] δόξα, like πνεῦμα (cf. I Cor. xv. 43-4; δόξα = δύναμις = πνευματικόν), means the nature of God and also of the angels.

[3] Dibelius, *Pastoralbriefen*[3], *ad loc.* Cf. Kittel, art. *Righteousness*, E.T. 60.

[4] As Calvin did, *In N.T. Commentarii* (ed. Tholuck, 1838), *ad loc.* For the meaning, cf. I. Cor. xv. 45; II Cor. iii. 6; Rom. viii. 11; Ezek. xxxvii.

[5] E. G. Selwyn, *The First Epistle of St. Peter*, 325, draws a parallel between the individual details of the confessions of faith in I Tim. iii. 16 and I Pet. iii. 18–22.

the formula expressed a Christology which made Jesus the Son of God only as a result of his ascension (Acts xiii. 33; ii. 36; cf. the subject of Mark ix. 3, 7). The Church put this schematically in the flesh/spirit contrast (κατὰ σάρκα/κατὰ πνεῦμα) and combined it with the view taken from official Judaism that Jesus was the earthly descendant of David. Paul improves on this by prefixing υἱοῦ αὐτοῦ to the whole formula.

Paul was not the first to use πνεῦμα to mean the sphere of divine glory, which the Redeemer enters when he is exalted.[1] The O.T. contrast between the holy Spirit of God and weak and sinful flesh (Isa. xxxi. 3) begins to take on Hellenistic traits, for which the ground was certainly prepared by the Apocalyptic and Rabbinic distinction between a "lower" and an "upper" world. While for the Jew the characteristic feature of this world is rebellion against God, or at least its transitoriness, for the Hellenist it is its material alienation from God.[2] Human existence is determined by the sphere, the magnetic field, as it were, into which it is inserted.[3] But if the sphere really determines existence, then entry into the spiritual sphere means entry into spiritual existence. Now Christ has entered this, therefore he is necessarily termed πνεῦμα, which is theoretically a statement about his material being, but is in fact a statement about his power, that is, his significance for the Church.

Paul accepts the Gnostic conception of the spirit-body of the ascended κύριος embracing all its members; for his unquestioning use of the phrase σῶμα Χριστοῦ (and also ἐν Χριστῷ) does not introduce this idea so much as presuppose it.[4] The same conception lies behind I Cor. xii. 13. That ἓν σῶμα is identified from the start with ὁ Χριστός in xii. 12 shows that in 13 it cannot mean just the objective which is achieved when all the limbs are

---

[1] Cf. Phil. ii. 9–11; Rev. v.

[2] I Tim. iii. 16 is probably closer to this, while Rom. i. 3–4 is far more Jewish in feeling.

[3] For a modern statement of this, see C. Michalson, *The Holy Spirit and the Church*, Theology Today, 8 (1951–2), 43–4.

[4] Yet it is quite possible that O.T. conceptions, and the thought of the Body which was sacrificed for us on the cross, also play their part. Cf. E. Schweizer, *Lordship and Discipleship* (S.C.M. Press, 1960), ch. 4.

organically united, but rather the already existing Body into which the believers are baptized.[1] This brings the various concepts together; they describe the spirit element with which the believers are united and with which they are given to drink (13β).[2] In 13α ἐν πνεύματι is probably to be taken instrumentally,[3] as in I Cor. vi. 11. But the power which makes membership possible is no less materially conceived, and corresponds to the frequent phrase ἐν ὕδατι.[4]

So far the relationship between Spirit (πνεῦμα) and the Body of Christ (σῶμα Χριστοῦ) is not yet made clear, but in II Cor. iii. 17 the Lord (κύριος) is identified with Spirit (πνεῦμα).

The interpretation of this passage is of course discutable.[5] The sentence has been taken as an explanatory note to the quotation, pointing out that the κύριος of the quotation means the Spirit (though on the analogy of Gal. iv. 25 we should expect τὸ δὲ κύριος); turning to the *Spirit* would then "lift the veil" and 17 would define this "Spirit" still more precisely as the Spirit of Jesus. The reasons advanced for this view do not hold water. Whatever else the sentence is, it is not a superfluous Christological digression. In iii. 6 and 8 the new service is described and determined not by γράμμα but by the πνεῦμα. It is then shown that unbelieving Judaism still lives under the "veil", which is only removed ἐν Χριστῷ (14). Only turning to the κύριος (=Χριστός 14, as always) can take it away. The statement that this κύριος is the Spirit brings the two series of statements together. Indeed, the identity of the ascended κύριος, to which Israel should return instead of to Moses (cf. Rom. x. 4–5, I Cor. x. 2), with the πνεῦμα, shows that turning to him also means turning to the new διακονία in the πνεῦμα. It cannot be maintained that Paul, even though he readily

[1] Lietzmann, *Kor.*[4] *ad loc.* M. Barth interprets it: "baptized into the body of Christ", *getauft auf den Leib Christi.*
[2] On the image of the out-poured Spirit, cf. Thornton, *op. cit.* 89–91. Water-drinking produces inspiration, Tatian, *Or. Graec.* xix. 3.
[3] Thornton, *op. cit.* 89.
[4] Therefore πνεῦμα can just as well be the causative power of Baptism as the new "element" (13β) which is transmitted through it. Cf. Flemington, *op. cit.* 69; 39, n. 2.
[5] Davies, *op. cit.* 196, n. 1: C. H. Dodd, *History and the Gospel,* 55–7.

ascribes the same functions both to Christ and to the
Spirit, nevertheless never makes the two equivalent (see
below).[1] It has already been shown (p. 57) that Rom.
i. 4 cannot be adduced as evidence for a second Pauline
conception.

It is clearly stated, then, that the Spirit ($\pi\nu\epsilon\hat{\upsilon}\mu\alpha$) is
the ascended Christ, and that turning unto him is union
with the realm of the Spirit. Whoever approaches him
enters the sphere of the Spirit. iii. 17β makes a distinc-
tion between Lord ($\kappa\acute{\upsilon}\rho\iota\sigma$) and Spirit ($\pi\nu\epsilon\hat{\upsilon}\mu\alpha$); but this
is only to clarify 17α, which does not assert the identity
of the two personalities, but only indicates by the word
Spirit the mode in which the Lord exists. "Spirit of the
Lord" is simply used as a periphrasis for his mode of existence, in other words for the power in which he encounters his Church.[2] When Christ is seen in terms of his
role for the Church and of his works of power within the
Church, he can be identified with the Spirit; but insofar
as Christ is also Lord over his own power, he can be distinguished from that power, just as "I" can always be
distinguished from the power which goes out of me. The
same conception is expressed still more precisely in I Cor.
vi. 17; for the basis of this passage is the concept of the
spirit-body of the ascended Lord, which includes believers
within itself. This organic connection of believers with
Christ is completely analogous to sexual union with a
prostitute; and to underline this, unchastity is reckoned
as a dire sin, precisely because it is consummated *bodily*
and so affects the relationship with Christ.[3] It is made
explicit in I Cor. xv. 45 that by his resurrection Christ has
become "the spirit that maketh alive" $\pi\nu\epsilon\hat{\upsilon}\mu\alpha$ $\zeta\omega\sigma\pi\sigma\iota\sigma\hat{\upsilon}\nu$.

[1] I Thess. i. 5; II Cor. xii. 9; Phil. iv. 13. See C. A. A. Scott, *Christianity
according to St. Paul*, 260. See further II Cor. iv. 10–11 and Col. iii. 4;
Gal. v. 25 and II Cor. iii. 6.

[2] The expression "Spirit of Christ" is very rare in Paul; though cf. Rom.
viii. 9; Phil. i. 19; Gal. iv. 6.

[3] This judgment is traditional (Prov. vi. 23–35; Lietzmann, *Kor.*[4],
ad loc.).

Moreover, on this depends the gift to the believer of a "spiritual body", σῶμα πνευματικόν.[1] The whole argument depends here upon the presupposition that Christ, like Adam, embraces the whole of humanity. Paul is faithful both to the Old Testament patriarch-idea and to Hellenism; he insists that the resurrection (or ascension) has removed Christ into the sphere of the Spirit, and that union with him assures the believer of the same spiritual existence, experienced as life in the Church.[2]

But Paul was also influenced by early Christian eschatology. For this, the important passage is I Cor. xv, where Paul's thought starts from the fact of the Resurrection. This is quite unlike the Gnostics, whose only use for the myth was that it arouses a memory of an already indwelling reality. For Paul it was a fact, a fact which had completely altered the situation. It is therefore no accident that Paul never uses Gnostic language about the "spiritual substance" of the pre-existent one. But on the other hand, he has no use for the concept of the "spiritual body" of the ascended Christ except for explaining to the Church the significance of Jesus' resurrection for their own raising from the dead. It is true that in I Cor. xv. 35–50 Paul starts from the Corinthians' own presuppositions. But he parts company with them precisely in his use of the phrase "spiritual body", σῶμα πνευματικόν. They understood it as something which is already given to the believer and simply survives death; but he sees it as something given once and for all by God in the Resurrection. Again, he does not talk about the "living Spirit", πνεῦμα ζῶν, which would be a kind of contagious life-force, but about the "Spirit which giveth

---

[1] Burton, *Galatians* (I.C.C.), 489; Selwyn, *I Peter*, 282–3, think that this is the body of the human πνεῦμα, which can do without an earthly body. This is impossible.

[2] Cf. J. Knox, *Chapters in a Life of Paul*, 128–40; C. H. Dodd, *Romans* (Moffatt N.T. Commentary), on Rom. vi. 6; J. Moffatt, *I Corinthians* (same series) on I Cor. xv. 44.

life", πνεῦμα ζωοποιοῦν, that is, about the creative power of the resurrected Lord.[1]

There is no trace here of the idea of a spiritual body underneath the physical body. In fact, Paul actually attacks this idea (xv. 46; 45 merely supports the proposition in 44β; and this is what 46 refers to, not anything in 45, so that the word to be understood is σῶμα). Paul is not warding off an attitude which sought to replace the eschatological coming of the Redeemer by a doctrine of a pre-existent original man: he is fighting a belief in the prime importance of the "spiritual" σῶμα as something belonging by right to man and therefore not first given to him at the Resurrection. 44β, it is true, seems to take it for granted that his opponents have no knowledge of such a thing, but 29 makes it clear that they nevertheless believe in a life after death. Their mistake is that they know of no "spiritual body" in Paul's sense, but only in the Gnostic sense of something hidden beneath the "psychical" body and simply surviving death. That is why in 49 Paul writes φορέσομεν. From the premise that Christ, like Adam, controls all humanity that belongs to him, it is a short step to the Corinthians' conclusion that all who belong to him *are* already ἐπουράνιοι. But for Paul they only "are" so by virtue of their faith in him who will one day make them so, and certainly not by virtue of their physical superiority over the "unspiritual".

There is another view according to which the place of σῶμα in the scheme is merely as the medium through which the change from "fleshly" to "spiritual" substance takes place. But this too is untenable. The particular position taken up by Paul is shown by the contrast between ψυχικός (xv. 44), which is characterized by φθορά (42, 50), ἀσθένεια and ἀτιμία (43, cf. Phil. iii. 21 ταπείνωσις), and πνευματικός characterized by ἀφθαρσία (42, 50) δύναμις and δόξα (43; Phil. iii. 21). Behind this formal thinking in terms of substances lies the O.T. contrast between weakness and strength.[2] Man remains dependent upon the creative power of his Lord, who

---

[1] A sharper distinction still is made by F. W. Grosheide, *Commentary on I Corinthians* (1953), 387, on I Cor. xv. 45, who thinks that Christ's whole life-work as Mediator, and not just his resurrection, made him πνεῦμα ζωοποιοῦν.

[2] Rom. vi. 19; viii. 26. δόξα is not a material light-flash, as is shown by II Cor. iii. 8–iv. 6.

will resurrect him.[1] The link between earthly and
heavenly body is forged by a miracle. The same goes for
xv. 47, where "earth" ($\gamma\hat{\eta}$) in the first phrase indicates the
stuff of which the "first man" is composed, while the
second phrase describes the "second man", not in terms
of the substance he is composed of, but in terms of
his origin. Consequently the $\sigma\hat{\omega}\mu\alpha$ $\pi\nu\epsilon\nu\mu\alpha\tau\iota\kappa\acute{o}\nu$ of the
Redeemer, as of the believer, cannot be understood
simply as something *composed of* $\pi\nu\epsilon\hat{\nu}\mu\alpha$ but as something
controlled by $\pi\nu\epsilon\hat{\nu}\mu\alpha$. Nevertheless, it must not be forgotten
that this is only true of Paul's own position. His termi-
nology betrays the fact that, like every Hellenist, he has a
material view of power (see above, p. 18 n. 2). Thus, whilst
Paul's doctrine is Jewish, his terminology is Hellenistic.

Certain other passages have the same implication:

(a) I Cor. vi. 14 starts from the fact of the raising up
of Jesus, and emphasizes that the bodily raising up of
believers lies in the future.[2] But this leads to another
point; the concept of consubstantiality between the
believer and Christ, which is apparently expressed by the
simile of sexual one-bodyness (see above, p. 60), is not
definitive, but is only another way of expressing the connection between two creative acts of God, the raising up
of Jesus and the raising up of all believers. $\sigma\hat{\omega}\mu\alpha$, then,
cannot here mean just physical substance; indeed it is
contrasted with $\kappa o\iota\lambda\acute{\iota}\alpha$ which does not qualify for the
promise of resurrection (vi. 13). Because $\sigma\hat{\omega}\mu\alpha$ can be
replaced by $\dot{\eta}\mu\epsilon\hat{\iota}s$ it is clear that for Paul the important
thing about the sexual act is that it is personal. In the
same way the association of the believer with Christ,
though it is thought of as bodily, is not just physical but
personal.

(b) In the same way Rom. viii. 11[3] starts from the fact
of the resurrection and presupposes that the raising up of
believers lies in the future, "because of" the Spirit that
dwells in them.[4] Nevertheless there is no suggestion here

[1] In this sense even the $\pi\nu\epsilon\nu\mu\alpha\tau\iota\kappa\acute{o}s$ belongs to the $\dot{\epsilon}\pi\acute{\iota}\gamma\epsilon\iota o\iota$ (xv. 48–9, 40;
E. B. Allo, in Rev. Bib. 43 (1934), 342. The aorist $\dot{\epsilon}\phi o\rho\acute{\epsilon}\sigma\alpha\mu\epsilon\nu$ should be understood in terms of the future $\phi o\rho\acute{\epsilon}\sigma o\mu\epsilon\nu$).
[2] An already accomplished "raising up" of believers is first taught in
Col. ii. 12; iii. 1, and even there is qualified by $\delta\iota\grave{\alpha}$ $\pi\acute{\iota}\sigma\tau\epsilon\omega s$.
[3] Cf. Kittel, art. *Sin*, E.T. 83–4.
[4] The accusative (twice in Origen, once in Tertullian) is to be preferred
as the *lectio difficilior*, since apart from I Cor. xv. 45 (where it depends on a
quotation) $\pi\nu\epsilon\hat{\nu}\mu\alpha$ does not mean creative power in Paul.

of a material guarantee,[1] but two ideas are combined: (i) the God who has raised up Jesus is already at work in them through the Spirit, and will continue so to work after their death; (ii) natural man, as a sinner, is subject to death (viii. 10) but he who is righteous owing to the work of the Spirit (see below, p. 71) will be resurrected (viii. 11).

(c) It is true also of II Cor. iii. 17 that the thought is not dominated by material categories. This is shown not only by the already mentioned shift to πνεῦμα κυρίου in 17β but also by the definite article with πνεῦμα. Paul starts from the already developed concept πνεῦμα (which certainly does not represent a miraculous substance, see below, p. 74) and then goes on to explain that the κύριος is this πνεῦμα. In other words, he takes over the popular view of the "spiritual body" of the ascended Redeemer, in order to express something which is right outside any material category.[2]

The decisive event thus has two moments: the raising up of Jesus, and the Parousia with the raising up of the faithful. Consequently the Spirit is to be understood, as in the early Church, as a sign of that which is still to come. Now that the Resurrection of Jesus has come to pass, the Resurrection at the End of Time is no longer a vague hope; the reality of the Spirit's presence is a guarantee of the reality of what is to come. Consequently Paul can describe the Spirit as the "first fruits", ἀπαρχή, of the still expected redemption of the Body (Rom. viii. 23), or as a "guarantee", ἀρραβών, for the new "house" which awaits us (II Cor. v. 5; i. 22.)[3]. Yet he is also able to adopt the view that the Spirit is the giver of extraordinary and miraculous feats.[4]

In I Thess. v. 19, for example, πνεῦμα, corresponding to προφητεῖαι, means a power which manifests itself in

[1] Cf. J. A. T. Robinson, *The Body*, 72.

[2] Scott, *op. cit.* 259–60, interprets thus: the κύριος (Christ) represents (i.e. means for the believer) the πνεῦμα.

[3] In all 3 cases, τοῦ πνεύματος is a Gen. of apposition (cf. Eph. i. 14), not a partitive genitive (Bl.-Debr. §167).

[4] The Gnostic would agree: but for him miracles are evidence for the new "spiritual" substance, while for the primitive Church, and especially for Paul, they are a foretaste of God's ultimate intervention.

exceptional ways.[1] The only question is whether the reference here is specifically to speaking with tongues; but II Thess. ii. 2 is certainly not to be understood in this way, since here the Spirit makes a particular statement. Eph. v. 18, it is true, probably refers to an ecstatic phenomenon, but v. 17 surely excludes speaking with tongues.[2] In I Cor. xiv. 37, as in xiv. 1 (cf. 12) πνευματικός is to be taken as a generic term, with προφήτης as one of its species. The same goes for I Thess. v. 19. Once (I Cor. xiv. 14–16) πνεῦμα occurs in antithesis to νοῦς as the miraculous power which bestows speaking with tongues; but then the emphasis lies only on the inadequacy of the νοῦς, and it may be that xiv. 15 is a way of expressing, not two alternatives, but (what was adequate for the congregation) the connection between πνεῦμα and νοῦς. In I Cor. ii. 4–5, ἀπόδειξις πνεύματος καὶ δυνάμεως is actually contrasted with σοφίας λόγοι and σοφία ἀνθρώπων, indeed in I Thess. i. 5 with λόγος altogether. In Rom. xv. 19 the δύναμις πνεύματος corresponds to δύναμις σημείων καὶ τεράτων.[3] In Gal. iii. 5 πνεῦμα corresponds to δυνάμεις.

In all this, the Spirit is consistently understood as something the possession of which can be demonstrated.[4] Thus Paul can count speaking with tongues among the activities of the Spirit just as much as gifts of healing or miraculous powers.[5] The formal similarity between these manifestations and the ecstatic phenomena of the heathen world is so far-reaching that Paul gives the Corinthians a criterion by which they can distinguish the activities of the Spirit of God from those which have a different source: the criterion is the confession of Jesus as Lord (I Cor. xii. 2–3).[6]

[1] Cf. J. Jeremias, *Unknown Sayings of Jesus*, E.T. 92.
[2] Dibelius, *Gefangenschaftsbriefen*[3], ad loc.
[3] It is possible that by a chiastic construction λόγῳ should be understood here; but not in view of I Cor. ii. 4–5; iv. 20; I Thess. i. 5. (cf. II Cor. xii. 12).
[4] Gal. iii. 2; Dodd, *Apostolic Preaching*, 51–2.
[5] I Cor. xii. 9–10, 28–30; xiv. 18–26. Cf. Bultmann, *T.N.T.* I, 154–5.
[6] The same problem arises in the primitive church at large. I John iv. 2 makes the formula more precise. Matt. vii. 16; Didache xi. 7–12 find the criterion in the moral conduct of the prophet. Hermas, m. XI, 7–16, finds it besides in his positive attitude to the Church. Both these last

That Paul presupposes the existence of phenomena of this kind in Thessalonica just as much as in Galatia, in Rome (where he did not found the church) just as much as in Corinth, shows that this is something much more alive than a mere survival of a primitive attitude. Paul is more naïve than Luke; in the strictest sense he reckons all miraculous phenomena among the manifestations of the Spirit, not recognizing the late Jewish and Rabbinic limitation to the "Spirit of prophecy". Indeed the frequent role of the Spirit as a guarantee, ἀρραβών, of what is to come is much more prominent in Paul than in Luke.

When we were considering the "Hellenistic" concept of the spiritual body, with its emphasis on the here-and-now of the Spirit, we found that it had been significantly adapted so as to safeguard the not-yet. We find the same adaptation here, though the other way round. Not only does Paul, like Luke, hold fast to the belief that all the members of the Church are endowed with the Spirit[1] (Rom. viii. 9), but, unlike Luke, he attaches the greatest importance to a consequence he draws from this, namely that the manifestations of the Spirit need not necessarily have an extraordinary character. That is why, unlike the Corinthians, he includes among these manifestations "help", ἀντιλήμψεις and "administration", κυβερνήσεις,[2] and in other places "service", διακονία, and "acts of mercy", ἐλεεῖν, "contributions", μεταδιδόναι, and

---

passages at the same time allow for direct and startling appearances of the Spirit as a positive criterion. Ps.-Cor. (ed. Vetter, 1894) iii. ff. has recourse to the authority of the apostle. Ps.-Clem. *Hom.* ii. 6–11, mentions the occurrence of forecasts of the future as a proof of authenticity, cf. *Recog.* iv. 21.

[1] In certain passages πνευματικός seems to be restricted to a smaller group. Yet I Cor. xiv. 37 and Gal. vi. 1 should not be understood in this sense. I Cor. ii 13–iii. 3 calls πνευματικοί not a group of "ecstatics", but those who understand the gospel of the cross, so that all that is expressed in iii. 1–3 is that the believer may always be tempted to become an unbeliever (Scott, *op. cit.* 147–8). Nevertheless, the view that πνεῦμα is something exceptional is still so strong that οἱ πνευματικοί does not become a term for Church members like οἱ ἅγιοι, οἱ ἐν Χριστῷ.

[2] I Cor. xii. 28. Their absence from 29–30 shows that they were not among the gifts aspired to by the Corinthians.

"championing", προΐστασθαι (Rom. xii. 7–8). Still more significant is his notable depreciation of speaking with tongues,[1] which the Corinthians regarded as the most exceptional and indeed the highest of the gifts of the Spirit. This means that extraordinariness is felt to be basically irrelevant as a criterion; it would do just as well as a criterion for the religious experience of pagans (I Cor. xii. 2). The real criterion for measuring the value or lack of value of the gifts of the Spirit is the confession, Jesus is Lord, and at the same time the edification, οἰκοδομή, the expediency, συμφέρον, of the Church.[2] But this brings us to a completely new understanding of Spirit. (See below p. 80.)

2. *Paul's personal interpretation*

The argument has now taken a very individual turn. Paul had adopted the Hellenistic line of thought, which offered for the first time the simple and attractive possibility of interpreting spirit (πνεῦμα) quite simply as the new existence, and at the same time of seeing this in terms of union with the Redeemer. Yet he corrected any statements that savoured of natural religion, and by a line of thought which started from the Old Testament, he made it quite clear that salvation is not at man's disposal for him to possess. Yet even here Paul had to make qualifications. If the New Creation were already present, the Spirit could not be a mere sign for what was to come; it could not be something merely exceptional; it must be a feature of the new existence as such.

His new understanding of the Spirit allowed for both these points of view; but it was also moulded by another factor: the event which, for Paul, was the ultimate scandal, he could also understand as the ultimate saving event— that is, the cross.

[1] I Cor. xiv—though he esteems it for personal edification.
[2] I Cor. xiv. 3–5, 12, 26; xii. 7.

The argument in I Cor. ii. 6–16 starts from the premise
that Paul has nothing to preach but Christ crucified
(ii. 2). It is true that in the same passage Paul defines
the Spirit as the miraculous power which transmits supernatural knowledge (σοφία ἐν μυστηρίῳ ἀποκεκρυμμένη,
ii. 7, contrasted with ἀνθρωπίνη σοφία, ii. 13); yet he
remains entirely true to that understanding of it for which
the ground was prepared in a church influenced both
by the Old Testament and by Hellenism. The miraculous
power of the Spirit determines both the content and the
form of the preaching, and is for that reason only perceptible to those who are "spiritual".[1] But what is the
content of this "spiritual" teaching? Paul's reply is
expressed in a way which is completely Gnostic: "the deep
things of God", τὰ βάθη τοῦ θεοῦ (ii. 10); but its meaning
is completely un-Gnostic: the saving work of God on the
cross. Thus the content is "the gifts bestowed on us by
God", τὰ ὑπὸ τοῦ θεοῦ χαρισθέντα ἡμῖν (ii. 12β); and the
Wisdom of God (i. 24), which is revealed through the
Spirit (ii. 7–10), is nothing other than Christ crucified
(i. 23; ii. 2; confirmed in ii. 8)—which is "foolishness"
(μωρία ii. 14) for the "unspiritual" (who are also those
referred to in i. 23).[2] A Christian Gnostic could only
have understood the cross as a tactical device for
deceiving the demons and preventing them from ob-
structing the saving event of the Ascension.

This marks a decisive step forward. The cross is
recognized as the crisis, now past, which separates the new
creation from the old. Paul is a Hellenist in so far as he
understands the Spirit as the power which releases men
from "this age" (I Cor. ii. 6) and places them in the next.
But at the same time he decisively redresses the balance:
the union of the believer with the Lord is not given in a

---

[1] That ὅμοιον is only known to ὁμοίῳ can be paralleled in Empedocles
fr. 109 (Diels[7], I, 351, 20 ff.); Orph. Fr. 345 (Kern); Gnostics: Lietzmann, *Kor.*, *ad loc.*
[2] Kittel, art. *Gnosis*, E.T. 40. Cf. Thornton, *op. cit.* 108–9.

material mode of spirit, but in the knowledge, given only by the Spirit, of him who was crucified for us.[1]

It is now clear how Paul was able to take over the concept of the "spiritual body" of the Lord. All that is meant by "substance" is a way of conceiving the power which, for the Israelite, was the one reality; and all that the idea conveys is the insight that the believer's life depends entirely on his indissoluble union with the Lord, κύριος, in whom God's saving work has taken place for him. Entry into the "magnetic field" of the spirit-body then has no meaning in practice beyond the believer's self-abandonment into the "magnetic field" of the saving events, that is, of the Church which lives by the cross and resurrection. But at the same time there is no relaxation of the Old Testament attitude that the bearer of the Spirit is always completely dependent upon acts of God. His life does not depend upon this new substance, but upon the action of God on the cross. Thus it becomes possible to conceive of the Spirit as the basis of the believer's very existence, and no longer just as an extra miraculous power; yet at the same time it does not become a material possession of him whose nature it is to be saved, φύσει σωζόμενος. We can now understand how the extraordinariness of the manifestations can cease to be the decisive criterion. The supernatural quality of the knowledge does not depend on its being ecstatically received, or learnt, or on its being logically or illogically framed. The miracle is that a man can believe that, in Jesus Christ, God is on his side. The content of this supernatural knowledge is not some disclosure of the secrets of the heavenly places,[2] but is the love of God fulfilled in his action in the

---

[1] Dodd, *Apostolic Preaching*, 146-7, rightly stresses that a share in the Spirit is a share in Christ and not just in one of his gifts: though the passages he adduces for this (Rom. i. 4; II Cor. iii. 17) are capable of a purely natural interpretation.

[2] ἡμεῖς (I Cor. ii. 12) can only refer to all believers, as also in 10 (cf. Eph. iii. 18, where βάθος also occurs). βάθη τοῦ θεοῦ are picked up in 11 by τὰ τοῦ θεοῦ, and in 12 by τὰ . . . χαρισθέντα ἡμῖν (aorist!): therefore they must mean the already accomplished act of God's grace, and not something

cross, or else (a result of this) it is the fact that the believer is a son of God.[1]

So it is that πνεῦμα, Spirit, can be referred to outright as the Spirit of faith, πνεῦμα τῆς πίστεως (II Cor. iv. 13). Possessing the "earnest of the Spirit", ἀρραβὼν τοῦ πνεύματος, means "walking by faith", διὰ πίστεως περιπατεῖν (II Cor. v. 5, 7). In contrast to all secondary characteristics, it is the recognition and confession of Jesus as Lord which in I Corinthians xii. 3 is the gift most typical of the Spirit as such.

> The expression in Gal. iii. 14 (and v. 5?) which makes the reception of the Spirit depend upon faith (διὰ or ἐκ πίστεως)[2] appears to contradict this, but this is only superficial. The expression is used continually in opposition to "the works of the law", ἐξ ἔργων νόμου, and only means that it is not human merit which has earned the Spirit.[3] In Gal. v. 5 the content of what is received is the expectation of the ἔλπις δικαιοσύνης, that is, in fact, nothing other than faith understood in the light of the righteousness which has come to pass in Christ. This shows that the Spirit is not just an initial event.[4]

When the whole tradition is considered, it is understandable that Paul should see the operation of the Spirit more vividly in a continuous and externally guided "believing", πιστεύειν, than in the preliminary act of belief, πιστεῦσαι.[5] In a different way from Rom. viii. 16 Paul in Gal. iv. 6 can attribute to the Spirit not just

---

particular that lies in the future. λόγοις (13) can only be understood if the discussion in ii. 1–5 is still being carried on; and iii. 11, 18–23 shows that the argument has been continuous since i. 18. So iii. 1–3 (along with i. 7; iii. 16 n.b.) is to be understood as the paradox of the believer so often not living out what he believes (cf. viii. 7 with viii. 1; Rom. viii. 12–14 with viii. 9). In ii. 1 μυστήριον is probably the right reading, in which case it must be the same as in ii. 7.

[1] Rom. v. 5; viii. 16.

[2] In Gal. iii. 14: Lietzmann (*Gal. ad loc.*) renders: "the (fulfilment of the) promise, which is the πνεῦμα."

[3] In Gal. iii. 2, 5, the peculiar phrase ἀκοὴ πίστεως (not ἀκοῆς πίστις) may be used instead of πίστις simply because it is the work of the Spirit.

[4] Thus the first endowment of the Spirit has the aorist, its continued activity only the perfect (Thornton, *op. cit.* 82, on Rom. v. 5). Cf. ἐκ πίστεως εἰς πίστιν, Rom. i. 17.

[5] Hence there is no statement that the Spirit " gives " faith.

the recognition of sonship but concrete living as a Son of God; by which he simply affirms that the Spirit is not only a mysterious power which appears before faith and explains the birth of faith, but is also the power which continually reveals itself in faith.[1]

Incorporation into the Body of Christ, and the believer being made to drink of the Spirit (I Cor. xii. 13), is in the last analysis only what is expressed in I Cor. ii. 12 or Rom. viii. 16: it is the event which reveals and promises to a man the saving act of God in Christ Jesus, the event which makes him a Son of God and gives him life.[2] Since inclusion in the Body of Christ and inclusion in the saving events of the cross and resurrection (i.e. justification, $\delta\iota\kappa\alpha\iota\omega\theta\hat{\eta}\nu\alpha\iota$) are ultimately the same thing, one can be ascribed to the Spirit just as much as the other (I Cor. vi. 11). The Name of the Lord justifies objectively, the Spirit subjectively. In the same way, being in the Spirit is synonymous with being in Christ. Both indicate the being of the believer. If he lives in contact with Christ's activity—who was crucified and resurrected for him—then he lives also in the sphere of the Spirit's activity, which reveals Christ to him and assures him of his salvation.[3] But since the Old Testament view made the believer dependent upon an always future act of God's grace, the gift of the Spirit appears now as a "waiting for the hope of righteousness" (Gal. v. 5), "walking in faith, not in sight" (II Cor. v. 7) a faith in the future resurrection (II Cor. iv. 13), a knowledge of the imminent redemption of the body (Rom. viii. 23), life everlasting ($\zeta\omega\grave{\eta}$ $\alpha\mathit{\iota}\acute{\omega}\nu\iota\sigma$ Gal. vi. 8).

[1] That in Rom. i–v $\pi\acute{\iota}\sigma\tau\iota s$ is predominant, and in vi–viii $\pi\nu\epsilon\hat{\upsilon}\mu\alpha$, shows that, contrasted with the works of the Law, $\pi\acute{\iota}\sigma\tau\iota s$ is the condition, and $\pi\nu\epsilon\hat{\upsilon}\mu\alpha$ the possibility, of the new existence.

[2] "Spirit-baptism" is therefore certainly not initiation into higher knowledge or equipment for special feats of strength (Flemington, op. cit. 56–7), but is subjection to God's saving act in Christ and so the foundation of all gifts of the Spirit (I Cor. xii. 4–11); hence it accompanies water-baptism. Cf. G. W. H. Lampe, The Seal of the Spirit, 56–7, 60.

[3] Rom. viii. 1, 9; cf. Bultmann, T.N.T. I, 334–6.

But if the Spirit is a divine power of which the main characteristic is not the extraordinariness of its activity, but the way in which it makes a man into a believer and governs his life as a believer, it can no longer be thought of as a power of magical operation, which a man is irresistably delivered over to.[1] It must be understood as the miraculous power of God which makes it possible for a man, who is separated from God, consciously and willingly to base his life on a power that is not his own.[2] But this indicates another line of development: although the two aspects cannot always be clearly distinguished, the Spirit is both the power which creates faith, and now also the norm of the life of faith. In so far as Paul wants to emphasize that the Spirit is entirely a gift of God, and not a potential of man himself, he conceives of it as power; but in so far as he wants to emphasize that it is the kind of power which summons to faith and not a substance which automatically makes a man divine, he conceives of the Spirit as the norm according to which the believer is called upon to live. This duality comes out most sharply in Gal. v. 25: "if we live by the Spirit, let us also walk by the Spirit". In the first clause it is established that the Spirit, as a superior power, determines a man's life; in the second clause the man is required consciously to recognize the fact and to allow his whole conduct to be governed by it.[3] Thus life in the Spirit has two sides. One, the negative side, is renouncing "the flesh", σάρξ; the other, the positive side, is laying oneself open to God and one's neighbour.

---

[1] In I Cor. xiv. 32 (cf. I Thess. v. 19) the believer is credited with control over the Spirit, in xiv. 1, 39 he is told to ζηλοῦν it, and warned not to κωλύειν it; in Rom. xii. 6 the prophet is obliged to follow the faith proclaimed by the Apostle. The Spirit does not exclude rational deliberation (I Cor. vii. 40), the self (Rom. viii. 15–16) or the natural function of συνείδησις (Rom. ix. 1); and in I Cor. xiv. 14 the co-operation of νοῦς is commended.

[2] In Pauline language, to renounce his καύχημα.

[3] Cf. the conjunction of ind. and imp. in Phil. iii. 16; Col. iii. 1, etc. Cf. Bultmann, T.N.T. I, 336–339.

(a) Renouncing the Flesh

The contrast between Spirit and "flesh" (σάρξ) originally, as in the Old Testament, means the opposition
between a force that is alien to man and man's own weakness.[1] That is why God, or the Lord, κύριος, his grace or
his pardon, appear in opposition to "flesh", and why in
Gal. iii. 2, 5 the Spirit is certainly understood mainly as
a miraculous power (see above p. 65). Now iii. 3 states
that the Galatians, having begun "in the Spirit" (πνεύματι)
were wanting to end "in the flesh" (σαρκί); this means,
in the first place, that they wanted to continue with their
own human strength. This is correct, but still inadequate;
for "flesh" corresponds to "works of the law", ἐξ ἔργων
νόμου, Spirit to "hearing of the faith", ἐξ ἀκοῆς πίστεως,
iii. 2, 5. If this antithesis is taken in its broad sense, and
not limited to moments of ecstasy and the supernatural,
the "Spirit" must at least be the power which determines the being of the believer as one whose life depends
on the fact of salvation. The meaning of "beginning in
the Spirit", πνεύματι ἐνάρχεσθαι, is then as follows. In the
indicative it expresses the certainty that a man's life
depends not on his own but on an alien strength. But
in the imperative it expresses a demand that he should
live his life relying upon that alien strength and not his
own, in other words that he should let the strength which
does in fact mould his life also be the standard at which
he aims. This comes out clearly in Phil. iii. 3. "Serving
the Spirit of God" (πνεύματι θεοῦ λατρεύειν) means "not
trusting in the flesh" (οὐκ ἐν σαρκὶ πεποιθέναι) and 4–6 go
on to define "flesh" as the totality of characteristics and
deeds which a man could boast of as his own, that is, "his
own righteousness from the law" (iii. 9). "Spirit", by
contrast, is God's power, and therefore Christ's power.
Living under this power means also living up to this
standard and so "boasting in Jesus Christ" (iii. 3)—

[1] Hence the opposite to πνεῦμα can also be ἄνθρωπος: I Cor. iii. 1–4;
Ign. Eph. v. 1 (Bultmann T.N.T. I, 153–54).

that paradoxical boasting of oneself which, when there is faith in Christ, leans only upon the "righteousness of God" given by Christ, and therefore esteems all personal advantages as refuse (iii. 8–9). In just the same way, we saw in I Cor. ii. 6–16 (see above) that the Spirit, when it is the miraculous power which gives to a man the knowledge of what God has done for his salvation, also demands from him renunciation of his own wisdom (ii. 1–5), indeed of all attention to human standards (14–15). Similarly, the Spirit in II Cor. iii. 6 appears mainly as the miraculous power which (in the future in I Cor. xv. 45 and so now in the present[1]) is credited with "making alive", ζωοποιεῖν. But iii. 9 shows that it is also the power which reveals to man what God has done for his salvation, enables him to live by it, and so gives him the possibility of not worrying about his own justification (see below pp. 91–2). Again, the phrase (Rom. ii. 29) "Circumcision of the heart in the Spirit and not in the letter" (περιτομὴ καρδίας ἐν πνεύματι, οὐ γράμματι) includes giving up all subservience to human criteria. Again, in Rom. vii. 5–6, "law" not only reveals or condemns sin, but actually provokes it, while the Spirit bestows the new "slavery" (δουλεύειν). The only difference (as comes out still more clearly in Rom. viii. 13) is that here that side of faith is emphasized which finds expression in concrete deeds (see below p. 77).

In Gal. iv. 23, 29 "he that is born of the Spirit" and "of the flesh" are opposed to each other. But in the second instance the word γεννηθείς is lacking, and in iv. 23 κατὰ πνεῦμα is replaced by δι(ὰ τῆς) ἐπαγγελίας; therefore there can be no thought of πνεῦμα as a seed-like material of generation, still less of a feminine spirit which bears children like a mother-goddess. δι(ὰ τῆς) ἐπαγγελίας is surely to be taken instrumentally. In iii. 18 ἐπαγγελία is explicitly contrasted with νόμος[2] and in iv. 29

---

[1] I.e. "proleptic", not "realized" eschatology (H. V. Martin, *Proleptic Eschatology*, Exp. T. 51 (1939–40), 88–90).

[2] Cf. Rom. ix. 8 where ἐπαγγελία, instead of the usual πνεῦμα, is the opposite of σάρξ.

ὁ κατὰ σάρκα γεννηθείς is one who stands under the νόμος; it follows that the point of this passage is not to describe a miraculous birth, but to establish the fact that one son's life depends on human potentialities, the other's on the gift of God's grace. Once again, in this usage, cause and standard are intertwined. πνεῦμα means the gift of God's grace proceeding from Jesus Christ which sets in motion a new existence; and at the same time, that which is the standard according to which man lives out this existence. Whereas πνεῦμα had been principally the miraculous power which reveals God's saving work and so lays the foundation for a new life, so here its equivalence to ἐπαγγελία shows it in a still clearer light as the objective power, given by the grace of God, which creates this life (cf. John's view, below, pp. 91–2).[1]

In Gal. v. 17, man is apparently regarded as the neutral battlefield between flesh and Spirit. But v. 16, 18, show that even here there is no question of irresistible pressure. It is especially important to give due weight to ἵνα in 17; the intention of both must come into account. This means that even when a man is a believer he stands under the threat of apostasy just as much as under the promise of the Spirit. But it does not follow that both must work in him at once, or that he is delivered up to both without choice or freewill. What he is given is precisely the possibility of "walking in the Spirit", πνεύματι στοιχεῖν, with his flesh crucified (v. 24–5, see below, pp. 77–8). At the same time flesh is not actually a power external to man, but is his own will. No more is said here than that the flesh *can* become dominant and threaten him.

The Spirit in the sense of standard of life comes out clearly in Gal. vi. 8. Here, what determines a man's life is whether he "sows to the Spirit" or "sows to his own flesh". Similarly, in Rom. viii. 4–5 the formula "walking by the flesh" or "by the Spirit" is picked up by "setting one's mind on things of the flesh" or "of the Spirit", τὰ τῆς σαρκὸς, τὰ τοῦ πνεύματος φρονεῖν. This certainly

---

[1] Cf. ζωοποιεῖ, II Cor. iii. 6. Nevertheless, Paul's thought is expressed far more trenchantly in legal categories (πνεῦμα = ἀρραβών, ἀπαρχή, its activity = μαρτυρεῖν, δικαιοῦν) than in biological ones. So too the πνεῦμα υἱοθεσίας of Rom. viii. 15 is defined as that which proves (not begets) sonship.

brings out the paradox once again: the liberating "standard" of the Spirit is nothing else but the fact that God has acted and has achieved what the law was incapable of. So, in Gal. vi. 8, the word "own", ἑαυτοῦ, which stands with "flesh", is characteristically omitted with "spirit". This is only another way of saying that the standard of the Spirit, according to which a man directs his life, is not a potentiality of his own, but is given to him from outside himself.[1]

These two aspects are not altogether on the same plane. "Walking in the Spirit" is man's "yes" to the power of God which he cannot control and which, instead of his own power, must now determine his life. Therefore it is no accident that in Rom. viii. 13 "by the Spirit", πνεύματι, which indicates the motive power of this new life, is contrasted with "according to the flesh", κατὰ σάρκα, which expresses the standard. Still more clearly, Phil. iii. 3 speaks of "serving the Spirit *of God*", πνεύματι θεοῦ λατρεύειν, in distinction to "trusting in the flesh", πεποιθέναι ἐν σαρκί. Living "according to the Spirit", and being released from the flesh, means therefore just this: living in God's saving "sphere of action"—except that here the emphasis is more on the decision of the believer than on what happens to him. Yet even this decision of faith is understood as a gift of God, not as a man's own accomplishment; it is the standard by which he decides, and in fact also the power of his decision. Hence the notable pronouncement in Rom. viii. 4 that in consequence of the saving event the requirement of the law is fulfilled *in* (not by) those who walk after the Spirit and not after the flesh.[2] Still clearer is II Cor. i. 12, where the Grace of God (χάρις θεοῦ) is the opposite of fleshly activity. (Cf. Rom. v. 2.)

Thus we find ourselves in a world quite different from

[1] Cf. C. H. Dodd, *Romans*, 136–7, on Rom. viii. 28 ff.

[2] It is clearly the believer's concrete actions which matter here, but equally clearly these are based on *God's* power. In what follows, "abiding" is interpreted by strong active verbs.

that of the Gnostic. The Gnostic is certainly aware of the same antithesis, but regards it as a datum of the universe; whereas in Paul it is something created by the act of God in Christ, in response to which man has to answer yes or no[1].

(b) Spirit as laying oneself open to God and one's neighbour

According to Rom. viii. 15, 26–7 and Gal. iv. 6, the characteristic activity of the Spirit is Prayer.[2] This connection is particularly underlined in Rom. viii. 27, where the Spirit appears before God on behalf of man, who left to his own does not even know what to pray for.[3] The Spirit is therefore the same in its "ethical" function as in its "soteriological": it proves to man his Sonship (which is assured through God's saving act in Christ) and enables him to live in it. Freedom from the old written code, παλαιότης γράμματος, nevertheless means serving the new code of the Spirit, δουλεύειν ἐν καινότητι πνεύματος. The sinful passions which were aroused by the law must be indulged no more (Rom. vii. 5–6). The requirement of the law is fulfilled in those who now live according to the Spirit instead of according to the flesh (Rom. viii. 4). Setting the mind on the flesh (φρόνημα τῆς σαρκός) could not be made to serve God's law (Rom. viii. 7); but thanks to the Spirit, those who believe put to death the deeds of the body (σῶμα, Rom. viii. 13). Living as a Son of God can be summed up as faith made concrete.

The best example of this is in Gal. v. 13–15, where 13 and 16 make it clear that walking in the Spirit (πνεύματι περιπατεῖν = ἐπιθυμίαν σαρκὸς μὴ τελέσαι) means being servants of one another through love, διὰ τῆς ἀγαπῆς

---

[1] W. L. Knox, *St. Paul and the Church of the Gentiles*, 99, 109, 127, takes this differently; but his view that πνεῦμα strengthens νοῦς (*ib.* 99) does not allow for I Cor. xiv. 14.

[2] Never in the Rabbis (Str.-B. III, 243).

[3] This is not the Gnostic πνεῦμα which groans in its material prison (cf. above, p. 21, n. 3), i.e. the innermost self of the "spiritual" man. Similarly, Phil. i. 19 is to be translated "support through the Spirit" (Dibelius, *Phil. ad loc.*). In this context it should be mentioned that in Rom. xiv. 17, χαρά is a gift of the πνεῦμα.

δουλεύειν ἀλλήλοις, and so at the same time fulfilling the whole law (v. 14).[1] Love, so long as it is outward-looking, is nothing other than life in the Spirit, which has shaken itself free from trusting in the flesh. It is "active faith" (Gal. v. 6). The concrete result of it is the ful-filling of the law, precisely because man is relieved of straining after his own righteousness (v. 14–18).[2]

In other words, living in the power of the Spirit, and by the standard of the Spirit, means living in freedom from the law, living altogether "by Christ", "by grace", "by the cross", and at the same time being open to love (ἀγάπη). This comes out with particular force in Gal. v. 19–23. Whereas the evidence for the activity of the flesh is works (ἔργα), for the Spirit it is only possible to speak of "the fruits" (καρπός).[3] Not that "fruits" are only interior, invisible; it is clear from v. 25–vi. 10 (and indeed from v. 21β) that Paul is thinking entirely of concrete actions. Nevertheless they are all actions which cannot be *demonstrated* as being the activities of the Spirit.[4] Again, in I Cor. xiii. 1–3, it is neither the mira-culous nature of the deed nor the superhuman degree of sacrifice which is an unambiguous mark of love and of the Spirit which is expressed in it; yet it remains a fixed pre-mise that the Spirit, for example in worship (I Cor. xii-xiv), expresses itself in concrete loving activity. In Gal. v. 22, love, ἀγάπη makes its appearance as the first of the gifts of the Spirit,[5] and it is clear from Rom. xv. 30[6] and

---

[1] The opposite of σάρξ, instead of πνεῦμα, is here ἀγάπη.

[2] The contrast is between σάρξ (13, 16), νόμος (2–4, 18), περιτομή (6, 11), δουλεία (1) and πνεῦμα (5, 16–18), Χριστός (2–4), χάρις (4), σταυρός (11), ἀγάπη (6, 13) ἐλευθερία (1, 13). Hence νόμος appears again in antithesis to πνεῦμα (18); and contrariwise the activity of σάρξ is shown in the oppression and destruction of others (15).

[3] In Rom. vi. 21 καρπός is used *in malam partem*. It means a fortuitous instead of a procured result.

[4] That is why the plural φανερά is not used! φανέρωσις τοῦ πνεύματος I Cor. xii. 7 is its activity in the Church, but that cannot be calculated objectively—at any rate not by its exceptional character.

[5] Kittel, art. *Love*, E.T. 57.

[6] If indeed the parallel phrase in Philem. 9 is to be interpreted with Gal. v. 22 and not Rom. v. 5.

Col. i. 8, and especially from I Cor. xiii, that love embraces all the others. But at this point it must be reiterated that love can only be understood as faith when it is directed towards others. In the same way, when the Spirit appears as the power of sanctification (Rom. xv. 16; I Cor. vi. 11, cf. II Thess. ii. 13) it is impossible to say whether Paul wishes to emphasize the Spirit as involving a man in God's saving activity and justifying him, or as enabling him to base his life on it in concrete obedience.[1] The two come to the same thing.[2]

At this point the difference in the Gnostic interpretation becomes particularly apparent. When the Gnostic, in ecstasy, possesses the Spirit, it destroys his individuality; all that matters is the divine substance within him. It also separates him from other men, who, if they are "unspiritual", are completely strange to him, and if they are "spiritual", only serve to lead him to the point where he finds himself (i.e. the same spiritual substance) in them.[3] For him, the highest ideal is *Gnosis*, that is to say, the apprehension of the divine substance within himself. And it is precisely this which cuts a man off from others (cf. I Cor. viii. 1–3). In Paul, on the other hand, knowledge (γνῶσις) is subordinate to love (ἀγάπη).[4] In other words, if the knowledge which is given by the Spirit is knowledge of the saving act of God, then it frees man from himself and in so doing lays him open to others. At the same time it restores to him anew his individuality, not in such a way that he can contemplate it and take his stand upon it before God and man, but as a means of existing for others.

Thus it is the concept of the Church which really

---

[1] The first is stressed in I Cor. vi. 11, the second in I Cor. vi. 19; II Cor. vi. 6; I Thess. iv. 7–8 (cf. Rom. xiv. 17).

[2] C. T. Craig, *Paradox of Holiness*, Interpretation, 8 (1952), 147–61. There is no neutral zone between flesh and spirit; therefore freedom from sin is necessarily obedience.

[3] Hence the "spiritual" Gnostic founds, at most, θίασοι, not permanent ἐκκλησίαι.

[4] Kittel, art. *Gnosis*, E.T. 43.

decides the matter.   When Paul speaks of being received
into the "Body of Christ" (probably adopting a Hellenistic expression) this serves to underline the unity of the
Body, which binds the various members together.[1]   The
value of spiritual gifts is not to be found in the fact that
they mark out their bearers as "spiritual people", but
that they build up the Church (I Cor. xiv).   It is true
that the building-up happens through the "spiritual",
but then *everyone* is "spiritual", everyone has his χάρισμα.
If individuals break away, they thereby show themselves
to be "unspiritual", σαρκικοί.[2]

It is true, then, that the Spirit is still the miraculous
power which proceeds entirely from God and breaks in
upon man's affairs in a way quite out of his control.   But
Paul has carried this to its logical conclusion.   Precisely
because it is the power of God, it cannot be exhibited in a
series of exceptional events.   If it could, man would be
able to appeal to his own religious and miraculous powers.
Basically, it is the power which involves him in the saving
act of God through Christ, takes away his independence,
makes impossible for him all confidence in his own
"flesh" (σάρξ) and lays him open to a life of love
(ἀγάπη).   All that Paul has done is to carry to their
logical conclusion the synoptics' interpretations of the
cross: sin-offering for many (Mark, xiv. 24, see above
p. 68); call to repentance, shattering all false religious
security (Mark xii. 1–12, see above p. 73); event which
makes possible the discipleship of service (διακονία, Mark
x. 45, see above p. 77).

This is different from the way in which Acts sees it;
certainly not because Paul introduces ethical categories;
nor yet because in Acts it is the outward history of the
Church, in Paul the inner life of the individual, which is

[1] Rom. xii. 4–5; I Cor. xii. 13–27; x. 17; Gal. iii. 28.   Being involved in
God's saving act means death to everything of which a man can boast and
which can separate him from others.
[2] I Cor. iii. 3–4.   Hence the Church is not subject to individual
πνευματικοί, but can pass judgment on them.

controlled by God; nor again because in Acts the possession of the Spirit can be ascertained while in Paul it is a part of faith; nor yet because the dynamic conception of the Spirit in Acts is in contrast with Paul's "being in Christ". At most these are superficial differences, underlying which we can see a deeper difference: the Spirit is the power of God which enables men to believe in the Cross and Resurrection of Jesus. This means that, when its other-ness needs to be emphasized, it can have the dynamic appearance of an extraordinary and miraculous power; but it can also be at the root of a permanent life in Christ. It can control both the outward fortune of the Church and the inner life of the individual; it can be visible or invisible, momentary or permanent. But in all this it is no longer merely an additional phenomenon, as in Acts; it is the power which determines the new life of faith as such.

3. *The Spirit and Christ*

In Rom. viii. 1–11, "the Spirit of God in you", πνεῦμα θεοῦ ἐν ὑμῖν (9), alternates with "Christ in you", Χριστὸς ἐν ὑμῖν (10), and "you . . . in spirit", ὑμεῖς ἐν πνεύματι (9), with "those who are in Christ" τοῖς ἐν Χριστῷ (1), without any apparent difference in meaning.[1] From the Hellenistic standpoint this can be explained as a matter of terminology; the ascended Christ has the substance of Spirit (cf. above p. 57); consequently, abiding in Christ here and now is equivalent to abiding in the Spirit, and in the same way Christ's abiding in us is equivalent to the Spirit's abiding in us. It can be objected to this that "in the Spirit" (ἐν πνεύματι)[2] often occurs in an instrumental sense; but this objection collapses as soon as it is realized that the concept of the substantial sphere which the believer enters is only Paul's formal way of

---

[1] Further parallels in W. D. Davies, *Paul and Rabbinic Judaism*, 178.
[2] Rom. xv. 13; I Thess. i. 5. Alternation between ἐν . . . and the dative: I Cor. xii. 3/xiv. 2 (cf. Eph. i. 13/iv. 30; v. 18). Dative for local ἐν: Gal. iii. 3; v. 5, 16, 25.

grasping the concept of power. However, it follows that this approach can only explain why this particular terminology is chosen. It cannot explain the reality behind it. In its context, "walking by the Spirit" (περιπατεῖν κατὰ πνεῦμα) or "having the mind of the Spirit" (φρονεῖν τὰ τοῦ πνεύματος) is referred back to "being in the Spirit" (εἶναι κατὰ πνεῦμα, 4–5, or ἐν πνεύματι, 9) and this in turn is referred to "the dwelling" of the Spirit "in you" (9).[1] This makes it clear yet again (cf. above p. 69) that Paul is trying to define the conception of the "sphere" in which the believer lives in terms of what it means to him, that is, as a power into whose range we have come, and which determines our thinking (φρονεῖν), our walking (περιπατεῖν) and our obedience to the law of God (ὑποτάσσεσθαι τῷ νόμῳ τοῦ θεοῦ).

This power is not something nameless and unknown. It is identical with the ascended Lord—so long as one does not think of the ascended Lord in himself, but only in his dealings with the Church.[2]   Paul is hardly touched by the metaphysical question how God, Christ and the Spirit are related to each other.   For this reason at least it is a mistake to see the root meaning of the word for Paul as "the third person of the Trinity".   The Spirit often makes a completely impersonal appearance (I Cor. xii. 13; I Thess. v. 19); it can alternate with Wisdom or Power (I Cor. ii. 4–5, 13).   The Spirit which is given to man can be referred to as "his spirit" or as the "spirit of sonship". The Spirit "teaches", "thinks", etc., but it shares this property with other words like "wisdom" or "flesh". The question of how far the Spirit is personal may be a

---

[1] From the O.T. point of view, this view is more surprising than the other, which is at least grounded on the concept of the Spirit "clothing" a man (L. Köhler).

[2] Paul is not the first to make this distinction (C. A. A. Scott, *Christianity according to St. Paul*, 141–5.   In Acts the Spirit is not only τοῦτο (ii. 33) in distinction from the Pauline and Johannine (John xiv. 26) ἐκεῖνος, but πνεῦμα and κύριος alternate (see above, p. 39 top).

false one,[1] for the simple reason that the word "personal" does not exist in either Greek or Hebrew. Paul shares with Judaism (see above p. 11) and with the early Christian Church (see above p. 36) the conception of the Spirit as the gift and power of the Last Age. His concern is not to replace the concept of "power" by the concept of "person", but to show that this power is not an obscure "something" but is the way and manner in which the Lord of the Church is present. For that reason the Spirit can be placed on a level with the Lord, or subordinated to him, quite indifferently (II Cor. iii. 17–18, see above p. 60).[2] For that reason also, Paul can occasionally use God, Lord and Spirit interchangeably, simply because their encounter with the believer always takes one and the same form.[3] The clearest instance of this is I Cor. xii. 4–6, not only because all three concepts there correspond to each other, but also because the Spirit, as it is manifested in the life of the Church, is defined precisely as the "manifestation of the Spirit", $\phi a\nu \epsilon \rho \omega \sigma \iota \varsigma \ \tau o\hat{v} \ \pi \nu \epsilon \acute{v} \mu a\tau o\varsigma$ (7), and is distinguished from the source of this activity.

A question remains about II Cor. xiii. 13. Is $\kappa o\iota \nu \omega \nu \acute{\iota} a$ $\tau o\hat{v} \ \acute{a}\gamma \acute{\iota}o\upsilon \ \pi \nu \epsilon \acute{\upsilon} \mu a\tau o\varsigma$ a subjective or objective genitive? Similar passages in I Cor. i. 9, Phil. iii. 10 suggest that it is objective, but the arguments for this interpretation are by no means convincing.[4] The nearest parallel in Phil. ii. 1 is certainly not to be understood as fellowship with the Holy Spirit of God; for $\kappa \upsilon \rho \acute{\iota}o\upsilon$ and $\theta \epsilon o\hat{\upsilon}$ are certainly subjective genitives. It is then open to question, whether the meaning is not completely parallel: "the $\kappa o\iota \nu \omega \nu \acute{\iota} a$ given by the Spirit". But this still does not help us to decide whether it is brotherly fellowship

[1] Cf. C. Welch, *The Holy Spirit and the Trinity*, Theology Today, 8 (1951–2) 33.

[2] Similarly it can be almost synonymous with $\theta \epsilon \acute{o}\varsigma$ (I Cor. iii. 16; cf. xiv. 25; II Cor. vi. 16) and yet be contrasted with $\theta \epsilon \acute{o}\varsigma$ (I Cor. ii. 10; Rom. viii. 26–7).

[3] E. Lewis, *The Biblical Doctrine of the Holy Spirit*, Interpretation, 7 (1953), 281–98 shows that both in O.T. and N.T. the Spirit is often replaced by God, Lord, etc., without any difference of meaning.

[4] Cf. J. E. L. Oulton, *Holy Spirit and Holy Communion*, 62–4; G. J. Jourdan, *KOINΩNIA in I Cor. x. 16*, J. B. L. 67 (1948), 116–18.

one with another which is in question, or fellowship with the Spirit. This last corresponds better with χάρις and ἀγάπη and would give κοινωνία the strongly active sense of the gift by the Spirit of a share in itself, in which case the first meaning would be included. In other words, it comes to the same thing if one explains the expression as an objective genitive. However, it is better to interpret κοινωνία τοῦ ἁγίου πνεύματος as a subjective genitive, so long as the complexity of the notion is grasped; for in fact the objective reality of this fellowship characterizes it just as strongly as the subjective power which bestows it.[1]

All these concepts occur again in Rom. v. 1–5, Gal. iv. 4–6, this time not in exact parallel, but all close together. These passages show that God's work in the Son or in the Spirit must always be understood as really the work of God himself, but that the question, how God, Lord and Spirit are related to each other, is not yet felt to be a question at all.

4. The Human Spirit

What Paul says about this is by no means consistent or even original. The Holy Spirit of God affects the whole man, and cannot be given a psychological explanation; a fact which enables Paul to take over popular conceptions without embarrassment. The thesis that Paul knows nothing of a human spirit cannot be sustained. Along with "body" and "flesh", "spirit" appears to be simply a general word for the functions of the human soul (I Cor. vii. 34; II Cor. vii. 1; Col. ii. 5?): thus it can be used as equivalent to "soul" (ψυχή, Phil. i. 27, see below p. 100) or, like "flesh" (σάρξ), can describe the whole man; the only difference being that in this case the soul is emphasized more than the body (II Cor. ii. 13; vii. 5; cf. vii. 13; I Cor. xvi. 18, always with personal pronouns). In closing greetings (Gal. vi. 18; Phil. iv.23; Philem. 25)

[1] Jourdan, op. cit. 119, 123–4. Cf. L. S. Thornton, The Common Life in the Body of Christ, 74–5.

"your spirit" means exactly the same as "you" (I Thess. v. 28). In the same way, in I Cor. ii. 11 "spirit" can stand for human consciousness and be distinguished from the Spirit of God which exactly corresponds to it; although in this case it is precisely the correspondence which determines the use of the words. So, too, in the famous passage I Thess. v. 23, spirit, along with soul and body, is to be taken as a component part of man, on the lines of popular psychology.[1]

Paul, therefore, has no scruples about taking over "spirit" as a psychological term from current Jewish usage. Yet even so he still regards it as being the spirit which is God's gift and so ultimately alien to man. He does not need to stress this point, and is capable of ignoring it altogether, but sometimes it comes out quite clearly. In I Cor. xiv. 14 the spirit which is given to a "spiritual" person—which is clearly distinguished from his mind (νοῦς)—can still be referred to as "his" spirit. In Rom. i. 9, too, the "Spirit" is the Spirit of God which is made available to the apostle personally.[2]

I Cor. v. 3–5 is not altogether clear. The spirit of the sinner, which must be saved, is certainly the "I" which is given him by God, and so a part of the Spirit of God; although it represents also the totality of the new man, the believer.[3] But at the same time it is not a *character indelebilis*; for Paul allows for the possibility that it may be lost, that is, if the judgment on the σάρξ is not carried out (does this mean illness? or death? xi. 30 cf. Acts v. 1–11). It is the new "I" of a man which would be lost if he gave up altogether being a Christian. To avoid this last, horrible, ultimate possibility becoming actual,

[1] Above, p. 22–3. The greeting is very likely traditional, if not liturgical, and so tells us little about Paul's conception of man (Dibelius, *Thess.*[3], *ad loc.*). The combination may be fortuitous, as in Deut. vi. 5 (W. Robinson, q. by J. A. T. Robinson, *The Body*, 27, n. 2).
[2] Cf. Rom. xii. 11; in Rom. viii. 10–11 the divine origin of the Spirit is strongly emphasized.
[3] It is certainly not simply the human soul; for Paul is never concerned with the saving of a mere soul. It is the man himself in the existence Christ has given him, not in his natural powers and potentialities (cf. iii. 15, αὐτός).

the purifying judgment on the σάρξ must take place.[1]   In which case the apostle's own spirit, both here and in Colossians ii. 5, must also be understood as the gift of the Spirit of God imparted to him, which guarantees his authority and reaches out even beyond his bodily presence.

It is significant that this spirit, which abides in a man, is not suggested as being in any way more than something that is both attached to him and related to God.   Moreover, it never means the soul completed by God's Spirit. It is true that Paul unthinkingly uses spirit almost in the sense of soul; but this is only common Judaic usage which he naturally cannot avoid using himself.[2]   Paul never says that the soul finds its completion in spirit.   Where he does actually mention the idea of an "organ" which receives the Spirit of God, he also calls it "spirit" and expressly describes it as something not belonging to man but given to him by God (Rom. viii. 15–16; I Cor. ii. 11).[3]   When Paul is being consciously precise, he contrasts, like the Gnostics, this individual, transcendent, essentially divine spirit with both soul and body.[4]   A positive advantage of this is that "spirit" is sharply distinguished from the human "mind" (νοῦς, I Cor. xiv. 14); and the negative side of it comes out in Paul's avoidance of the word "spirit" when he wants to describe the profoundest "I" of pre-Christian man.[5]

At first sight this state of affairs is bewildering, but it becomes clear when it is realized that Paul's thought proceeds entirely from the *activity* of the Spirit of God, and that he regards the whole existence of the believer as

---

[1] The σάρξ which is destroyed is not Sin (F. Grosheide, *I Cor.* 123, *ad loc.*). Cf. I Pet. iv. 1, 6, 17, and below, p. 102 (iv).

[2] The human spirit is never thought of in the Stoic sense as an offshoot of God's Spirit, although Gen. ii. 7 might have suggested this.

[3] Cf. Odes of Solomon vi. 7.

[4] See below p. 87 ; N. H. Snaith, *The Distinctive Ideas of the O.T.* 184–6 ; F. C. Synge, *The Holy Spirit and the Sacraments*, Scottish J. of Th. 6 (1953), 68–69.   The dualism of immanence-transcendence is superseded by the πνεῦμα which comprises both.

[5] For which he uses ἐγώ or νοῦς (Rom. vii. 17–23).

determined by it. For Paul, the Spirit of God is no
extraordinary magic power; it reveals to the believer the
saving work of God in Christ, and enables him to give
responsible and informed assent to it (see above p. 67 and
especially p. 72). Consequently, the Spirit remains
entirely God's, and is never merged in the Spirit which is
given to the individual;[1] yet at the same time it can be
the deepest "I" of the man whose life no longer proceeds
from his own being , but from God's being on his behalf.

Appendix: πνευματικός

Paul's language becomes pointed when he contrasts
the πνευματικοί with the ψυχικοί. In I Cor. ii. 13–15
πνευματικός means the man who in the power of God's
Spirit acknowledges God's saving work (see above pp.
68–9), while the ψυχικός is blind to it.[2] This contrast is at
its sharpest here, because Paul does not recognize any
neutral existence. If you do not have the Spirit of God,
you are controlled by the spirit of the world, πνεῦμα τοῦ
κόσμου.[3] There is an equally pointed distinction in
I Cor. xv. 44–46 between the σῶμα πνευματικόν and the
σῶμα ψυχικόν (cf. above p. 62) which shows that even
before Paul these terms had been coined and were
current.[4] It follows from what has just been said that
πνευματικά can be the content of the knowledge which is
only given through the Spirit of God, that is, heavenly
things inaccessible to the νοῦς, in other words the gospel
of Christ (I Cor. ii. 13; ix. 11; Rom. xv. 27). In these
two last passages, earthly things are subsequently mentioned as carnal (σαρκικά) though without any connota-
tion of evil. They are simply what promotes the
natural life but does not unite with God. Thus even
ordinary foods and drinks are contrasted with the

[1] Rom. viii. 16, cf. Bultmann, *T.N.T.* I, 206–7.
[2] So Jude 19 (see below, pp. 102–3).
[3] A mythological expression, as in Eph. ii. 2. On iii. 1–3 and I Cor.
xiv. 37, Gal. vi. 1, see above, p. 66, n. 1.
[4] Cf. above, pp. 22–23.

"spiritual" ones which come directly from God's world and bestow divine power (I Cor. x. 3). There is no idea here of the elements bearing the Spirit, as is shown by passages using similar language[1] and also by I Cor. x. 4β.[2] In I Cor. xiv. 1 πνευματικά means the totality of spiritual gifts.[3] In Rom. vii. 14, the law (νόμος) is referred to as πνευματικός; this is to make it clear that it is God's law, νόμος θεοῦ, and proceeds not from man's world, but from God's.[4]

D. JOHN

1. *The significance of eschatology*

While the saying handed down in John xxi. 22 still represents the conviction of Mark ix. 1; I Thess. iv. 17, that some people will live to see the Parousia, and while the scoffers are already beginning to scoff (II Peter iii. 4; I Clem. xxiii. 2–3; II Clem. xi) and their opponents are simply deferring the time of the Parousia (II Peter iii. 8–10; I Clem. xxiii. 4–5; Barn. xxi. 3),[5] John on the one hand is firmly convinced that the consummation is still to come,[6] but he also proclaims, more clearly even than Paul, the present actuality of the salvation which is one day to be consummated. So that the first difference from the synoptics and from Paul appears in the greater consistency with which the old concepts are subjected to revision.

[1] I Pet. ii. 5. Also Barn. xvi. 10 ("spiritual" temple contrasted with one made with hands, perishable, 7, 9); Did. x. 3 ("spiritual" food and drink contrasted with ordinary ones); Ign. *Eph.* v. 1 ("spiritual" relationship with the Bishop). Cf. C. F. D. Moule, *Sanctuary and Sacrifice in the Church of the N.T.*, J.T.S. N.S. 1 (1950), 34–5 (spiritual=repudiation of external ritual).

[2] The "Spiritual Rock" is unearthly, miraculous, proceeding from God's world.

[3] Also xii. 1. Cf. Rom. i. 11.

[4] Rom. vii. 22, 25. Similarly Eph. i. 3. On all this see also Selwyn, *I Peter*, 281–5.

[5] C. K. Barrett, *The Holy Spirit in the Fourth Gospel*, J.T.S. N.S. 1 (1950) 2–3; *idem*, *The Gospel according to St. John*, ad loc.

[6] vi. 27; xii. 25; xiv. 2–3; xvii. 24. xi. 24, though inadequate, is not contradicted. Cf. E. Schweizer, *The Reinterpretation of the Gospel by the Fourth Evangelist*, Interpretation, 8 (1954), 387–96. On the whole question cf. W. F. Howard, *Christianity according to St. John*, 106–128.

In John there is no conception of a sudden appearance of the Spirit or of the exceptional character of its manifestations, or indeed of ecstatic phenomena or miracles altogether.[1] Jesus, again, never appears as a man of the Spirit. His inspired discourse and his miracles are never ascribed to the Spirit.[2] The way trodden by Luke is not adequate for John. He abandons completely the concept of inspiration, since it only serves to express a basic separation between God and Jesus which must ever be overcome by a third entity, namely the Spirit. But if the Christ-event is really to be understood as the turn of the era, then it is all-important that it is the Father himself, and not just a gift of the Father's, which is encountered in Christ. It follows naturally that the stories of his conception by the Spirit, and of his endowment with the Spirit at baptism, are left out.

> The first one is corrected straight away in i. 13;[3] though the verse shows that for John conception by the Spirit does exist, not for the Son, but for believers. The descent of the Spirit on Jesus in i. 33 is mentioned only as a proof, not as a cause, of Jesus' Sonship.

2. *Spirit as opposed to "flesh": a sphere*

Other differences from Paul are not fundamental but arise from the fact that John's thought is cast less in the categories of Rabbinic than of a heterodox Judaism. To the latter belongs the pre-Pauline usage (cf. above p. 57) by which "spirit" and "flesh" distinguish the divine from the earthly sphere (iii. 6; vi. 63). While iii. 6 speaks of "being born of the Spirit", iii. 3 and i. 13 speak of being

---

[1] Pentecost happens without tongues of fire or rushing winds, xx. 22–3 (Barrett, J.T.S. 1950, 3–4). And in xvi. 13 there is no trace of the old view that the main gift of the prophetic $\pi\nu\epsilon\hat{\nu}\mu\alpha$ is foresight (Barrett, *St. John, ad loc.*).

[2] E.g. vii. 28, 37; xii. 44; v. 8; vi. 11; ix. 6–7; xi. 43. Again, in xi. 33; xiii. 21, it is not the spasm of a "spiritual" man which is described; $\pi\nu\epsilon\hat{\nu}\mu\alpha$ is purely psychological $= \dot{\epsilon}\alpha\upsilon\tau\acute{o}\nu$ (xi. 33, cf. Barrett, J.T.S. 1950, 3). In xix. 30 it means the physical life-force.

[3] Howard, *op. cit.* 66–8.

born "from above" or "from God". The opposite of "being of God" ($\epsilon\hat{\iota}\nu\alpha\iota$ $\dot{\epsilon}\kappa$ $\tau o\hat{\upsilon}$ $\theta\epsilon o\hat{\upsilon}$) is being "of below" ($\dot{\epsilon}\kappa$ $\tau\hat{\omega}\nu$ $\kappa\acute{\alpha}\tau\omega$), "of the devil", "of the world",[1] just as the opposite of "born of the Spirit" is "born of the flesh" (iii. 6). In other words "Spirit", "above", "God" seem to correspond to "flesh", "below", "devil", "world".

iv. 24 states the equation: God is Spirit.[2] In this sentence John proclaims that the eschatological hour, in which "above" and "below", spirit and flesh, God and the world, meet together—that this hour, however much its consummation is still pending, has already struck.[3] Greek and Gnostic thought envisaged an ultimate union between the divine substance and the originally similar substance buried in mankind. John proclaims the exact opposite, namely that it is in the historical man Jesus of Nazareth that God calls us to faith and comes to meet us. Worshipping God in Spirit and in truth no longer means worshipping in the consciousness of one's own "spiritual substance", still less in one's own spirituality as opposed to anything external; it means worshipping in the divine and no longer in the worldly sphere, in reality and no longer in the sphere of appearances. But this sphere is only to be found where God himself enters the world, that is, in him who is the true God, $\dot{o}$ $\dot{\alpha}\lambda\eta\theta\iota\nu\dot{o}s$ $\theta\epsilon\acute{o}s$ (I John v. 20).[4] There were many objections to ritual worship;[5] and to put it in a neat formula, one could say that

---

[1] viii. 23, 42–7; xv. 19; xvii. 14, 16.

[2] Yet John avoids the expression $\nu o\hat{\upsilon}s$, and gives to the term $\pi\nu\epsilon\hat{\upsilon}\mu\alpha$ a completely new meaning by opposing it absolutely to $\sigma\acute{\alpha}\rho\xi$. This radical other-ness of God over against everything human is O.T., not Greek, in feeling.

[3] Cf. Barrett, J.T.S. 1950, 6. *Idem, St. John, ad loc.* understands $\pi\nu\epsilon\hat{\upsilon}\mu\alpha$ here as life-giving power of God, whereas $\dot{\alpha}\lambda\acute{\eta}\theta\epsilon\iota\alpha$ stresses the connexion with the historical Jesus. It would be more exact to define it as the power which forges union with God's world (and is therefore life-giving).

[4] Cf. i. 9; vi. 32–35; x. 11; xv. 1; x. 30; xiv. 9–10. In fact, xiv. 26 (not the D reading!) and xvi. 12–13 give us the key: the Spirit is the elucidation of the Incarnation (O. Cullmann, *Early Christian Worship*, E.T. 72).

[5] I Kings viii. 27. Cf. Sen. *Epistulae*, xli. 1–2 (cf. lxvi. 12). "Do not lift your hands to heaven . . . God is near you, with you, in you . . . a holy spirit dwells in you."

John iv. 24 orientates true worship upon the flesh and blood of Jesus.[1] Spirit consequently does not mean the soul and the understanding of man, what is "nearest to God in man" something immaterial, "completely inward".[2] Like "truth," it means the reality of God. In form, it is Hellenistic and substantial; but in fact it is completely suffused by the knowledge that this reality is only to be found in Jesus. Seeing the truth means seeing in Jesus Him who is truly God (τὸν ἀληθινὸν θεόν viii. 32; xvii. 3). "In Spirit" (ἐν πνεύματι) therefore comes to the same as Paul's "in Christ". The sovereign act of God's revelation in Jesus has marked out the area in which true worship takes place. Consequently any cult which is not a gift resulting from this act of God— however "spiritual" it may be—is condemned as not taking place "in the Spirit".[3]

3. *Spirit as opposed to "flesh": a life-giving power*

As in John iv. 23-4, so also in iii. 3-5 "Spirit" appears as the divine world which is inaccessible to man so long as he does not live "in the Spirit", ἐν πνεύματι. But here this life is connected with "being born of the Spirit".[4]

The decisive question in John is this: how does one obtain *life*, ζωή? Paul too could ask this question and, like John, he could answer that only the "Spirit" πνεῦμα, is responsible for making alive, ζωοποιεῖν (John vi. 63;

---

[1] Hoskyns, *Fourth Gospel*, ad loc.

[2] Howard, *op. cit.* 61; G. H. C. McGregor, *John* (Moffatt N.T. Commentary), *ad loc.* On ἀλήθεια see Bultmann, *T.N.T.* II, 18–19.

[3] The opposition between the spirit of truth, knowledge, light, and error, malice, darkness has its roots in pre-Gnostic Judaism. See above, p. 15ff. and Test. Jud. xx. 1; *Damascus Document*, ii. 13 (ii. 10). πνεῦμα ἀληθείας ought not therefore to be taken in in the O.T. sense: "Spirit of faith" (cf. *contra* N. H. Snaith, *The Distinctive Ideas of the O.T.*, 181).

[4] The Spirit is begetter, not mother, i. 13; I John iii. 9. This corresponds to the Aristotelian proposition, that every nature begets its own substance (*M.M.* I, 10, 1187a, 31). It is not simply an extension of Rom. vi. 3–4; I Cor. xv. 45, or a transference of Ps. ii. 7 from Jesus to believers (cf. *contra* C. F. Burney, *Aramaic Origin of the Fourth Gospel*, 45; Howard, *op. cit.* 198). On the question of new birth, cf. Dibelius, *Past.*[3] on Tit. iii. 5; *idem, Jak.* on i. 18; C. H. Dodd, *Fourth Gospel*, 303–4.

II Cor. iii. 6). But Paul thinks in the Rabbinic category of justification, δικαιοσύνη,[1] and consequently defines life, ζωή, straight away in terms of "righteousness", δικαιοσύνη, as opposed to "judgment", κατάκρισις (see above, p. 71). For John, on the other hand, life, ζωή, consists in knowing, γινώσκειν, God (xvii. 3).[2] Therefore he does not follow Paul's line of thought all the way, for this would imply that the Spirit gives (a) life (because it communicates the knowledge of God's redeeming act on the cross, see above p. 69), and therefore (b) freedom from boasting (καύχημα) (see above, p. 73), and therefore (c) openness to one's neighbour (see above, pp. 77–81), in short (d) δικαιοσύνη in its largest sense. Consequently John can make far more direct use of the concept of the life-giving Spirit (which was originally conceived along quite different lines) without thereby saying anything fundamentally different from Paul. As in Paul, the originally substantial conception is completely superseded. The only difference from Paul is that union with the Redeemer itself entails the abolition of the separation between God and man,[3] and for this reason Spirit—more than in Paul—refers to God's world (as opposed to σάρξ) as the sphere from which man is controlled in his new existence. John therefore has less embarrassment than Paul in ascribing birth, γεννᾶν, to this world of God's. But this no longer means any change in the substance of the soul;[4] it now means the God-given knowledge that in Jesus God himself has come into the world; and this is made a reality by faith. iii. 3–5 is a statement of the theme that knowledge of this kind can only be a gift of God and in no way a possibility for man on his own: it is also a challenge to Nicodemus to stop worrying about

---

[1] Kittel, art. "Righteousness". E.T. 72–3.

[2] The noun γνῶσις does not occur at all, presumably in opposition to "Gnostic" usage. But the verb is frequent.

[3] Hence the Cross is not seen primarily as expiation, but as the consummation of the Incarnation, in which God's loving approach to the κόσμος is completed (cf. Dodd. op. cit. 441–2).

[4] A. L. Humphries, The Holy Spirit in Faith and Experience, 235–6.

what is possible *for him* but to lay himself right open to
the gift of God—in other words, to believe.

In iii. 8 πνεῦμα means *wind*.[1] Nevertheless the wind,
being intangible and uncontrollable, corresponds to the
Spirit of God. But it is important to see that it is not the
Spirit, but the bearer of the Spirit, who is described in this
way. Special emphasis is now laid on the "strangeness"
of him who is born of the Spirit. The believer, whose
going and coming is unknown to the world,[2] is no longer
accessible to human knowledge, and although faith will
certainly express itself in acts of love (ἀγάπη), nevertheless "being born of the Spirit" does *not* mean moral renewal. It is something unobservable, whether in its
activity or its appearance, whether in its suddenness, the
spasm of repentance which precedes it, or the feeling of
liberation. It is that happening which the world can
now neither measure nor judge.

In vi. 63 (cf. xv. 3) πνεῦμα, in contrast to σάρξ which
profiteth nothing, is credited with a γεννᾶν which proceeds from the words spoken by Jesus as the Son of
Man. It follows from vi. 51–8 that σάρξ here can only
mean the flesh of the Incarnate One which becomes
most scandalously visible in the Eucharist in its saving
necessity for men. Nothing is said of the identity
of Jesus' σάρξ with the Eucharistic elements. What is
emphasized is only that in the Eucharist the individual
must take concrete advantage of the sacrifice of Jesus as
it is proclaimed in the saying over the Bread. For John,
the one purpose of Baptism and Lord's Supper is to give
evidence for the Incarnation.[3] The force of vi. 63 is then
that this σάρξ is only profitable when the πνεῦμα gives the
knowledge that it is precisely in this σάρξ that ζωή is to
be found.[4] Following viii. 15, the explanation now runs

---

[1] Linguistically, from *πνεϝω. In LXX, cf. Jonas iv. 8; Jer. iv. 11.
Another view: T. M. Donn, *The Voice of the Spirit* (John iii. 8), Exp. T. 66
(1954–5), 32.

[2] Cf. vii. 27–8; viii. 14; ix. 29; xv. 19.

[3] It is certainly true that for the believer this scandal is converted into
grace and help (Barrett, *St. John, ad loc.*).

[4] Cf. *contra* McGregor, *op. cit.* 161–2, who sees material communion in
51γ–58, spiritual communion in 63. Dodd, *Fourth Gospel*, 342, n. 3 sees
the solution in the unity of deed and word.

as follows: if men look only to the σάρξ of Jesus, his Incarnation as it is proclaimed and offered to them for their salvation in the Eucharist, then οὐκ ὠφελεῖ οὐδέν. Only when the words of Jesus, in which the πνεῦμα is at work, make them see the δόξα of the father in this σάρξ, only then ζωοποιεῖ (cf. xiii. 10; xv. 3). This is true for the aggravation of the σκάνδαλον in the ἀναβαίνειν of Jesus on the cross, as much as for every Eucharist, in which men naturally react just like Peter in xiii. 6. It is certainly not meant by this that one must not stop at the outward element, but must conceive of it "spiritually"— this could be suspected of being a deliberate evasion of the σκάνδαλον; but equally certainly it is not meant that one should find Life *in* the element. The point is more that in face of the scandalously visible flesh it is only in the strength of the Spirit that we can discern the δόξα and therefore the ζωή. This emphasis on the Word, and this demand for faith in response to it, shows that any connection between ζωή and the (sacramental) substance is even more consistently repudiated in John than it is in Paul.

The meaning of the sacraments in John has been seen[1] in the unity of spirit and matter. Just as water is first concentrated in a canal and then irrigates the country in a network of channels, so the Spirit which is principally concentrated in Jesus runs over into the sacraments; the fruits of Jesus' death are the elements, water and blood, which survive from the substance of his life and have the ability to be united with the Spirit (xix. 34–5). But this view collapses on the objections that in John σάρξ certainly does not mean matter; that the Eucharist is here understood as an aggravation of the σκάνδαλον, that is, as a challenge to faith; that in vi. 63; xv. 3 ζωή is derived from the Word alone (cf. v. 24; vi. 68; viii. 51; xii. 47); that in iii. 6–8 ὕδωρ is not referred to; and that in iv. 23–4; xx. 22–3 (otherwise than in Matt. xxviii. 19) the sacrament is not mentioned at all. In other words, the sacrament may keep its value for John, but it is certainly not central.[2]

---

[1] E.g. by Cullmann, *Early Christian Worship*, passim.

[2] Cf. Howard, *op. cit.* 147; Bultmann, *T.N.T.* II, 58. Barrett, *St. John*, 75, stresses that the sacrament does not transmit the Spirit, but the Spirit is the power which gives blessings.

The same point comes out of vii. 38–9,[1] where, as far as substance goes (there is nothing about sacrament), all that is said is that the Spirit, as the Church's life-giving water, will pour forth in the subsequent preaching by word and deed. But what is new here is the statement that the Spirit will only come after Jesus' death. This certainly corresponds to the historical facts, but takes on a special meaning for John, as the Paraclete-sayings will show.[2]

In John's account of the bestowal of the Spirit (xx. 22),[3] the Eleven are the representatives of believers in general.[4] It is possible to take this scene as a flimsy fulfilment of the Paraclete-sayings, or as a device to make good the necessary absence of Pentecost in the gospel. But this is a misunderstanding. For John, Life ($\zeta\omega\dot\eta$) consists in the knowledge of the true God ($\dot\alpha\lambda\eta\theta\iota\nu\dot o\varsigma$ $\theta\epsilon\dot o\varsigma$) in Jesus, and the Spirit ($\pi\nu\epsilon\hat u\mu\alpha$) is none other than the power of evangelism which leads to this knowledge. Hence the authority of the preaching is all important.

4. The Paraclete

It is no accident that the Paraclete is called the Spirit of truth, $\pi\nu\epsilon\hat u\mu\alpha$ $\tau\hat\eta\varsigma$ $\dot\alpha\lambda\eta\theta\epsilon\dot\iota\alpha\varsigma$ (xiv. 17; xv. 26; xvi. 13), for he seems to represent reality as opposed to every kind of appearance.[5] The divine world is present in him,

---

[1] If these verses originally belonged together. Some (e.g. J. M. Thompson, Exp. VIII, 14 (1917), 221–2), believe 39 is a gloss.

[2] The idea in Acts ii. 33 (derived from Rabbinic theory?) may have been the origin of this statement (Knox, Acts, 85–6), but is no longer of any importance for John.

[3] Barrett, St. John, ad loc., points out the reminiscence of Gen. ii. 7; Ezek. xxxvii. 9; Wisdom xv. 11: it is life-giving new creation. On the peculiarity of this passage compared with the usual Johannine attitude, cf. Dodd, Fourth Gospel, 430.

[4] Cf. vi. 63; vii. 38. If they are to be regarded only as holders of an office (J. H. Bernard, St. John (I.C.C.), 672, 676; cf. 575 on xvii. 18; L. S. Thornton, in The Apostolic Ministry, ed. K. E. Kirk, 108–9) then the same must go for the whole of the farewell discourses, including the command to love one another. The correct view: R. N. Flew, Jesus and His Church [2], 173–4.

[5] Just as $\dot\alpha\rho\tau o\varsigma$ $\tau\hat\eta\varsigma$ $\zeta\omega\hat\eta\varsigma$, vi. 35 (cf. 33, 50–1) = that which gives $\dot\alpha\lambda\dot\eta\theta\epsilon\iota\alpha$ and is $\dot\alpha\lambda\dot\eta\theta\epsilon\iota\alpha$. On the Paraclete promises in general cf. W. M. Firor, Fulfilment of Promise, Interpretation, 7 (1953), 299–314.

just as it was present in Jesus, and will now continue to be present in his Word (xvii. 13–17).[1]   It is said of him, just as of Jesus (xiv. 20), that he is in the disciples; but it is the disciples, not the world, who know him (xiv. 17) as they know Jesus (xvi. 3).   Both are sent by the Father (xiv. 24, 26) and proceed from him (xvi. 27; xv. 26); both teach (vii. 14; xiv. 26), bear witness (viii. 14; xv. 26) convict the world of sin (iii. 18–20; xvi. 8–11), and at the same time do not speak on their own authority (xiv. 10; xvi. 13).[2] Thus he is only the "other Paraclete" after Jesus (xiv. 16); indeed one might be tempted to say, that there is really no place in John for the Spirit.[3]   In the Paraclete Jesus comes himself (xiv. 18); and yet the Paraclete is not simply identical with Jesus; he only comes after Jesus has gone (vii. 39; xvi. 7) and whereas Jesus was only with his own for a time and will one day be with them again (xiii. 33; xiv. 3; xvi. 4; xvii. 24), the Paraclete will always be with them (xiv. 16).   Jesus can be seen and yet not seen, heard and yet not heard (vi. 36; v. 37–8), he can be excluded by unbelief.   Indeed, in a sense the same is true for his own, so long as he is with them (xiv. 5–11).   It is only the Spirit, coming to the Church in the Word, which "brings to life"; the historical Jesus as such is the "flesh", which "profiteth nothing" (vi. 63, see above, p. 93). Only the Christ of the preaching is the Redeemer;[4] therefore it is only the Spirit of truth which really reveals Jesus to the disciples (xiv. 26; xvi. 13) and which "glorifies" him (xvi. 14).   The words of the historical Jesus are almost repeated in the words of the Spirit (vi. 63; xiv. 26; xvi. 14) and this is how the historical words first gain their

---

[1] Howard, op. cit. 74.

[2] Cf. the juxtaposition of Paraclete and Jesus sayings: xiv. 15 ff. and 18 ff.; xiv. 25–6 and 21–24; xvi. 12–15 and 16–24.   For the exegesis of xvi. 9, cf. Barrett, St. John, ad loc.

[3] E. F. Scott, q. by J. G. Simpson, The Holy Spirit in the Fourth Gospel, Exp. IX, 4 (1925), 293.

[4] Hence John does not make him say "I will come to you in the Spirit". Cf. Simpson, op. cit. 294–7.   There is no theorizing here about Trinitarian inter-relationships.

power (xvi. 8–11). Hence it is here that the concept of an advocate, a helper, first makes its appearance, a concept which has wider implications than that of "revealer". Yet those very words of the Spirit are none other than those which are spoken in the authoritative preaching of the Church (xx. 22–3; xv. 26–7).[1]

Once again, therefore, it becomes apparent that John regards the Spirit as nothing other than the power of the proclamation of Jesus as Redeemer, a proclamation in which man encounters the divine world.[2] True life, ζωή, is only to be found with God, in the sphere of Spirit (this had long been the answer of a church under Hellenistic influence). God is Spirit, not flesh, and can only be approached by one who is himself in the Spirit. But what is this Spirit? In heterodox Jewish circles two quite different answers were current: (1) a heavenly substance, which is imprisoned in matter; or (2) an angel which is at work in the Good. For John, as for the whole Church, the Spirit could only be the power which makes it possible for man to recognize Jesus as the Redeemer, in whom he encounters God. In this way, in John as in Paul, the Jewish answer is given a new twist: the Spirit is the Spirit of prophecy; but this is not a phenomenon of remote ages, but is the power of God now present in the preaching of the Church, moulding the life of the Last-Age people of God and so challenging and judging the world.

e. OTHER NEW TESTAMENT WRITERS
1. *The school of Paul*
(a) *Ephesians*

Here the Pauline language is already somewhat diluted. The Spirit is in general the power by which the Church grows (iii. 16) and in particular the power of prayer (vi.

---

[1] Two different witnesses are not meant, naturally; it must be understood like viii. 18; III John 12 (Hoskyns, *Fourth Gospel, ad loc.*). ἐστε, instead of ἦτε, shows that the witnesses are those of all times. Cf. K. Barth, *Church Dogmatics*, E.T. IV, i. 647.
[2] Cf. Barrett, *St. John*, 76–7.

18) but, as in Paul (see above, p. 68), it is also especially the power of revelation (i. 17; iii. 5). But here we can see the influence of the primitive Christian view, in so far as the revelation concerned is thought of as a special one which is given to apostles and prophets, or can be besought for again and again by the Church, but not as the basic apprehension of the Christ-event.

> vi. 17 is a fairly traditional expression of the Spirit as working mainly through Scripture. On the other hand, in v. 18 the emphasis is rather on the ecstatic element (see above p. 65). It is probable that in iv. 4 the truth about human nature: "one body, one spirit" (ἓν σῶμα, ἓν πνεῦμα), is transferred to the Body of Christ, σῶμα Χριστοῦ, which embraces all its members within itself, so that the Spirit which works in all of them must be the one Spirit, the Spirit of the Lord (κύριος). This is surely how two further passages, ii. 18, iv. 3 are to be understood, and not in the manner of Phil. i. 27.

In other words, Ephesians comes much closer than Paul to Gnostic thought, though at the same time it approaches the views of a "pre-Gnostic" Judaism (see above pp. 15ff.). In ii. 2 the "evil spirit" makes its appearance,[1] which is at work in the damned, along with the "spiritual hosts of wickedness" (πνευματικὰ τῆς πονηρίας vi. 12) which reign in the air; moreover the typical expression, "grieving" the holy Spirit of God which is given to men, occurs in iv. 30. The Pauline conception of the Spirit as the "surety of the coming inheritance" ἀρραβὼν . . . κληρονομίας) turns up in rather sharper form in the idea of the *seal* (which is also a guarantee?) (i. 13[2] and 14; iv. 30, cf. II Cor. i. 22),[3] though there is no thought here of a substance which cannot be lost (as in James, see below p. 101).[4]

[1] See above, p. 24.
[2] τῆς ἐπαγγελίας stresses its eschatological bearing, as in Gal. iii. 14.
[3] Cf. Ezek. ix. 4; Lampe, *Seal of the Spirit*, 3–18.
[4] iv. 23 (ἀνανεοῦσθαι τῷ πνεύματι τοῦ νοὸς ὑμῶν), is uncertain: it is more likely to be an instrumental dative (so that νοῦς simply defines the area of the holy Spirit's activity) than dative of respect ("in your spirit" cf. Rom. xii. 2), in which case νοῦς would specify πνεῦμα as the human spirit.

(b) The Pastoral Epistles

A completely un-Pauline feature of these is the fact that Spirit only occurs six times, and one of these in the sense of "spirit of error" (I Tim. iv. 1). Out of these I Tim. iii. 16 (see above p. 57) and II Tim. iv. 22 (see above pp. 84–85)[1] are stereotyped phrases. I Tim. iv. 1 is a wholly traditional way of speaking of the prophetic Spirit. II Tim. i. 7 is close to I Cor. iv. 21. Does this mean that the Pauline conception of the Spirit as not essentially out of the ordinary has led to activities of the Spirit being replaced by Hellenistic lists of virtues? It is more probable that the day-to-day self-authentication of the Spirit had to be insisted on in the face of enthusiasts who could only see the exceptional character of their spiritual gifts. A new thought appears in Titus iii. 5 (see above p. 91 n. 4).[2] It is in good Pauline tradition that in this expression no miraculous powers are named as activities of the Spirit, but rather the new birth which admits one to justification and hope.[3] But at the same time the author himself has probably understood this as something ethical (iii. 1–3).[4]

2. Hebrews

Here the linguistic usage is complex, though strongly under Jewish influence. "Spirits" (xii. 23) are the departed (as in Judaism).[5] xii. 9 shows that behind this there is a dualistic world of flesh and spirit. This is a

---

[1] This has no reference to the grace of vocation (Dibelius, *Past.*[3], *ad loc.*).

[2] Whether πνεῦμα is taken as dependent on both phrases or only on the second makes no material difference. "The bath of a rebirth and renewal effected by the Spirit" is the most likely rendering. In any case ἀνακαινώσεως must be taken parallel with παλιγγενεσίας, not λουτροῦ.

[3] This is also a repudiation of all Hellenistic apotheosis theories (Dibelius, *ad loc.*). On the difference from Paul cf. B. S. Easton, *The Pastoral Epistles*, note *ad loc.*; E. F. Scott, *The Spirit in the N.T.*, 176–7. Another view: Flemington, *Baptism in the N.T.*, 103–4.

[4] Flemington, *op. cit.* 101.

[5] Eth. Enoch, xxii. 9; xli. 8; ciii. 3 (Wisd. iii. 1; iv. 14: ψυχαί); C. Spicq, *L'épître aux Hébreux*, II, *ad loc.*

long way from the idea that we are sons of God by virtue
of our "God-given nature". All that is said is that God
is not merely the father of mortal flesh, but also of that
innermost "I" which will one day be answerable to him.
In i. 14 angels are referred to as spirits.[1]

In iii. 7; ix. 8; x. 15 there are completely traditional
references to the Spirit speaking through scripture. In
iv. 12 "spirit" and "soul" are distinguished in purely
psychological terms, as two closely interdependent parts;
in other words the distinction is a cliché.[2] ii. 4; vi. 4–5
belong to earliest Christianity (see above, pp. 54–5) in
seeing the activity of the Spirit principally in miracles.
The first of these passages is dominated by the conception
that the Spirit of God can be divided and distributed to
individuals in different ways.[3] In the second passage the
Spirit is seen especially as a foretaste of the Age to Come.[4]
The Spirit of Grace ($\pi\nu\epsilon\hat{\upsilon}\mu\alpha$ $\tau\hat{\eta}s$ $\chi\acute{\alpha}\rho\iota\tau\sigma s$ = Zechariah
xii. 10 LXX) in x. 29 must not be taken as a means of
salvation (despite its association with the Blood of the
Covenant); it means the Spirit as a sign of the eschatological grace of God. ix. 14 is difficult. "Christ has
offered himself unspotted to God through the everlasting
Spirit ($\delta\iota\grave{\alpha}$ $\pi\nu\epsilon\acute{\upsilon}\mu\alpha\tau\sigma s$ $\alpha\grave{\iota}\omega\nu\acute{\iota}\sigma\upsilon$)". Here, too, as in xii. 9,
the contrast with flesh seems to be dominant (cf. ix. 13):
in the Old Covenant the offerings were always perishable, earthly things in the sphere of Flesh, but now
One offers himself who comes from the sphere of Spirit
and possesses the Spirit, and thus brings a redemption
which lasts far longer than the flesh.[5] "Through" ($\delta\iota\acute{\alpha}$)
means "the ways and means" of this offering.[6]

[1] $\pi\nu\epsilon\acute{\upsilon}\mu\alpha\tau\alpha$. Paul regards angels as conquered powers of the enemy:
here we are once again on orthodox Jewish ground.

[2] Spicq, op. cit. I, 52–3.

[3] $\pi\nu\epsilon\acute{\upsilon}\mu\alpha\tau\sigma s$ is gen. obj., since $\alpha\grave{\upsilon}\tau\sigma\hat{\upsilon}$ refers to $\acute{o}$ $\theta\epsilon\acute{o}s$ (J. Moffatt, Hebrews,
I.C.C. ad loc.). The idea can be found in the O.T.

[4] The punctuation is uncertain: the easiest is to take $\delta\omega\rho\epsilon\grave{\alpha}$ $\acute{\epsilon}\pi\sigma\upsilon\rho\acute{\alpha}\nu\iota\sigma s$
and $\pi\nu\epsilon\hat{\upsilon}\mu\alpha$ $\acute{\alpha}\gamma\iota\sigma\nu$ as parallel synonyms, which are then explicated in
$\dot{\rho}\hat{\eta}\mu\alpha$ and $\delta\upsilon\nu\acute{\alpha}\mu\epsilon\iota s$. Differently, Moffatt, ad loc.

[5] Moffatt, ad loc. compares vii. 16 and especially Midr. Ps. 31 (Str.-B.
III, 741): "formerly you were redeemed with flesh and blood . . . wherefore your redemption was temporal. But now I will redeem you by myself,
who live and remain for ever; wherefore your redemption will be eternal
redemption."

[6] Bl-Debr. §223.3. [Cf. C.F.D. Moule, Idiom-Book of N.T. Greek, 57.]

3. *The General Epistles*

(a) *James*

Apart from the purely psychological sense (ii. 26) Spirit is only spoken of in iv. 5 and there it is probably the spirit which God bestows on a man and then simply requires of him again. In point of fact, wisdom (σοφία) in iii. 17 is identical with this spirit.

(b) *I Peter*

Here there is a richer content. i. 11 follows tradition in limiting the prophetic Spirit to the O.T. prophets and the apostles,[1] to whom it was sent from heaven. But the difference between the time of the prophets of Scripture and the time which followed Easter is evened out: even in those days it was already the Spirit of Christ.[2] In i. 2 the Spirit is in very general terms the power of salvation.[3] iv. 14 corresponds to Jewish thought and confines the bestowal of the Spirit to the Martyrs (see above p. 27).

iii. 4: ἡσύχιον πνεῦμα has turned into a cliché.

ii. 5, see above, p. 88, n. 1.[4]

iii. 18–19 and iv. 6 present difficulties. Just as in iii. 18 (see above, p. 57) so in iv. 6 one can find two spheres mentioned, in which judgment and salvation are brought to completion, and which are certainly characterized by the substance of the body and of the Spirit which transcends the body.

There remain some questionable points.

(i) Is πνεύματι the antecedent of ἐν ᾧ (iii. 19)? Surely not, if this means that in the days of Noah Christ

---

[1] Overlooked by H. A. Guy, *The N.T. Doctrine of the Last Things*, 95, when he takes this here and in Acts to mean the breaking-in of the Eschaton.

[2] The B reading (omitting Χριστοῦ) is a later attempt to remove the sting. There is something similar in Barn. v. 6; Ign. *Mag.* ix. 2; Just. *Apol.* lxii. 3–4.

[3] = II Thess. ii. 13. Corresponding to θεοῦ πατρός and Ἰησοῦ Χριστοῦ, πνεύματος (I Pet. i. 2) can only be taken as a subjective genitive. The triadic formulation has progressed a long way; but even so the Spirit still comes before Christ. See below, p. 108, n. 3.

[4] Selwyn, *I Peter*, following E. Lohmeyer, sees the Eucharist in the "spiritual sacrifices". Cf. *contra* F. W. Beare, *I Peter, ad loc.* Cf. also R. N. Flew, *Jesus and His Church*, 160.

was already preaching in the spirit to those who are now
in prison (cf. Ign. *Mag.* ix. 2).   A possible idea would be
that Christ, after the crucifixion, went as a disembodied
spirit to the spirits, but it is fairly certain that here, as in
i. 6; iv. 4 ἐν ᾧ only means "and so".[1]   In which case the
Resurrection is not to be distinguished from ζωοποιηθῆναι
as a second event, but rather the fact of the Resurrection
is explicated in the descent into hell and the ascension
into heaven.   It remains to ask whether both come to
the same thing, in other words whether the φυλακή is to
be thought of as being "under way" in the air.   If it is
correct to reconstruct an old formula from this passage,
then this was the original sense.   In the present context
the two are separated from each other.

(ii) Are the πνεύματα demons or the departed?
Since iv. 6 cannot be separated from this passage, they
must be the departed.   However, it is possible that in a
rather obscure way the demons (perhaps at work in their
successors) are included too.   But would they be placed
in Hades?

(iii) Who are the νεκροί in iv. 6?   Despite the combination of literal and spiritual meanings of "living" and
"dead" in Hermas, s. IX. xvi. 3-6, it is very difficult to
refer the word here to those who are still alive on earth
but spiritually dead, particularly because the formula in
iv. 5 can hardly be interpreted in this way.   But it is
also highly improbable that deceased Christians who
heard the Gospel during their lives are meant.[2]   Along
with iii. 19, one must take them to be the πνεύματα
who are named there.[3]

(iv) In which case, what is σάρξ?   When iv. 6 is
compared with iii. 18 and I Cor. v. 5 (see above, p. 85),
it can only be a judgment in the earthly sphere, i.e.
death, which is in question.   κριθῶσιν (iv. 6) must therefore be understood as a pluperfect.

(c) II Peter and Jude

Here the Spirit is by now only the inspired power of the
now canonical Scriptures (i. 21).   In Jude, on the other

---

[1] [Cf. C. F. D. Moule, *Idiom-Book of N.T. Greek*, 131-2.]

[2] So Beare (*I Peter, ad loc.*) against Selwyn (*I Peter*, 338-9).

[3] The *Gospel of St. Peter*, 41, suggests the deceased.

hand, it is, in Gnostic fashion, the mark of the "un-psychic", coming out especially in prayer.[1]

(d) I John

The Spirit is understood principally in a primitive Christian way as the visible sign of the great turning-point; but the new factor which is recognized by this is no longer simply the breaking-in of the Eschaton but is the abiding of Christ in believers (iii. 24; iv. 13).[2] This explains why once again there is no emphasis on the extraordinariness of the gifts of the Spirit. It is true that the Spirit is clearly grasped as a gift from outside, which is in no sense innate (iv. 13);[3] nevertheless, as in John, the Spirit again bears witness; in one place it is said to do this com-prehensively in "water" and "blood" (v. 6) but it also, in a narrower sense, is independent of these (v. 7); that is, when it is the power of preaching, which, after the sacra-ment, is to an especial degree an activity of the Spirit.[4] The same conception of the testifying prophetic Spirit appears in iv. 1–6; but here the Johannine concept (see above p. 97) is combined with that of the two mutually hostile spirits,[5] and the result comes to precise expression in I John iv. 6. Fully Christian is the naming of the opposing force as Antichrist (iv. 3) and especially the confession of the Incarnate Lord as a criterion of manifestations of the Spirit (see above p. 65). Animistic concepts

---

[1] On 19–20 see above, p. 87. In 20–1 the πνεῦμα ἅγιον is subordinate to θεός and κύριος ἡμῶν Ἰησοῦ Χριστοῦ (see below, p. 108, n. 3).

[2] This is of course the eschatological fulfilment; but it is understood in a way very different from that of the primitive church, cf. Guy, op. cit. 171.

[3] The Spirit is still superior and generic (ἐκ).

[4] But here the Sacraments do not carry the Spirit, though they are important precisely because it is through them that the prophetic πνεῦμα proclaims the Life and Death of Jesus as real events. That the Baptism in Jordan was the real moment of redemption, and that the death of Jesus only had the function of making the Spirit which had been received there available to believers (Flemington, op. cit. 89–91), was acceptable to Gnostic opponents. But the author means more than that, as i. 7 shows.

[5] Test. Jud. xx. 1: τὸ τῆς ἀληθείας καὶ τὸ τῆς πλάνης (πνεῦμα). Cf. above, pp. 17–18.

have left a somewhat deeper impression here. Nowhere else in the New Testament is there such an emphasis on trust in the Spirit which is at work in the Church, which dispenses with all official authority, and which bears true testimony in bringing, not new, unheard-of revelations, but the old message.

4. *The Apocalypse*

That the Apocalypse occupies a place of its own in the New Testament is true also in respect to its theory of the Spirit, which has clear affinities in "pre-Gnostic" Jewish circles. Both here and in popular Judaism,[1] unclean demon-spirits appear as "spirits", πνεύματα (xvi. 13–14; xviii. 2), and the pure vital life-force as the "Spirit" given by God, or, it might be, by a demon (xi. 11; xiii. 15). But the dominant concept is that of the Spirit of Prophecy (xix. 10). This is evidently thought of as an abnormal phenomenon; the state of "being in the Spirit" is distinguished from an habitual state (i. 10; iv. 2). The Spirit is the power which bestows a countenance which a man does not normally have. It can "lead him away" (xvii. 3; xxi. 10) into miraculous places which the natural man does not see.[2] Therefore in xi. 8 "spiritually" (πνευματικῶς) means in prophetic, as opposed to normal, language.[3] But this Spirit has not merely been at work in the past. It speaks to-day. Its task is not just to recall the promises of scripture; it gives them

---

[1] See Eth. Enoch, *passim*; E. F. Scott, *The Spirit in the N.T.* 212. Without the Apocalypse we would not know how primitive the conceptions of the Spirit were in the Christian community. But is the lack of a *doctrine* of the Spirit not due to the fact that here, as throughout primitive Christianity, all the stress is laid on the future, not on the presence of the Spirit?

[2] Yet cf. ἐν (contrasted with Mark i. 12, where the reality of the change of place is unambiguously stressed).

[3] The interpretation "allegorically" is impossible. A text referring to Sodom or Egypt is not transferred to Jerusalem, nor is Jerusalem given an allegorical disguise. No, Jerusalem is seen with prophetic eyes and identified with the Biblical Sodom and Egypt.

new expression (xiv. 13). Consequently its superhuman divinity is felt so strongly that the human speaker can drop out altogether.[1] In the Apocalypse, the Spirit always speaks to the Church, and the person through whom it speaks is of secondary importance. To this extent, the Spirit is associated with the Church and not with the individual.[2] But the Spirit—and this is decisive—is none other than the Ascended Lord himself (ii. 1 = 7, 8 = 11 etc.), even if it is the Ascended Lord in his function of speaking to the Church: for only as the Spirit is he with his own. (Such a thing is never said of the Lord ($\kappa\acute{v}\rho\iota o\varsigma$) himself;[3] he is entirely in heaven.) That is why in xxii. 17 it can be said that the Spirit and the Bride say "Come". When the Church, in the power of the Spirit,[4] calls for her Lord, it is ultimately not her own power and piety, but the Lord himself, who calls. Yet at the same time the Spirit, as the power proceeding from the Lord, can be distinguished from the Lord himself (see above p. 60).

This tension comes clearly to light once again in the strange notion of the seven spirits. From the point of view of the history of religion, they are simply the seven archangels.[5] In the Apocalypse, they stand between God and Christ, and Grace and Peace proceed from them (i. 4);[6] they stand like lamps before God's throne, as the angels do (iv. 5);[7] they are sent out over the whole earth as messengers of God and Christ (v. 6); together with the angels of the churches (i. 20), they are in the hand of

---

[1] ii. 7; xiv. 13; xxii. 17.

[2] Lohmeyer, *Apok.* on ii. 28.

[3] *Idem ibid.* 186; cf. the Johannine Paraclete.

[4] On the parataxis cf. Acts v. 32; John xv. 26–7.

[5] Tobit xii. 15. Another view: G. H. Dix, *The Seven Archangels and the Seven Spirits*, J.T.S. 28 (1927), 233–50, who suggests the influence of the 7-branched candlestick (iv. 5). For the number seven cf. Zech. iv. 2, 10 (Rev. v. 6); Philo, *Op. Mund.* 99–128.

[6] The passage is certainly not interpolated (*contra* Lohmeyer, *Apok.*; R. H. Charles, *Revelation*, I.C.C. *ad loc.*).

[7] viii. 2; cf. Syr. Baruch. xxi. 6; Ps.–Clem. *Hom.* viii. 13. Differently Str.-B. III, 788.

Christ (iii. 1). Thus they represent the Spirit of God in its fullness and completeness,[1] while at the same time they represent the angels of the throne and correspond to the angels of the churches.

This can only be understood against the background of "pre-Gnostic" Jewish thought. Exactly the same concept, perfected by Gnosticism, can be found in Valentine. There the angels are simply Christ himself, but now it is the individualized Christ, the Christ who comes to the individual, and who is at the same time the alter-ego of the human spirit ($\pi\nu\epsilon\hat{\upsilon}\mu\alpha$).[2] The only essential difference is that the Apocalypse is a Church book and ascribes the Spirit, not to the individual, but to the Church.[3] By now, the process was already complete by which the Spirit of God had become that individual spirit which is given to each man as "his" spirit, and similarly the identity of this spirit (which proceeds from God) with the newly-given "self" of a man was well established. But since the thought of the Apocalypse begins with the Church and not with the individual, the "seven churches" correspond with the "seven spirits" which are just as much the "new, grace-endowed self" of the Church, as they are the works of the Spirit, proceeding from God, with which the Church is endowed; and in their totality they are nothing other than the one Spirit of God.

That the Spirits are thought of as angels no longer presents any difficulties. The two are frequently interchanged.[4] It is already the case in heterodox Judaism that the figures of angels have almost the same rank as God or as the Messiah.[5] The angel appears as a mediator

---

[1] As *Spiritus Septiformis*, Isa. xi. 2. The Hebrew text knows only six gifts of the Spirit, LXX and Syrian versions arrive one way or another at seven. Cf. Charles, *Revelation*, on i. 4.

[2] See above, p. 21. Cf. G. Quispel in Eranos Jbch. 15 (1947), 264: "L'ange est le Christ rapporté à l'existence individuelle de l'homme spirituel". Cf. also Cl. Al. *Exc. Theod.* xii. 2 (angels = $\pi\nu\epsilon\acute{\upsilon}\mu\alpha\tau\alpha$ $\nu o\epsilon\rho\acute{\alpha}$).

[3] Loh. *Ap.* on ii. 28.

[4] See above, p. 17, n. 1; also Herm. m. XI, 9; Rev. xvii. 3; xxi. 10.

[5] IV Ezra v. 43; Eth. Enoch xxxix. 5–7.

between God and man, who intercedes for men and brings their prayers before God.[1] That is why the triad, God-Christ-angels, is so common, even in the Apocalypse.[2] Just as it is true throughout the Apocalypse that God's activity is represented in concrete, personal forms, and yet remains his own activity, this is true also of the seven angel-spirits, who are simply the personal activity of God.[3]

[1] Test. L. v. 6–7; D. vi. 2; cf. R. H. Charles, *Apocrypha and Pseudepigrapha*, II, 307, 335; Tobit xii. 15

[2] Luke ix. 26; I Tim. v. 21; Rev. iii. 5.

[3] Cf. also M. Kiddle, *Revelation* (Moffatt N.T. Commentary) on Rev. iv. 6.

APPENDIX: THE APOSTOLIC FATHERS

In the period that immediately follows, the development can be followed under three heads.

(i) The Gnostic-substantial tradition (see above, pp. 20–23). That Christ is composed of a spiritual substance becomes more and more important. It is true even of the Pre-existent One (see above, p. 61 and II Clement ix. 5; xiv. 2, Hermas s. IX, i. 1). Ignatius, although he maintains the Jewish doctrine of resurrection in opposition to Gnosis, nevertheless reveals a tendency to think along Gnostic lines: the union of spirit and flesh-substance in Christ makes possible the resurrection of the flesh of the believer (*Eph.* vii. 2; *Mag.* i. 2; *Sm.* iii. 2–3; xii. 2).

(ii) The ecstatic tradition. The Spirit is replaced by extraordinary psychical phenomena (see above, p. 65 n. 6).[1] In due course it comes to be thought that these are a kind of reward for exceptional faith (cf. I Clem. ii. 2).

(iii) The official Church tradition. It is no longer so, that a man whom God marks out by the gift of the Spirit is appointed to a particular ministry, but rather the man who is duly appointed to an office is guaranteed to possess the Spirit of God along with it. II Tim. i. 16 is corroborated by I Tim. iv. 14; i. 18. Ign. *Phld.* vii. 1–2; *Mag.* xiii. 1; I Clem. xli–xlii (but. cf. xlii. 4) are more doubtful. Irenaeus is the first to put it unequivocally: *qui cum episcopatus successione charisma veritatis certum . . . acceperunt* (*Haer.* IV, xxvi. 2).[2] Nevertheless the Kerygma of the New Testament preserves its power, and in the succeeding centuries it will again and again make new conquests.[3]

[1] Herm. v. I, i. 3; II, i. 1.
[2] Cf. W. D. Davies, *Light on the Ministry from the N.T.*, Religion in Life, 21 (1952), 267–8.
[3] On the question of Trinitarian formulae see further Ign. *Mag.* xiii. 1–2. In the repeated ἐν (xiii. 1) and in the expressions in I Clem. xlvi. 6; lviii. 2. there is discernible a slight hesitation in making the Spirit fully equal to God and Christ.

INDEX OF REFERENCES